PRAIRIE VISIONS

Prairie Visions

A Personal Search For The Springs
of Regional Art and Folklife

By Robert Gard

HEARTLAND PRESS

PRAIRIE VISIONS contains materials previously published by Stanton and Lee of Madison, WI. Permission to reprint sections of Robert Gard's earlier books has been generously provided.

Published by Heartland Press,
an imprint of NorthWord, Inc., Box 128, Ashland, WI 54806.

Library of Congress Catalog Number: 87-61245

ISBN 0-942802-54-3

Edited by Tom Klein

Designed by Moonlit Ink, Madison, WI.

Printed and bound in the United States of America.

For Hazel von Jeschki

With appreciation
of her loyalty and humor

CONTENTS

PREFACE

I N THE SUMMER OF 1969, AS NEIL ARMSTRONG WAS taking a giant step for mankind, Robert Gard was walking his patch of real estate somewhat more casually. Somehow I had a feeling that Bob's strides on familiar Wisconsin earth were as significant as Neil's on strange moon craters. More, perhaps.

It was during that salubrious season I first ran into Robert Gard. He was conducting a seminar on writing. Yet, I knew at once, it was more than that. Just as I immediately sensed he was more than a teacher, though he was wondrous at it. He was acquainting us, Wisconsinites and outlanders, with the magic of our surroundings. It was as though Thoreau were showing us around and about Walden. In his knowing this territory, *his* territory, we, strangers no more, came to know it: its prairies, rivers, nightwoods. "When I seek to rediscover the Wisconsin prairie," he writes in one of his evocative journals, "I seek to rediscover my own soul." I've a hunch he has eminently succeeded.

A feeling for place—a you-can-put-your-hand-on-it place—is what Bob Gard is all about. A place that is like no other, because it's yours. In springing forth this feeling, this awareness, Bob awakens it in the rest of us.

Never in our history has this longing been as keenly felt as it is right now. In this high tech time, in this franchised time, our benchmarks, our regional uniqueness, appear to be going, going, gone. Almost.

Consider your arrival at the airport. Any airport. See those Golden Arches? You've seen them elsewhere, haven't you? See those "inns," ironically called Holiday? Familiar? See that neon wilderness where Crazy Charlie or Madman Earl offers you his shirt as well as a spiffy car? Can you tell if you're in Cleveland or Alberquerque? Or, God help us, Dallas?

It is a feeling of lostness. And no compass.

Consider, then, Bob Gard. "It's a funny thing: when I'm out in the woods at night, it is as if the whole world is mine. If there is a small moon over the woods at night, and night sounds all around, something inside of me takes over. I am me, but I'm not me. I am like everybody I ever knew and they are right there beside me. People are mortal, but still, they're not in the way they think they are mortal. When I die, I would like to recall all the beautiful things I have seen all my life. That's some kind of immortality; that's the way I figure that folks are in their imaginations. That's why people are immortal, to be able to see and feel all in one moment everything they are, or what the land is, or has been."

Perhaps that's why, especially at this moment in the life of our species, Bob Gard's vision is so precious to us all.

Studs Terkel
Chicago, Illinois

INTRODUCTION

OWADAYS, THEY OFTEN CALL ME A "FOLKLORIST." I LIKE to hear that, but more accurately, perhaps, I like to be called a "folklife specialist."

From early on it was my hope to sometime weave the stories and legends of American places and people into plays and other kinds of literary efforts.

My experiences in Eastern Kansas stimulated my imagination, and awakened me to tales of Jesse James, John Brown and a host of local characters who bit by bit assumed for me images that were larger-than-life. I carried these impulses toward story-making with me wherever I went. The Kansas boyhood experience was very important in setting the dimensions of my vision.

In central New York I learned what it was to translate local regional material into creative form. I became associated with the New York Plays

Project, where Professor Alexander M. Drummond of Cornell University had begun to draw wide public attention to local and regional stories. Often, on a hill above one of the long, slender Finger Lakes, he recited to groups of his students sagas of the country. After I wandered this area myself, and began to understand some of the things that motivated the land's people, I attempted to transfer some of these yarns into plays and books. In 1940 I published a first book with Professor Drummond, *The Lake Guns of Seneca and Cayuga*, a collection of New York State plays.

Later, using some of these same gathering resources, I had the opportunity to collect native materials in Western Canada. I found that many of the early pioneer settlers of the Alberta country were still living. The tales they told I wrote down in my notebooks, and I published my first regional book of prose, *Johnny Chinook*, in 1945. During those years I also learned of the potential literary importance of climate and geography on people. The vast and silent short grass plains of the southern parts of the Province, which had bred a state of morose loneliness in many settlers, women especially, left alone in small isolated dwellings, had great emotional meaning for me. So did the Chinook Arch, a unique cloud formation, which often preceded a mid-winter thaw, and brought a breath of spring for a little while, puffing down over the great mountains onto the flatlands. "The greatest next-year country on earth" was what the local people called the Alberta land; and I understood their hope, a faith maintained in the midst of drought, hail and wind.

Yet, it was the heartlands of America which drew my greatest enthusiasm and attention. When I came to the place I now call home, I found that Wisconsin is a kaleidoscope of change.

My sense of regional value matured in Wisconsin, where I have lived for more than forty years, always on the search for tales of regional and literary interest. Most of the material included in this book reflects my personal effort to interpret regions, and the people who live there and are influenced by the flavors of regions. Most of what I have written is related to the heartlands, but actually, everything might be applied to places and to people everywhere.

I am sure that every sensitive person has his or her own favorite "homeland," or choice memories of other regions where they have lived. I recognize these regional voices echoing near and far. I am devoted to the traditions of the prairie and the heartlands. The "visions" I have experienced have a constant relationship to the past and present of the land where I have lived, and over the years there has grown a mystical affinity between the land and myself.

My reasons? I love the land. I recognize the regional voices in the wind, in the burn of the sun, in the sweeping cold, in the history-making rivers such as the Fox and the Wisconsin, and the Mississippi. This homeland country possesses a wide-ranging heritage which includes settlement by Yankees and Europeans and York-Staters of agricultural lands in the southern portions of Wisconsin. The same kinds of peoples also took lands in Minnesota, Iowa, Nebraska and the Dakotas. On prairie, lakes, and hill, they established traditions that are many and colorful. Especially, the tales and imprints left by lumberjacks who cut the mighty white pine forests of northern Wisconsin are probably without compare.

Generally the stories I like to tell are ageless in a way; because the land the people cherish is ageless. Many Wisconsin people live on old farms that have been in the same family for more than a hundred years. I believe that Wisconsin now has more than 8,000 of these Centennial farms. Family roots are very deep, and many times it becomes hard to distinguish the land from the dreams.

For many years I have tracked heartland countryside and have learned to appreciate the whole process of settlement and of the transformation of the land. There remains despite the thousands of farms in places where prairie and marsh once bred a deep wilderness, a sensation of the past. There persists still in place a sense of unending forests, of explorers and voyageurs; of the cries of new settlers, elated at finding new homes; and of ancient Indian peoples who left a definite spell upon the land.

Over the years, I have seen so many examples of art and craft arising from the land, and I have tried so hard to encourage these things. I have been in so many communities, teaching, seeding the idea that art can arise from within people.

Prairie Visions is the recording of my quest. . . .

AUTHOR'S NOTE

The arrangement of materials in this book is a result of an awareness of the traditions and heritages of people and of the places in which they live. I have tried to follow a trail of experiences and encounters from the time of my young manhood to the end of my odyssey in Wisconsin. The trail, I find, shows a sensitivity to the theater that is always present in folklife.

In PRAIRIE VISIONS there are sections from previously written and published works.

RECOLLECTIONS
OF KANSAS

THE RIVER

UT OF YOUTH, RESTLESSNESS, AN AFFINITY FOR SEARCH, emerges the first of my visions. That dark and early Depression dawn in Kansas, I had no expectation of where the events of the next hour or so would lead me; far from home, with such anticipation and fear. Who can tell where his Odyssey will carry him, or how far?

I believe that every person has within him or her the seeds of wanting to discover a home place that means more than any other. Also, the telling of the tale of the journey, which carries one from place to place in time and reality until the goal of a home place is found, is a possibility for every person. Thus it was with me.

I think of the prairies and understand that the prairie was a major theme in my young life. It grew more so as I further understood what the prairie represented. My father journeyed west from his boyhood home in eastern Illinois because of the prairie and its indefinable call that moved so many young people. Perhaps it was the grass and the images of the grass and the movement and freedom and openness of the grass and the falltime migration of the birds that motivated him.

The prairie indeed has a dark and hidden vision. When I seek to rediscover the prairie I seek to rediscover my own soul. I was a lad (young-for-my-years) of nineteen, and in a certain darkness after midnight on a June night in the 1930s I was asleep in my room in our tall, narrow, Kansas farmhouse, and I was awakened by my mother who placed her hand nervously upon my shoulder and propelled me awake. I felt her hand very hard, desperate, shaking me and she was saying, "Bobby, wake up. Dad hasn't been here all night. I'm sick with worrying."

It took me awhile to get enough awake to figure out where I was and who it was shaking me; and then I heard what she was saying, and I began to feel scared. She kept shaking and talking, "He's been gone since suppertime. Get up, please Bobby, go out and look for him."

"Now? What time is it?"

"It's about two."

"My gosh, he'll come back, won't he?"

"I don't know. Please."

"He shouldn't go off alone like that."

"I guess he's sick. Hurry, Bobby."

"You got any idea where he went?"

"Well, probably over toward the Neosho River. That's where he usually goes. You know that."

"Yeah, I know. Well, I'll try to find him."

"He might be hurt."

"I doubt it."

I got up, not hurrying, but feeling uneasy. I knew there wasn't any reason for it, but I began to get images of him lying out somewhere in a field, hurt or dead, maybe, and how I would feel and what I'd do if I did find him. I saw the whole picture all the way through; stumbling over the body, seeing that he was dead, maybe, if I could really tell; then running as fast as I could back to the house to tell my mother. Then the calls for help, the lanterns lighted and carried by hurrying neighbors, and all of us running and muttering to each other while my mother stayed at home with a neighbor woman or two looking out after us from the back porch, crying for us to hurry. . . .

I pulled on my overalls and blue shirt, fumbling for the buttons. The upstairs hallway light was on, but my mother hadn't turned on any light in my room, and I had to search for my heavy shoes back under the bed. I laced them up, and stood, ready to go, but not feeling much like it, except that the urgency of my mother now standing in the doorway made me hurry a little.

"Do you want to carry a lantern, Bobby?"

"No. It'd just be in the way."

"Be careful, don't you get hurt."

"Nothing to hurt me."

The old house was so tall and narrow that the stairs seemed to go straight up. As I stumbled down them, feeling for the wall on one side and the rail on the other as I'd done ever since I was big enough to go up and down by myself, I was reminded of the game I played when I was little—seeing how many steps I could jump down from the top. But tonight my mother followed me anxiously. I went through the downstairs hall, through the dining room and the kitchen and out onto the back porch. It was screened in and the screen door always squeaked when it was pushed open as I did it now, and I went down the three steps, the bottom one loose, and stepped onto the flagstone walk that was laid to the barn.

The night sky was clear, there wasn't any moon, but in the early morning, before dawn in Kansas, there is a night light in the open sky that illuminates the fields. Eastern Kansas is a land of wind and rolls of small hills, and creeks and slow rivers. It was open prairie land once, but no longer, and on about every side around our part, there were cornfields running right up close to many farmhouses. And there was a cornfield behind our barn.

I went through the gate and across the barnyard, smelling the manure, and saw that the work team, Jack and Pet, were over in a corner of the yard. I could hardly see them; they were there, faint against the starlight, but it was comforting to know that the horses were near. Horses are comforting in the night, especially if you know them as well as I knew those two. I thought for a moment of putting a bridle on Pet and riding her bareback out to look for him, but then I decided I wouldn't, because there were fence gates to open and it'd take more time and she'd be a trouble, actually, in getting through the corn.

I cut across the edge of the cornfield, trying to not step on the new corn too much. It was coming up good, and would be indeed knee-high or better by the fourth. It was due to be cultivated soon.

Beyond the cornfield there was the railroad track with tight barbed wire fences on both sides of the right-of-way. I knew where to get through the fence and I slid down under and down the embankment. I crossed the Santa Fe track, the rails glistening and going away, away, north toward the town of Iola and south through Humbolt and Chanute and Independence, and on down to Tulsa. I'd never been down that far and someday I thought I would set out to walk down the track, maybe catching onto a freight train as it came past, and riding some and walking some, clear down to Tulsa, and maybe clear on down to Texas. I had never been away from home for any time and felt the urge to go, to leave, and had a funny kind of thrilling feeling in my guts when I thought of myself all alone, walking on the railroad, or maybe out on the high road, just ambling from place to place, not caring, free and easy, just me to worry about. Not like now, with a worry on me and the uneasiness of my mother driving me, and I not knowing what to expect.

It isn't easy to find somebody in the early morning hours; not out in a country of cornfields and pastures and small ravines and woods and rocks. It isn't easy to know where a person will go alone in those hours;

but I knew something about how a certain person would go and where, especially if the person is your father and you like him real well, and if you are worried about him, too, no matter what you have told your mother. Your father hasn't been acting just normal lately, maybe, and he has done some strange things like sit at the dining table and not say much of anything at all during a whole meal, and this is strange because he has been very talkative most of the times you sat with him at the table. He has sat there staring at nothing special, eating a few mouthfuls and then he cries out, "Damn it, God damn it," and this isn't like him, because he has always been very considerate of Mom. He would never let a hired man swear in front of her. She was so particular about the name of God, the way all of the Baptists were in that part of the country about swearing. But here he was shouting the name of God right out and looking as if God had done a bad thing to him. It was shocking and I couldn't forget it, really, though it was buried down inside me somewhere. But here I was in the night walking out across the fields looking for him, and I was really scared. I know my mother was thinking that he had lost his mind or something, though she had said so often that there had never been a breath of insanity on either side of the family.

By the time I had crossed the little creek that never had much water except in flood time, and had crossed the pasture where our cows were still resting . . . I almost stumbled onto them in the dark and one rose, I guess it was Anabell, as Dad called her, big, red-spotted, and she gave out a loud grunt when she got up. I circled around the herd and went through a grove of trees that was near our south line fence and went off across the big alfalfa field. There was a heavy dew on the alfalfa, and I felt the wetness sopping my overalls and seeping through my shoes. It wasn't cold at all, just wet, and I never had paid any attention to wetness really. I just took wetness and dryness and temperature as they came. That was the way I felt about everything. I didn't care. I just went along. But now I did hurry, because it was as if something was driving me beyond my mother's fear and my own uneasiness.

I started to trot, keeping close to the line fence, and I guessed I would follow it along until it got close to the river, and then I would turn north, because that was one way that he did like to walk sometimes. There was an old burying ground over that way near the river, and the grass in there was pretty high. I never did understand why he liked to go over that way, but it was a favorite hike of his, and one on which he hardly ever took anybody else along. It might be where he was now, I didn't know, and if he was dead or something, then I figured that he might be in there in the tall grass among the old graves that had been there ever since the country was settled back in the 1850s and 60s. One thing that Dad liked to do was talk about that old graveyard, and he could sure interest me in it when he told how it seemed to him. Dad had something special in him, that was sure. When he got to talking it was really something, and neighbors of ours who heard him talk about earlier times and about some of his ideas said they'd never heard anything like it.

Dad was self-educated. Maybe, all added up, he had the equivalent of a high school education, and he was a member of the Kansas Bar and practiced law as well as farming. He used to say that he didn't get much schooling in Illinois after the Civil War. But he had all the words he needed to say whatever he wanted to say, and he read anything that was good: he had a set of the *Encyclopedia Americana* that he had read from Volume One on and just kept reading and studying it, and there was something else he had, that my mother said was like he was gifted with poetry or something. She said he was like a wind-harp that could play any kind of music that the wind decided. But you know it's not easy to live with somebody like that.

Every now and then as I moved along through the wet grass I yelled out for him, but I didn't get any answer, and my voice sounded loud and strange in the silent early morning. The birds weren't even awake, and there just wasn't any sound at all as I stood and listened. I thought I might hear him coming, or walking, through the grass, the way shoes sound in grass when it is wet, a soft slushh-shushh, but I didn't hear that sound at all.

I turned north and went across a plowed field that had some hickory trees and oaks growing around the edge. At the far edge of this plot was the old burying ground. I headed for it. I hadn't been that way for a long while—the place was kind of eerie, actually. It sat all alone at the far edge of the plowed ground, a little island there, just something left over; but I had to go now, that was sure. I kept calling and getting no answer; but as I got closer to the tall grass I thought I saw a little flicker of light and I hurried up a little, running now, breathing hard, stumbling along over the rough earth. What I saw might have been just my imagination, because I wanted so much to see a sign of Dad. It could even have been a flicker of a will-o'-the-wisp that I had heard him tell about so often.

But when I got near to the grass and came up to the edge. I could see that there was indeed light shining out from the middle of the plot. My heart started to beat really fast, because I was sure, then, that I would find Dad in there and that he would be dead or something. So I called "Hey, Dad, Dad," and pushed into the grass.

He was there all right. He was lying back, his head on a piece of old log, and he was sprawled out, his legs and feet stretched wide, lying back with the lantern beside him. And he didn't say anything when I came up beside him. I did, though. "Hey, you got Mom really worried. Why'd you stay out here all night?"

"I was told to come out here."

"Who told you? Who could tell you?"

"All of them."

He was getting old, you could see that. In the yellow light of the kerosene lantern his face looked thin and his body seemed very small and tired. He lay there with his hat back from his forehead. I was really worried now, because I thought sure that he was sick, or had lost his mind. I didn't know what to do or say. It would be bad enough if this was somebody you didn't know at all, but to be confronted with such behavior suddenly, in your own father, who had always seemed so ahead of other people. That is hard.

"I heard you yelling." He whispered.

"Why didn't you answer?"

"I didn't want to spoil it."

"Spoil what?"

"Why, all this. And it's a good thing you came to find me. Because, boy, you are the last of the wandering Gards. It has to be up to you, boy."

"What has to be up to me?" I asked nervously.

"You'll find out."

"Come on back home with me."

"Sit down. I've got to talk. Your mother thinks I'm running out of time; or that I'm crazy, maybe. Do you think I'm crazy?"

"Nope. But you've been acting awful funny."

"Is it funny, boy, to see the way things are?"

"I don't follow you, Dad."

"Sit over here. Here, sit down on this log. You and I always been pretty good friends, haven't we?"

"I guess."

"And we've reached a time when things have to be evened out, when the Gards have run out of time. Not just me. All of us. All of us Gards. We moved west joint by joint, we just kept pressin' on and on, and all of us had something we saw that we had to have. And now we've come to the end."

"To the end of what?"

"To this land here. To this grass. This tall grass here. So tall you couldn't see me, or hardly see my lantern. Look how this grass sets here in the middle of the land ready for growing. Everything's gone. All that I saw here is gone. Do you know what I'm talking about, boy?"

"Not really."

"I'm near seventy years old. You're young. Nobody else had the vision. But you got to have it. You are all the chance I got left."

I unhinged myself down beside him on an end of the log. I knew we ought to be getting back to the house; that Mom would be worrying sick, that she would think that both of us had got into trouble, or hurt. I felt nervous, and the wind had come up a little bit and I heard the wind in the trees that weren't far away.

"Let's go home."

"Nope. Not yet. What I've got to say might be the most important thing I ever said. Because you are my blood, boy. You are my chosen messenger, the one who can save my dreams for me."

He reached over and took hold of my ankle. I felt his hand, very strong, an old man's strong hand shaped by years of labor. It was the first time he had ever really touched me that I could recall. We Gards were never folks who touched and showed our affection for each other that way. But he held onto my ankle, like the claws of an eagle I thought. He pulled on my ankle and my leg, and sat up, scraping his heels into the grass in front of the log. He kept hold of my ankle, squeezing harder, and I let him do it; it was a strange sensation being held so hard by my father, and he used my leg to pull himself over so he could get his feet under him. He rose, very stiffly, letting me go as he stood. The grass in there was about shoulder high, very coarse prairie grass, and we couldn't see much in the dark, though by that time the sky was just beginning to lighten. He looked like a dark shadow in the wavering grass and in the dim lantern glow, for he left the lantern sitting on the ground. He took hold of my arm when he got straightened up, and I stood up too. He pulled me beside him and started to move out through the grass.

"Come here. I want to show you."

"Mom'll be excited. We ought to be going."

"She's waited and waited for me. She'll wait some more. She isn't like me, boy. Her family isn't like mine. Hers is religious. They put a lot of store by God and how he tells them what to do. The Gards ain't that way. We go by God, but we go the way we got the strength to do. The way the wind goes; the way the clouds go. Come over here."

He pulled me along with him to the edge of the prairie. At the edge of the grass he stopped. The edge of the unbroken grass was higher than the plowed ground. We couldn't see very far out into the field, just a little way, but you could feel and tell that there were two different things: the prairie and the plowed ground, and I began to get a feeling that we were really all alone out there, and that maybe we wouldn't be able to get away. He kept holding my arm, harder now, and I thought of his hands, the way a man's hands get as he grows old, when you feel the hard bones and the muscles. My arm ached, but he didn't let up.

And strangely, he began to put into words what I was feeling before about being alone, unable to leave.

"We been cast up here," he said. "Cast up on this shore. This is an island in the whole ocean, and we are castaways, you and me, boy. No ship brought us here, but our wandering selves brought us here. This is the island of the Gards. And the Gards made the ocean, too."

I kind of knew what he meant. He'd told me many times when we were sitting out in the yard on a Sunday afternoon, when Mom had made a big pitcher of lemonade and Dad was sitting in his old wicker rocker that Mom had bought at the 1893 World's Fair in Chicago. I'd heard him tell plenty of times how the land was when he came out to Kansas in the 1880s: all prairie grass, hardly any plow-broken, and the prairie flowers and plants all growing. Mom said Dad should have been a poet or a writer or something, and she couldn't see how he got the talent to talk like he did; because there had never been a poet or a writer in the Gards as far as she knew. But now he just kept holding me, and he began to talk like he did out in the yard; but this time I seemed to be a real part of it.

"You know, boy, we saved this prairie grass here in the old burying ground, because we never wanted to disturb these graves. I don't know who these people are who're buried here. They were buried long before

28

I came. But when the plow was turning the new sod, and the roots were breaking, when they drove the teams up to this part here they always stopped. Never broke this. Broke all the rest, and year after year we grew crops. Now this is all there is left, and the dream of the Gards is ended. You see why I come out here in the night and stay all night while your mother stays up at the house and worries about me? You see why I do it?"

"Not really. You ought to go home; you might get sick out here."

"Boy, it ain't sickness that is worrying me. Your mother wouldn't know. But I am worried about the death of dreams and the death of a country. I'm out here in the night because this is all there is left."

He stood for a moment, and with his left hand he grabbed at some of the prairie grass and jerked it loose. He held the grass over against me, so I could feel it and smell it. It had a dew-grass-acid smell, sort of pleasant.

"Here, take the grass. Ball it up, roll it around, tear it apart. Put it in your mouth, taste it. Chew on it."

I tried to do what he said, getting more nervous all the time because what I wanted him to do was go home with me across the fields over to the house. I wanted to get him inside, into bed so Mom could watch out for him; and what I really wanted, I guess, was to get rid of the responsibility of him. But he wasn't going. I put a blade of the grass into my mouth and chewed on it. The juice was a taste I knew because I often grabbed spears of grass when I was walking along a fence or railroad and put them in my mouth. The taste always made me think of spring, somewhere about May, when everything is blooming in the fields in Kansas, and the new grasses are well up. There's a taste and spirit about fields and woods, and tastes of greens you can cook, and dandelions out in the yard, and meadow flowers and wild onions . . . all that came to me as I chewed on the prairie grass that night with Dad holding onto my arm.

"Now you look," he said, "this grass here, this old burying ground that I have kept for you, boy, nobody else; this piece, this acre or so, is not of our time, neither yours nor mine. It belongs to itself: the wild, the grasses, the roots, the fermenting soils; the wild things, the bugs, the people who used to live here—they all own this grass. I don't own it, and you don't own it. And look, how these grasses have browned and brittled in the fall, and laid rotting under the snows. Look how the new shoots of the grasses push up in the spring out of the rot, and their roots are down in the rot, but the grasses taste sweet. You got to know how to listen. How to listen, boy."

He stopped talking and I was afraid to answer him right then, for fear I would start him going again, and we had to get home.

"Listen to the wind," he said. "Listen to how she breathes out, over the long grass; listen to how it is in August when she swirls out the corn leaves. Feel the wind file the corn leaves against your cheek, boy, you've felt that, and so have I, and listen to the sound of the wind in the August corn. Listen to the wind the way she whirls up the dust along the road and settles it down over the hedge rows, and how she sways the sunflowers in the fallow field and lightens up their yellow with the white dust. You got to know how to listen to the wind in these tall grasses, and how it stirs up the grasses outside you and inside, too, and breathes the day, and the sunup and the evening. You got to know how to listen to the shadow of the past, and to the way this prairie grass was left here."

He was talking about the same way he talked on Sundays to Mom and me out in the yard; or to neighbors if they happened to come by. I was kind of cold now, I hadn't worn any jacket, just my work shirt with sleeves rolled up, and I shivered a little in his grasp. I guess he felt me shiver; he pulled me around to face him. He wasn't near as tall as I was, but he was a little bit heavier, sturdier built than I. I wasn't near as strong. Even now when he was old, I could feel the strength of him coming down in his hand. He came around a little now and looked me more directly in the face. I saw his face dimly, but it was sharp, like a hawk's bill, I thought, because he seemed so tense and eager, like a bird coming down out of the sky. It was when he was talking about the prairie and the way things were that he got tight and kind of desperate.

"I was there in the night, and the tall grasses were everywhere, weaving the wind, and I walked out into it, just me, alone, feeling something I never felt before, like this was the beginning of the world. The Creation. The Genesis. And like I was God himself, mastering over all, calling on all. My voice heard above the wind and up to the clouds. And I was young then. And I had come out seeking, searching, like my father and his father, never stopping, ever searching on and on. And I found tall grasses—the roots of man and the roots of grass are all the same, and both of them require freedom to live and to be."

I felt like I was in some kind of a crazy play, and that I was playing one of the parts whether I wanted to or not. I tried to get away, but Dad was awfully strong, and I couldn't break his hold. He kept saying, "Don't spoil it, boy. Let it be. I want to show you how it was."

"We haven't got time. We got to go home."

"We'll go soon. I got to show you this, then I have something to ask you."

"What?"

As he spoke the words came out like little poems, and I remembered the time when my older sister was in high school and had to give a little talk about how the southeastern Kansas country looked in the days when the settlers came into it. She told her English teacher what Dad said and the teacher made her ask him to come to the school and give a little talk to the students about the early days. My sister didn't much want him to come, because she was afraid that he wouldn't change his clothes, and might shame her, I guess, but he did clean up real good after the morning chores were finished and went up to school and came right into the classroom and sat down in a back seat until the teacher asked him to come up to the front and talk. Mom heard all about it from the teacher, because my sister never did get it so she could tell what happened. But

31

the teacher called up Mom on the telephone and said that Dad was the greatest poet she ever heard, and that Walt Whitman never made any better poems. Mom tried to get him to tell what he said but he never would and the students, like my sister, never could describe it either. But I guess he was pretty wild when he was talking.

"God, boy," he suddenly continued, "you never held the handles of a sodbreaker. You never had the experience, as I did, of hearing the roots of the sod cutting and breaking; then it was a happy sound to me, like a million fiddle strings snapping; the cut of the blade of the plow, and the slow strength of the horses. Look, boy, get hold of the plow handles!"

He made me lean and take hold of imaginary plow handles, and he yelled, "Hey! Gitup!" to imaginary horses, and I swear I felt something in my hands and arms, the power of a plow cutting through sod, the grasses bending over and breaking down; the turning under, the fall of the heavy strips of cut roots and grass. I felt it, and as he yelled at the horses, I was there in the old days with him, walking along behind the plow. I felt unreal and foolish, too, and I couldn't get completely into the game he was playing with himself and with me. I knew it was a game and I think he knew it was a game, too, but in some way he was living over his life.

We came to the edge of the grass and he stopped, and forgot the game and the imaginary horses all at once. He took hold of my hand.

"Boy, you've got to help me. I raised you up to understand. It's the time for you to go seeking as I did. You never yet met the Stranger, and you never felt the roots and the body of the grass as I did. And I broke all the sod that I could get that was mine. It's gone. The tall grass is gone, and you ain't going to find that. But you got to find something. There's something out there for you that is like the grass was to me. I come searching for it. And you got to find out what they left in place of the grass, because I am an old man and I have to know before I die. I can't go, because I have no youth left in me. But you go. You go, boy. You go searching and find a Stranger in the grass like I did; unless you

32

do, boy, my life is over and all that I found in the middle of the grass is nothing. All the Gards will be dead. You go. Go, boy go."

"Where do you want me to go?"

He grabbed me hard by the arm. "Say you'll go."

I wanted to humor him, and I didn't have any idea what he wanted me to do. He said he wanted me to go somewhere, nowhere, where there was a stranger, whoever that was, standing in the middle of a big field of prairie grass. He had never mentioned a stranger before. I guessed that in his mind he could go anywhere or do anything. There wasn't any limit. But I was different. I couldn't talk like he could, and make everything seem like a story or a play. I couldn't do any of that and hadn't, even though sometimes I'd wanted to try. And I didn't want to go wandering away without knowing where I was headed. The Depression was a tough time to go anywhere, anyhow. All the tramps and hobos were drifting through the country, and you could see them anytime as you stood along the Santa Fe track, riding in the coal cars, or maybe on top of the boxcars. Dad just expected me to start going, looking for some more prairie grass that wasn't out there anymore. Well, I wasn't going to do it. But I said, "Oh, sure I'll go. I'll go if you'll come home with me. Mom'll be crazy with worry."

"When will you leave?"

"Oh, I don't know, soon."

"Tomorrow."

"I can't tomorrow. But soon, I promise if you'll come home."

"Go tomorrow if you can," Dad said. "Go tomorrow if you can, boy. You got a long way to go."

He let go of my arm and walked into the grass to get his lantern. The light wavered and dimmed and then got strong again as he lifted the lantern above the grass and turned up the wick. The light was growing in the sky, and the morning Kansas wind was rising. The grass lay bent over, combed out by the wind, and I shivered in the early morning coolness. I couldn't make a thing out of what had happened. I just had the feeling that something tremendous had happened to me, and I wanted to get home. And as far as going away was concerned, I would forget about that, because I was sure that he would forget it after he'd had a good rest, and we'd let him sleep in the morning. I would do all the chores myself, and maybe Mom would help some. But I wasn't going anyplace, no matter what. He was an old man and talked a lot, and needed to calm down, from what, I didn't know. I knew that he was excited and that he figured something had gone sour with his world, and that there wasn't any more wild prairie. That much I understood, but I was awfully tired.

He took hold of my arm as we started across the plowed field. "You got an awful lot to do to get ready to go," he said.

LEAVETAKING

I REALIZE NOW WHAT I ALSO KNEW THEN—THAT I HAD to leave my Kansas home. Still, I tried every which way to get out of leaving, but I was blocked by Dad every time.

Soon, I also came to understand how the idea of a Stranger that one meets by chance, coincidence, or predestination became more and more a part of the search I was making. And so began one of the great landmarks that ever happened to me. That's the way it almost always goes. You get, for the first time, a feeling that you have an indication of your own span of time, and that all along it are things that happen . . . things that influence you for the whole rest of your existence. That's the way it was with me when I left home that time. The world opened up.

I guess I didn't exactly find Dad's vision: a great, vast sense of the nation in development, always on the edge of an ever-changing frontier;

of tall, waving grasses, where a man could carve out his own life, but I found something.

It seemed as though in one summer I covered the whole world. I thought my Dad, and the way he arranged for me to go, was unconventional, too, but I did make a great attempt to find what Dad sent me to discover. I went west and north, survived many new adventures, became terribly conscious of the Depression and the turmoil and movement of humanity in those days. I had no sense that my odyssey was going to lead to anything, and that I would meet persons who would make all the difference. But the way I left home in Kansas was something I dwelt on for years and years, and, in a curious backwards and forwards in time, had made my later experiences possible.

Maybe you have had thoughts about going away from home the first time on your own, and you get to thinking that you might not ever come back again, or that you might not ever come back again in the same way when you left. A lot of people have had those thoughts, and I sure had them the night before I left. I really loved our part of Kansas. I guess I didn't feel deeply about it like Dad did, but I had wandered all over and knew every fence corner, almost, in our whole part of the country. Our river, the Neosho, would sometimes be very shallow and muddy, with little rills here and there and a few deep holes that were fine for swimming; but it wasn't a big, always-flowing river. In drought times the catfish came up to the surface in the holes and gasped for oxygen, and sometimes we went over and scooped out some fish and put them into tubs of clear water to wash the mud out. They always tasted kind of muddy, even so.

But in flood times the river really got savage and spread out over all the flatlands, and looked like one big lake from our upper windows. That was the way the country was; we had too much water, or we didn't have enough. And the people always seemed like that too. They were really happy when things were going well, and there was a good corn year, and the price for pigs was good. But in the 1930s, prices were just terrible, and folks were sad. And when there would be a flood they'd watch the waters rise and cover the bottom-land cornfields and they wouldn't say much, just stand and watch. The smells, the feelings, about everything I knew, were right there at home. Well, I went to sleep the night before I left home, thinking about things like that, and I really felt homesick and nervous.

Mom came into my room about half-past four in the morning. I was lying with my head away from the door and didn't hear her come in. She must have stood for a while at the head of the bed, not saying anything, and I must have sensed her there or something because I woke up and turned over.

It was going to be hard, leaving Mom. She and I had always been close. She didn't want me to go either; yet someway I suppose she knew I had to go. I sure didn't want my parting from Mom to be too abrupt or matter-of-fact. I felt deeply about her and she did about me, too. Only we just weren't all that demonstrative. Coming and going had to pretend to seem ordinary and matter-of-fact.

"You better get up. Dad's got the car ready to go."

"Up awful early."

"I put some underwear and clean overalls and a blue shirt in the old alligator valise. It's not too big to carry. I put some sandwiches in too."

"Thanks, Mom."

"You'll let us hear from you, I reckon."

"Sure."

"Well, I put some postcards in the valise too. Let me know where you are."

"All right."

"I still don't understand what's going on. More of your father's impractical nonsense. We'll have to hire somebody to help with the corn. Maybe we ought to just give the farm up."

"I won't be gone so long."

"I hope not. But not to know where you're going or anything. It's crazy."

"Don't worry. I'm big enough to take care of myself. Dad wants me to find a great thing. A stranger or the wild prairie or something."

"Sometimes your Dad's a stranger to me!" she said.

I got up and put on the clean overalls she had laid out for me the night before. Mom had baked pancakes and fixed sausage, and when I went down to the kitchen Dad was sitting at the table, finishing up. He was real cheerful, said good morning and asked how I felt, and I said I was feeling kind of sleepy but otherwise okay. Dad got up from the table and took my valise and started for the door.

"I'll put this in the car. Better hurry along. The boys probably won't wait, and we got to be in town pretty soon."

The "boys" were a couple of local characters named Zill and Harry. There was always local talk about their doings.

Mom kind of turned away. "Those awful fellows. Does he have to ride with them?"

"It'll be fine," came the response from the door. Mom said something that sounded like "huh!" and didn't say anything more.

"I'll be coming right away."

"I'll turn the cows into the barnlot while you're finishing. Got hay down for them so they're all ready to come into the barn. We'll do the chores when I get back."

There wasn't much more for Mom and me to say. I got up from the table and she said, "Well, son, we'll be thinking about you. You'll be fine. You've got good blood in you. I guess you got to go sometime, somewhere."

"I'm going to miss being home," I said, and there was a strange feeling across my stomach, an excited feeling that I'd never had before. It was like something great or big was going to happen, and I didn't know what it was and could hardly wait for it to happen. I gave her a hug and went out into the yard. Dad had come back from the barnyard and was standing beside the car, an Overland touring model that we had had ever since Dad got rid of our old Overland a few years before. This Overland wasn't much of a car, and it was getting pretty old now too, but it ran okay. I walked to the door on the driver's side because I wanted to drive into town for the last time, and we didn't much like to have Dad drive anyway. He was an okay driver but getting unsure of himself every now and then, or maybe he just got to thinking about how things used to be and forgot where he was.

"You feeling excited?" Dad asked. "I sure remember how excited I felt the morning I left Illinois more'n fifty years ago, boy. There's nothing like going away, first time."

I got in to drive and he got in beside me. Mom came over to my side of the car just before I started the engine, and slipped some money into my hand. She really didn't want Dad to see her do it, and he hadn't said a thing to me about any money. Maybe he knew she would give me some. I didn't know how much she'd given me, but I couldn't see how it could be very much. She just didn't have it to give. She leaned into the car and gave me a kiss on the cheek, and I sort of gave her one back. It wasn't that I didn't want to give her a lot more affectionate goodbye. It was just that our family didn't do it, or couldn't do it. We just took it for granted that we felt deeply about each other.

"Well, here we go," Dad shouted. I rammed the car into reverse and backed around the kind of circular drive we had. There was a silver maple tree growing right in the middle of the place where the drive circled in front of the house; I missed the tree all right and shifted into first gear as we started grinding out toward the road. I waved back to Mom and she waved at me, and that was the last I saw of her, because we struck the road then and turned north toward Iola and the courthouse square where we were supposed to meet Zill and Harry.

It never occurred to me to wonder why Mom hadn't come to town with us, but it wouldn't have seemed right if she had, because it was Dad's operation all the way, and she knew it. She wouldn't break in on it for anything. One there was no doubt about, though, she didn't care for Zill and Harry. She considered them outlaws and criminals.

There was a thing I felt about my mother, quite different from Dad. It was connected with blue blossoms rooted in small memories so far back I could hardly draw them out of the murk. When I was a little kid there were blue flowers growing along the Santa Fe railroad track back of our house, and Mom had often taken me for walks along the track in the summer. The sun melted the tars on the cross ties and the rails shimmering off the great summer heat; the flowers, creeping almost to the tracks themselves, swayed faintly and hung down a bit in the shimmer. When I broke one off, reaching and pulling, a whitish stickiness came out of the broken stem and when Mom took my hand again the milk welded my hand into hers. The blue flowers clutched at my legs when Mom and I crossed the right-of-way, climbed through a fence strung with taut, barbed wires, and went into the woods. And as we walked Mom said something about the flowers that sounded like a poem—she said, "The blue, the blue, the wild blue," and a peaceful sense, a tiny, remembered sense of the blue came over me, and when I sought her in pain or trouble the blue feeling of the railroad flowers moving so breathlessly in the waves of summer heat was always there. I went into the remembered sensation of the blue flowers with a security of unspoken peace. I took that with me as the Overland rumbled its way to Iola and the courthouse square.

From our farmhouse in eastern Kansas it was about three miles into Iola, the County Seat, and the road was all country. Off the road, on both sides, were hundreds of places where I had rambled so many, many times. For instance, back up Elm Creek about a mile was a cave in the limestone ledge where old John Brown was supposed to have hidden out in the days just before the Civil War, and sometimes a gang of kids from town played John Brown and the Missourians, because the ruffians from Missouri were after him for killing some of their folks; and there was another place still further up the hill from the cave where Jesse James was supposed to have had a hideout.

One thing I knew I would sure miss, though, were the wild roses which were just beginning to bloom. There absolutely isn't any flower that I have ever seen that I like as much as wild roses. I guess I got my liking for flowers from Mom, because she always told me how her father had made the very first flowerbed in their part of eastern Kansas (Bourbon County), because he thought the neighbors ought to be able to see some beautiful flowers, set out like they did it in the East.

Along the way, Dad and I didn't say anything to each other; though I could tell that he was about bursting to talk. I didn't want him telling me what to do and how to act. Now that I was going, I wanted to do it the way I saw it. And I guess he understood how I felt, because he kept still. The road winded up to the top of a little hill, and we could see the clock steeple of the Allen County courthouse. A shaft of early sunlight was striking it, and it looked awfully big and impressive, rising up in the middle of a collection of low buildings and small houses. The courthouse had always seemed to me like the biggest building in the world, and once when Dad and I climbed up to the windows where the clock was, I felt as if I could look out over the whole country. In fact, it seemed like I was looking at the whole world.

The courthouse was a red brick building, square, with a tall steeple and big clock. All around the courthouse square was four-inch pipe railing. In older days, quite a while before I was born, they had struck a big field of natural gas all around Iola, and there was a kind of boomtime which Dad told us how as a young lawyer he helped to start. They eventually piped the gas into this railing around the park, boring holes every six feet or so. Every night, all night long, the lighted gas flared from the holes. Dad said it was a symbol of the vast wealth of the earth which Allen County folks figured would last forever. They wanted people everywhere to know how rich Allen County was, and how they were going to stay that way; but when the gas suddenly petered out the railing became just a hitching place for horses.

As we rolled up to the courthouse square the big clock began to strike six. I tooled the Overland around the south side of the square, and noticed there wasn't a single person in sight. The birds were beginning to sing in the great old elms planted in the park, and that was the only sound. We came around the east side and saw a Model T Ford coupe parked near the old horse water trough. Though not many horses drank there these days, the trough was kept full of water. The town board wanted to remove the trough, but the folks in Iola still felt sentimental about the old days and wouldn't let them.

The Model T was an old one, about a '23 or '24 model I thought, and it was as dirty as it could have been. There was even chicken manure on the hood and top, because Zill had probably parked it under a tree where the chickens roosted by his shack. The body of those old model T's was very high, as if they had sat a high box on a little raft and then had put on a low turtle in the back and a small, low hood in the front. One of the windows on the driver's side was busted, too.

Zill and Harry were waiting on a bench beside the water trough. They looked about like the car, sort of unwashed and partly hooked-up. Zill, the biggest, had only one suspender of his overalls hooked, and Harry looked bashed-up some with a scar over his right eye. They were clean enough, I guess, but just sort of casual. They wore straw hats, the working kind, with big brims. The first thing that Zill said was, "Hey, kid, where's your hat at?"

I never knew how to take Zill. He had a reputation for being mean. I'd seen him hanging around town a lot, and everybody knew he was a bootlegger, but there were plenty of them then on the square on a Saturday. He was smiling now in a funny, snotty way, as he and Harry got up and came over to our car.

"I ain't met this kid," Harry said. He stuck his hand into the Overland and we shook. "He's a right big guy, ain't he?"

"Going to jam us up in the Ford," Zill said. "Well, hell, we been cramped up before. Well, get your stuff, kid. We got to be moving." I got out and removed my valise from the Overland's backseat. Dad moved over into the driver's seat. So far he hadn't said anything. But now he did.

"Where you headed, Zill?"

"Damned if I know, Sam."

"Well," Dad said, "this boy is a hard worker. But he don't know a damned thing."

I got hot in the face and wanted to answer Dad back and to tell him that I knew a hell of a lot more than he thought I did, but I didn't say anything because it would have been embarrassing. Anyhow, I didn't know what it was he thought I didn't know anything about. I knew our farm about as well as he did, and could do about everything he could do, and some things, like taking care of machinery, I did a lot better than he did.

"Bob don't know a damn thing about being alone," Dad said.

"Well I be dang," Harry said.

"You don't know a damn thing, kid," Zill said. I just didn't like the way he said it, like he was trying to imitate or mock Dad, but I didn't reply to him. I did begin to get mad, though, down inside.

"We'll try to teach him something about that, Sam," Zill said.

"You teach him what to do when he's alone. Nobody to help him," Dad said.

"Sure. We'll do that. We'll teach him a lot of tricks."

Zill sure knew tricks. The year before, when he was about to get arrested for bootlegging, the sheriff came to his place to find the still he was using. Only that same night Zill hauled the still into town and put it on the front lawn of the judge's house, so they never did get the evidence on him. Anyway, what Zill did caused the judge to take a lot of joshing, and everybody knew Zill was the one who left the still, but they were never able to catch him. Dad seemed to think it was quite humorous.

"The kid know anything about gals," Harry said.

"I don't suppose so," Dad said. "But it's probably time he learned something." He took his hand out of his pocket and held out a bill to Zill. "Here's ten dollars. When you figure you're run out about that much, kick Bob out. I want him to know what it is to be on his own."

"Ten bucks, ten miles," Harry said.

"Here's two bucks for you boy," Dad said, and shoved the bills into my hand. "That's a dollar more than I had when I started out. A dollar was hard for my mother to get then, and it isn't much easier today. Damn, I wish I was going with you."

Dad opened the car door and got out and stood there with the car door open, and by the look that was coming on his face I knew that he was about to say something that'd sound pretty strange to Zill and Harry. To me he seemed like he was in the grass a couple of nights before, but to strangers Dad would probably sound kinda crazy. I shifted around and started for the Ford's door, but Dad had started to talk and it was too late.

"I want to go myself. Look at me, boys. I came to the tall grass and went into it. In those days you could grab a big armful around you. It was that tall. Ride a horse into it you couldn't hardly see the horse at all. And then we tore it open, boys. We tore it open for the heavens to wet down our corn. And we raised some crops, I tell you. And you should have seen the prairies when I come here. You never seen anything like the prairie flowers. Prairie violets, alumroot, them shooting stars, and that tall blue indigo, and the roses, the little wild ones, they were everywhere. Oh it was a sight. And it was mine. I came into it and made it mine, boys."

I looked at Zill and Harry to see how they were taking Dad and what he was saying, and they were sure paying close attention, I will say that. Zill had his mouth about half open, and Harry's eyes were wide and big. I guess they'd never in their life heard anybody talking about how pretty wild flowers were, at least not right out loud. Folks in our part of Kansas didn't say much about pretty things, and one farmer we all knew, who lived away south of us in the river bottoms, had his wife put in the insane asylum at Osawatomie because she tried to write some poems. That's the way it was, mostly. Women folks were supposed to do whatever fixing up there was done, but the men didn't mess into that kind of thing—flowers and all that. It wasn't supposed to be manly. Dad was that way, too, I mean, the men were supposed to have all the big ideas, and do all the adventuring. Dad wondered why Mom didn't sew more, and do women stuff, but he sure didn't object to her coming out to the barn to help with the milking. But whatever he thought he sure loved to rant away about the way things looked . . . always through his eyes, of course.

"You own all this country once?" Zill asked Dad, mocking.

"No, I didn't have to own it. It was mine because I understood what kind of country it was. And I got my plow into it. That was when I made it belong to me." Zill tried to act kind of unconcerned, but he was interested, I could see that. He kept looking at Dad, and the two guys edged over toward the Ford, and Zill said he guessed we'd better be going. The far-away look disappeared from Dad's eyes, and he came and actually shook my hand.

"There ain't much left for you here, boy. Better you go, and I'll be here when you come back home. Guess you'll know where to look for me. And find the Stranger for me, boy!" And when he said "Stranger" he gave me a special look, as if he and I had a secret.

I knew where Dad would be all right, and that was where I sure would look when I came home. Just then I could still feel the tall grass out there in the prairie when I went looking for him, and the sound of the wind combing through it. I knew, though, I wouldn't find any Stranger, whoever that was. And probably no grass, either.

"You set in the center, kid," Harry said. "If you was to see a gal along the road you might jump right out the winder. Then you wouldn't likely see Bob again," he said to Dad. "This kid will give the women hell."

I edged in, sliding over on the torn seat.

"You come looking for me," Dad said to me, "I'll be here waitin' for your voice."

Well, you know how it is. Sometimes you get a kind of flash all at once, and I got one right then. I knew Dad cared a lot about me. He looked like he was going to cry. As I got settled in the car and turned away, Dad just stood there with his hand on the Overland's door. Anyway, that was all we said to each other.

Zill had taken my valise and put it into the turtle at the Ford's back. I heard the turtle door slam down, and Zill came around and cranked the Ford, yelling at me to pull on the wire that goosed her, and she caught, finally. Zill got under the Ford's wheel while Harry squeezed in beside me. It was a tight fit, too. I took up quite a bit of the seat and Zill was about as big as I was. Harry was smaller, and we had him smashed into the side. It was a good thing the weather was warm and the windows could be wide open, because we would never had made it in that Ford coupe. Harry groaned and swore and Zill and I squirmed around until we got fairly comfortable.

Zill pressed down on the reverse foot pedal and the old coupe rolled slowly backwards, popping and snorting a cloud of blue smoke. I didn't really think we would make it to the corner of the square, but the Ford took ahold in a moment and we were off. I twisted around a little so I could get a last look at the square, and maybe of Dad. I saw him standing there, still with his hand on the Overland door, and he never waved or anything, but I didn't expect him to. That wasn't the way he did things. I had a kind of funny feeling leaving Iola, and the square, and I thought of the many times I'd walked around on a Saturday night when almost everybody was in town. There was usually a band concert on Saturday night, but I didn't hear the music much. The old folks had their cars parked up close to the railing, and when the band finished a number they would honk their horns. The young ones, though, walked around, looking for girls or boys who might make a date or go for a ride if there was a car. I had our Overland sometimes, and I occasionally hauled a load of kids around the square, yelling and honking. I looked back one more time, and I saw that Dad had come out into the middle of the street and was gazing after us. I pretty near made Zill stop so I could get out of the Ford car and go back. Seeing Dad standing there affected me that much.

ROLLING OUT

RAMPED INTO THE OLD FORD COUPE, ZILL, HARRY AND I crossed the Neosho River bridge on that Kansas June 1930's morning and headed west, the old car bumping and rocking on the gravel road. Along the way there weren't any sizable towns to speak of, in fact no towns of any kind except a "crossroads" which Dad said had at one time been a lot larger. Nearby was a hill that we thought was awfully high and hard to get up, especially since the Ford almost didn't make the Picqua Hill. Zill and Harry kept whooping and hollering for the Ford to stay with it and she did, coughing and sputtering and blowing blue smoke up to the top. It was about the only hill anywhere around and beyond the hill the land flattened out and ran for a long ways, with nothing more than a few little ripples here and there. Once the prairie grass had grown tall out there, but it was plow broken now. I wondered what it would have been

like to have been rolling out in a covered wagon. Mom had actually ridden into Kansas from Missouri in a covered wagon, and she used to tell us how it felt, but I never had given it much thought. Probably a lot more comfortable than a Model T Ford coupe on a hot morning in June, crowded, and on a rough gravel road.

"You got some hard muscles kid," Harry said, and his fingers probed around on my upper arm. I suppose I made my biceps hard, too, maybe to show Harry that I did have hard muscles and that he'd better be careful. But he said, "Got a arm like a horse's leg. Ain't this kid got hard muscles, Zill?"

We were pounding along pretty good now having thumped through Yates Center. It wasn't a very big place, but it was a county seat, and I had never been over there before. That's how close we stayed at home in those Kansas days. Harry still had hold of my arm and I squirmed around, hoping that he'd let go. But he didn't.

"Ever done any wrestling, kid?" Zill asked.

"Just played around with it at home. Nothing much."

"Any kid of Old Sam's should be a good wrestler," Zill said. "Ol' Sam usta own all this country once."

I didn't answer for a moment. I knew they were kidding me, but even so I hadn't ever heard anybody say anything mocking about Dad. It really shocked me.

"What do you mean?"

"Mean about what, kid?"

"What you said about Dad."

"About ownin' all this country? Why he was braggin' himself about how he come out here."

I made a violent move. I was really upset. They were just poking fun at me to get my goat. I'd been kidded plenty of times before and it didn't bother me. But I guess I was sensitive about Dad and his way of talking.

Harry eased up on my arm. It was real hot, and I was sweating. I had never felt so uncomfortable. I wanted to get out of their car, but I didn't see how I could manage it.

"Ol' Sam never told you nothin' about his gal friends, either, I bet," Harry said.

"Dad didn't have any girl friends," I said.

"Hell, everybody does, kid. An' they'll get you into trouble. I was shot in the rear over a old gal I knowed down by Coffeyville. Usta hear it said that birdshot didn't hurt none when it went into you. Heard it was goin' too fast to hurt. That's a lie, buddy."

"Ever been shot, kid?" asked Zill.

"Nope."

"Well, you got a lot of time."

"Birdshot hurts aplenty when it goes into your rear," Harry said.

Harry slewed around and got hold of my arm again. I decided that maybe he felt more comfortable when he was talking, if he had hold of something. I let him go on holding my arm.

Suddenly, Harry let out a loud whoop and grabbed me hard. I pretty near broke my head on the car roof. I guess I hollered and slammed over against Zill and he almost lost control of the Ford. It ran off the road and into some weeds in the ditch. But the ditch wasn't deep and Zill swung the car back, skidding across the gravel. I was scared and didn't know whether to laugh or be mad. I didn't know why they wanted to tease me like they were doing, and nobody had ever grabbed me sudden like that before. Never.

I got hold of Harry's hand while the car was skidding around. Zill swore and hollered for us to set still, and the Ford straightened out for a moment, then she started sidewise again and corkscrewed down the gravel. Zill yelled and tried to get his foot onto the brake pedal, but my feet were in the way. The old car was gaining speed because Zill had forgotten to shove the hand gas-feed up. In all the excitement I near broke Harry's hand. He yelled real loud when I twisted it back. I was so upset I didn't know what I was doing, really. It all happened very fast. I've never been one to make really fast adjustments. I was a strong, country boy in those days, and I must have really put the pressure on Harry because he yelled in misery. Zill finally got his foot onto the brake and coughed the Ford down to a stop right in the middle of the road. I held onto Harry's hand. I wasn't going to let him grab me again.

"Zill," Harry yelled, "Help! He's bustin' my hand!"

Heavy dust and blue exhaust smoke caught up to us and came in through the windows. I could feel the sweat run down my armpits and down along my sides. We were really packed in there, I tell you, and I wouldn't let go of Harry's hand. It was about the only security I had. As long as I had hold of Harry, he wasn't going to do anything, but I sure couldn't see how it was all going to end. I was getting scared, and I wondered whether I had made a mistake by not going ahead and taking it all in good humor. But I knew that I had gone too far now.

"I'll twist Harry's hand clear off if he doesn't let me alone."

"Zill, make the kid let me go. He's made a figger eight outten my wrist."

"Now hold on a minute," Zill said, grinning. "Bob has got somethin' special comin'. Old Sam told us we got to teach him some things."

He sprung open the door and it squealed a little on rusty hinges. That coupe had a ruffled old pocket stitched onto the side of the door and Zill reached in there and took out a pint of stuff I guess was moonshine liquor. He pulled the cork with his teeth, took a long, long pull and breathed out hard. He stood looking into the car, grinning, and I hadn't realized until then how big he was, and I hadn't noticed his heavy beard. He hadn't shaved for three or four days. I hadn't noticed that at all before.

He reached in under my feet and pulled out a tire iron, the busted piece of spring that was used so much in those old days to change tires. After you got the wheel jacked up you had to get one of those irons in under the tire and pry it off the rim. I watched Zill spit and heft the iron and I knew what was coming. I really bore down on Harry's arm and he hollered fit to bust. Then Zill rapped me pretty hard across the toes with the tire iron.

"Get out, Bob." He looked really cheerful, but he hit me hard, anyhow.

My foot hurt and I was gasping with pain. I didn't know how or what to reply to Zill. He was standing there in the road holding the tire iron, and I didn't know what he would do. I sure didn't want to get hit across the head with it; things had gone a lot further than just teasing.

"I won't."

"Yes you are, too. Get outta there. You and me are goin' to have a little scuffle."

"I don't want to fight."

"Get out or I'll break your leg, Bobby."

I could see that he would really do it. He had a funny look on his face. Everybody knew he enjoyed hitting people. I slowly let go of Harry, who began to fumble for the door latch. I slid under the steering wheel since I knew I had to get out. I thought probably Zill would start hitting me with the tire iron as I was getting out, and I wondered how I could do it fast enough. I stuck my feet out first but Zill didn't do anything, so I came all the way out of the car and stood there on the running board, quite a bit above him, because the running board on those old Fords was pretty high.

The weeds in the ditch were quiet in the heat. The sun was beating down, and the whole scene, the Ford in the middle of the road, Zill standing there grinning and feeling the tire iron, and me standing up high on the running board; the whole thing was laughable almost, though nobody laughed, and Harry kept groaning on about his twisted wrist. He would mutter a few swear words then give out a loud groan. He was really overdoing it, because I was sure I hadn't hurt him.

I asked Zill, "What you want me to do?"

"Get on offa there, Bob. You'n me are goin' wrestle. I ain't had a good wrestle-match for a long spell."

"You give ol' Bob a good lesson, Zill," Harry hollered. "You give it to 'im good. He needs a good hurting. You do it to him for me and for his ol' man."

I had never thought about Dad giving me that kind of a lesson. He had never laid a finger on me. Ever. But he had abandoned me to Zill and Harry. Maybe he did want it their way. Or maybe it just got out of hand.

"We can't wrestle in the middle of the road."

"Why not?"

"A car or something might come along."

"What do I care?"

Zill tossed the tire iron down in the gravel and put up his hands. The heat was wavering across the fields in front of me, the way it does in Kansas, and away down the road I could see some dust rising, another car, maybe. I had plenty of reason to be mad, but I wasn't mad, exactly. I just knew that I didn't want to have any trouble with Zill. He was making a sucking sound, sucking on his lips, just waiting for me to get down so he could bust me. I never thought twice then about what I was going to do. Something just took over, that was all. I jumped into the air and kicked out at Zill's face, and my right shoe popped him on the jaw. It must have been a lot harder than I had meant it to be, if I meant to hit him at all, because he fell over backwards, sprawled out on the gravel; and I was so shocked that I was right on top of him. His straw cady came off and I grabbed his hair and pulled him over onto his face. I got a hammerlock, or what it was around home we called a hammerlock, when you bend an opponent's arm up behind at the elbow and keep lifting until the other guy hollers. It wasn't a real legitimate wrestling hold, but I didn't have the time to think about that. I guess I pushed it up pretty hard because Zill hollered loud. He turned his head over and to my surprise spit out some blood. It was the first time I had ever drawn blood out of anybody. It didn't give me any pleasure. It was kind of terrible, actually, but I had to hold onto him. I knew that if he got up, if I let him go, he would come after me, and he just might kill me as he had several people in fights. Harry shuffled near us now, sort of circling around, and I guessed that in a minute I'd have two of them to fight. Maybe then I'd have to take off running across the country to get away from them.

"What'll I do, Zill," Harry yelled.

"Pick up a rock and whack him."

Harry couldn't find a rock. He must have been looking for one, but the road gravel pieces were too little. So he limped over to where the tire iron was and picked that up. He started towards me, and I put a lot of leverage on Zill's arm again. He hollered real loud and scrabbled around in the road trying to break my hold, but I held him desperately. I must have come pretty close to breaking his arm and I yelled at Harry, "If you come after me I'll bust his arm off!"

Harry stopped and Zill swore louder than ever. There we were in a nice little standoff. Harry could have busted me with the tire iron and maybe I wouldn't have had time to really break Zill's arm, but Harry wasn't too bright and probably never thought of doing that. He just stood there, and I kept on straddling Zill and holding his arm. None of us heard the old Buick touring car, loaded with sacks of bran, coming up on us from the east side. The car stopped behind the Ford and an old Kansas farmer got out and came up and stood alongside me and Zill. He just stood there for a little while chewing tobacco and looking down at us. Finally he spit out some juice.

"What in Hades is going on?"

"This kid's busting Zill's arm," Harry yelled, hopping around.

"What you want to bust his arm for?" the farmer asked.

"They jumped me in the car. It wasn't my fault."

"He busted my hand," Harry said.

"Yeah. And what were you doing to me? I should have killed you."

"We was giving you some lessons. Like your ol' man said."

"He never meant that way."

Harry limped around behind me, and I put some more pressure on Zill's arm. I was even afraid that I would bust it, and I suppose Zill thought so too, because he hollered and cussed and flopped around in the road. But I had helped Dad and others handle big hogs many times, holding them down, or helping load them into a dealer's truck to take to market. I knew something about holding onto a struggling animal, and that's what I was doing to Zill. I guess the little bit of wrestling I'd done helped, too.

Harry edged up closer to me, holding the tire iron, and I tried to look around at him, to watch what he was doing. When I turned around, Harry jumped back a piece. But he didn't stay there. Zill kept yelling for Harry to do something, and before I could let go of Zill and tackle Harry, he came up behind me again. Harry swung the iron at me and I dodged it. He hit Zill on the shoulder, instead of me. That caused more hollering, and it might have been funny, except we were all too busy to laugh, especially when Harry came up fast again and swung the iron at me. It hit me across the side of the head. I saw a lot of stars and shooting lights. I must have let go of Zill and fallen over in the road. That's the last I knew until I came to, and I was lying in the road. The old farmer was bending down over me.

ON MY OWN

I GOT UP, SITTING IN THE ROAD, FEELING MY HEAD, AND looked around for Zill and Harry.

"They've went," the farmer said. "They give you a bad whack. It ain't right to whack you that-away with a tire iron."

I looked for the Ford, not really understanding what he said; but the Ford was gone. I saw my valise sitting in the middle of the road.

"They've went all right," the farmer said. "You want me to take you where you can call for the sheriff to get after them?"

"No, No." I got up feeling kind of dizzy and walked over to my valise. I leaned down to pick it up and saw the ten dollar bill lying there in the road. I don't know why they ever left Dad's ten dollars. Maybe they thought he would come after them in the court or something, or maybe they thought they hadn't earned it. They had some reason for leaving it, but most likely it was just that they didn't want anything more to do with me or Dad.

Well, I wasn't going back home, that much was sure. I wouldn't go back there for anything and tell how my going away was such a joke. I was just going right on west, even if I did have a really sore head. The farmer said I could ride with him for a few miles he was going, and then I'd have to walk or hope somebody else would pick me up. He said that some guys were like Zill, just mean. He added that he had known some men who just had a mean streak in them, that was all. The guy asked me my name and said that he heard of Dad. I don't know whether he really had, or was just making talk. He let me out at a crossroads, and I walked on.

My valise wasn't heavy, and I was really enjoying being by myself, taking it easy, walking on the road which wasn't heavily traveled at all. After a while I came to a little grove by the side of the road, and I figured I'd rest a bit and give my throbbing head a break, too. There were three cottonwood trees on the bank of a slough, or a dried-up creek, and the grass on the bank was still kind of green. I went over there, sat down on the bank, and opened the valise. I was going to have one of the sandwiches Mom had packed for me. I opened the valise, a real old one made of alligator hide that Dad had owned for a long time with one end ripping out, and found that Mom had not only put in sandwiches, ham and a couple of beef ones, but had also included a little thermos bottle we had—it was full of lemonade. I enjoyed my lunch, and as I ate I never gave another thought to what had happened. Later on my head hurt worse, but it didn't bother me too much and the blood had dried anyhow. Plus, it still wasn't too late in the morning, giving me plenty of time to get a long ways west before night.

I still couldn't see any relationship between Dad and the tall prairie and what had happened to me so far. That's what he had seemed most interested in. But as I sat in the shade of the cottonwoods I tried to recall exactly what Dad had said.

One Sunday, when we were sitting and talking, Dad said that the tall grasses were the symbol of all the fruit growing and of all heat and decay and death. That's the way he put it. When the grasses browned and withered in drought and became hay, their greenness went off with the hot summer wind. And the years of the seasons revolved, he said, and the years of great growing and strong crops overcame the years of drought. It was like hearing a Baptist preacher read a chapter from the Old Testament, almost, the way Dad spoke that day. And when he came to Kansas, Dad said he knew that the days of the tall grasses were almost over. He saw all the changes come to the prairie, and he said that as time went on a lot of the plants that had been on the fields when he came disappeared as the plows broke open the sod. Then the cattle came upon the land and when they did, and grazed upon the grass, the prairie flowers began to go. He said the prairie was a sea of violets and scarlet painted cup and something he called alumroot and wild lupine. The little prairie roses, he said, were across the whole prairie world in the spring; a great rug of roses in the spring and they came out five-petalled, pink, with a yellow center, and they were there amongst the trees, and in spring the dogtooth violets and the Easter lilies came in the shade, wooded, rocky places and on the sides of the little cliffs along the streams, the wild columbines grew amongst the little crannies. He said he walked out on the land and in the ravines and he thought he was in a paradise; now he said, there were a few of the old plants left, especially along the railroad track where the growing things weren't much disturbed. That's about the only place you could see the real prairie as it was, he said, except in that old burying ground on the river.

My head ached a lot, and there was a big bump now above my ear. Harry had hit me with the flat side of the tire iron. I guess I could have been hurt worse if he'd have hit me with the edge. I couldn't believe he'd wanted to hit me hard anyhow—if he had there would have been a larger cut, and I might have had to get stitches and all that. Funny thing, I wasn't really mad at Zill and Harry. I even though about laughing. It was as if they didn't care whether anything was right or wrong, as long as they wanted to do it.

I started out walking again, and after a while a young short guy in a Dodge sedan came along. He stopped, yelled at me real friendly, and invited me to ride along with him. He said he liked taller guys, and that he was on his way to a religious meeting at Estes Park, Colorado. He was a YMCA man, worked for the Kansas City, Missouri "Y" and was on his way out there to be part of a bunch who were working on a plan where there would be peace for everybody in every country. He said that it would be a Christian world one of these days, and then there wouldn't be any more trouble, and times would get better because everybody would love and care about everybody else. He asked me where I was headed, and I said I didn't know, but if it was all right with him I would just ride on for a ways.

As we rode over the straight gravel, with stones banging up and clacking on the Dodge's fenders, he told me that he figured bad trouble was abrewing. The World War that had ended in 1918 just wasn't anything compared to the hell that would someday be let loose on the world. It was foretold in the New Testament that fire would come out of the sky and lap up everything, he said, and all the wickedness of the world would be burned up. He figured that these hard times, with everybody out of work and all, were just the beginning to a time that would lead right up to the mouth of hell.

In fact, he said he knew a prophet in Kansas City who predicted how the USA would come mighty close to bein' done away with, burned up, scratched out. People would lose their morals, and there would be nude women in all the theaters, right on the movie screen, and on the streets, even. The prophet guy said the day was coming when people would do almost anything right out in the daylight, on the street, in the park, on the stage. He said that there would even be laws passed that would make it legal to have pornographic books in stores, and these laws would weaken the government until finally there would be a big explosion and then a great leader would come to save the country.

He added that he believed, personally, that this leader, the prophet the Kansas City fellow was talking about, was really Jesus Christ himself; but a guy he knew said no, that it was probably Alf Landon of Independence, Kansas who was coming on strong in the Republican party and who would get the country back on the right track if he would get elected president some day. Then he gabbed on about how there were forces in the world that were shaking things without folks knowing. "Influence," he yelled once. "Influence is what will get you there."

"Where?" I asked.

"Wherever you want to go. You got to be on the inside."

This YMCA guy talked all the time, seemed like. He didn't speak nearly as interesting as Dad, either. I just kind of half-listened to him. Anyway, the YMCA guy had it all fixed up good. He said there were just two kinds of folks, good folks and bad folks. He could tell by looking close at me that I was one of the good kind and that I had never done any wrong things. I asked him how he knew that, and he said that there was always a kind of special look to a guy who had been raised a Puritan. He could also tell by the way Puritans talked and shied away from subjects that weren't totally pure. He said that he hoped I would stop by the Kansas City, Missouri, YMCA some day, and if I did he would show me around and introduce me to guys who could maybe help me. He added that he knew a guy in Kansas City who was an expert on handwriting and could tell right off what a man was fitted to do and what his course in life was likely to be. That interested me because I thought the handwriting guy might tell me what Dad wanted me to be looking for. Well, I never thought I would ever actually see this YMCA guy in Kansas City, anyway.

We rode on and on. The YMCA guy said his name was Charlie Gribble. He talked most of the time, all of the time. I didn't feel like talking.

Through the hot, dusty June afternoon we rolled west. We passed a lot of guys out on the road, too, and they all seemed to be heading west. Some of them carried bundles or maybe an old suitcase, and the Y guy, Charlie, said that in Kansas City times were sure hard, and that there just wasn't any work for anybody.

There seemed to be an atmosphere about the Depression that plunged into the hearts of everybody. It was certainly like no other time America had experienced. There were wounds upon the land caused by the erratic seasons, by the strong winds, and by puzzling floods at certain times as well. The drought drained the moisture out of people as well as out of the land, and when the wetness returned it was in sudden spurts, far-spaced. I felt the spirit of the Depression as we drove, and would have liked to express it in words, but it was a spiritual thing, an unutterable misery of silence.

"Unless there is a change of president," Charlie warned, "there will, before long, be a revolution in the country." Folks were talking that way in Kansas City, at least. He hoped that there would be a peaceful change and that Franklin D. Roosevelt would be elected president. He thought the Democrats would have a better chance of cleaning house in Washington, and that some changes could be made to put guys back to work. Otherwise, every man in the whole country would become a hobo, just drifting around; graft would get worse and worse.

Even though he talked non-stop, Charlie also seemed real interested in me and my finding a job. I'd never had to find a job, really, and always had plenty to eat at home. I heard what Charlie was saying, but it didn't mean very much to me. I was a lot more interested in the kind of country we were going through. It wasn't like our eastern part of Kansas; it was a lot flatter and you could see a lot further. Mom had always said that Kansas was the prettiest state in the whole nation. She was always quoting a poem called "The Voice of the Prairie," which we all, Dad included, liked particularly well. He sometimes asked her to speak the poem at the dinner table, and when she came to the part about *"the voice of the prairie calling, calling to me,"* she would sometimes stop and tell how one of her relatives, Uncle Lloyd, and his family had gone out to western Kansas and got a homestead and built a house out of the prairie sod. Uncle Lloyd had later become a banker, but he always wanted, she said, to go back to western Kansas and live in that sod house. He told a minister once that if he had to make a choice of going to heaven or to western Kansas, he really didn't know how he would choose.

Well, the Kansas land was pretty flat; you could see the heat shimmer a long, long way, and the windmills, more and more of them, as we went on west, sticking up here and there on the flat lands. And there was a feeling about the whole country that I couldn't describe; it was widening out and opening up. There were still just about as many farms and houses; but a real difference from eastern Kansas was the way the land looked in browns and greens and then the sky taking over. I could sure see what Mom meant about Kansas, and I sensed that maybe the country did have a voice like her poem said. I suppose a lot of people would have said that Kansas was just hot and flat and would want to get across it as fast as they could. But if you're born and raised in Kansas, you sure got a different idea.

When we came to the outskirts of Wichita, we passed a crowd of people gathered in an open field. Once we saw they were crowded around an airplane, Charlie stopped and said we should go over and see what the excitement was about. My head had just about stopped hurting; the lump hadn't gone down, but I felt all right. We went across the field and into the crowd. A big guy was standing beside the little plane and was giving a lecture about how fast it would go, how it would roll and climb. Charlie asked who he was and somebody said he was a flyer from Kansas City named Art Goebel. We stood and listened to him for a little while before he finished talking. Then Art Goebel started up the plane's engine, got in, and the crowd hurried back out of the way. He gunned the motor, and the little ship traveled down the field only a hundred yards or so, and then seemed to spring right up into the air. It climbed very fast.

We all cheered, and people all around me were talking about how Wichita was going to come into its own pretty soon. They were going to make airplanes at Wichita, and everything there would be fine, if just Herbert Hoover would get re-elected. Charlie heard that remark and decided to stay and argue about it. He walked right up to an old man who was wearing overalls and a straw hat, and said, "Say, didn't you ever hear of Franklin D. Roosevelt?"

"I heard of Teddy," says the old man, "but who'n hell's Franklin?"

"Savior of America," Charlie says.

"Christ is the only Savior we recognize out here in Wichita," the old man says.

"Yes, Christ is the *big* Savior, but Franklin D. Roosevelt is the Savior of America."

"What's he done to prove it? Ain't the country in a hell of a fix?"

"And who put us there, friend. Herbert Hoover."

"It weren't Hoover. Was the Communists."

"The commies never had a thing to do with it. It was greed. Just plain greed. And our morals got rotten. That's what it was. Don't you know what happened to Sodom and Gomorrah? Do you know what it's like in Kansas City?"

"Hey, are you a preacher?"

"No, I'm not a preacher. But if I was one, I would tell all you people that you are going to hell. Roosevelt knows that. He'll take the country into a new day; the Democrats will do that."

"Ain't Roosevelt going to hell, too? Same as us?"

And so it went. Charlie really enjoyed the discussion. But the folks got tired of arguing after a while, and we set out going west. Not far outside Wichita we began to pass larger and larger wheat fields. The grain was mostly golden ripe, but here and there in the fields there were still some green spots. I could see the wind start at the far edges of a field and cross in strong, circular billows until the whole field would seem to be matted with bending stalks of wheat. I don't know what it was about the wheat and the wind, but I got a feeling as I watched; maybe it was the color, or the hot kind of dust-colored sky, or the way and land was opening out. I felt something, that was sure, like I wanted to go out into the fields and stand and take hold of the heads of the grain. Maybe it was like the grass of the prairie calling to Dad and Mom. It was all tangled up inside of me, all that feeling, and I still had a headache, too, and maybe that was part of the strange way the whole country looked to me. Anyway, Charlie never stopped talking.

"I believe in God, my friend. I believe in One Creator of Everything. How about you?"

"I guess I do."

"Chripes, you got to *know*, son. Hey, are you saved?"

"I dunno. I been baptized."

"You were? Tell me about it."

Well, I sure wasn't going to tell any stranger what happened in the church back home when they baptized me. I wasn't going to say a thing about it, but it sure ran through my memory. I had figured Dad was going to spare me from being baptized because he didn't hold much with going to church. But he never said a thing to stop Mom.

I remember that it was a cold Christmas Eve and the small church wasn't heated very well by the Round Oak stove that stood in a front corner. The baptistry was opened at the side of the pulpit. It was a covered tank set into the floor, about the size of a small, stock-watering trough. When they were going to baptize somebody they just took off the cover and then you could use the wooden steps leading down into it. Mom had laid out my new long underwear. "I want you to look clean, at least," she said "when you go down into the holy water."

"What will I wear?"

"This underwear, of course."

"Oh, no."

"Of course. Everybody does. When Mr. Benson up at the bank was baptized, he went down in his long underwear."

"In front of all the people?"

"Certainly."

"I don't want to."

"Now no more foolishness."

"I wish I wasn't being baptized."

"Hush."

But it happened. They brought me out of the Sunday school room, where I had undressed, into the full view of a couple of hundred folks who were in church for the Christmas Eve service, and the preacher motioned for me to enter the water. I went down the steps with the cold water creeping up higher and higher on my long underwear until it was above my waist. At least, I thought, they can't see much of me now. Then the preacher came down the steps in his best suit and I could see the large gold watch chain across his vest. I thought about how unfair it was that I had to go into the cold water, but I didn't think long because the preacher grabbed me by the shoulders and the head and pulled me over backwards. All I could think of then was that it was Jim Rayburn who had got me into it.

For Jim had come to our town and set up a large, wooden tabernacle in the courthouse park. And there, every night for a whole month, he preached and raved and told how he'd been a pro ballplayer and had seen a vision one day and become an evangelist. Always Jim's success was great and after each sermon people flocked, really ran, up front as the congregation sang the revival songs: "Throw out the Life Line" . . . "Just like a tree . . ." and they were converted.

Even then I wondered about that minute when they were converted, whether all the people really felt a great new change in their lives, or whether they walked up just because everybody else did. I wondered whether it was really possible for one moment in all of the time in a person's life to be so immensely important, so far outrunning the other countless moments a person knows, like when they walked out in early spring, for instance, and went into the woods, where they found, beneath the damp and quiet, last year's leaves, the first dogtooth violet blooming, or the first Dutchman's Britches growing in the shade, or later, the first of the yellow wild violets.

But Jim Rayburn's business was the conversion of souls and not the discovery of early wild flowers. So when, under Mom's pushing, I walked, hidden among a flock of converts, to the front of the tabernacle, I wished I wasn't there. But I was, and I imagined that I really thought I felt a mighty spiritual change when Jim put his arm around my shoulder, and said in a confidential voice, "Boy, so you want to be a Christian?"

"I reckon so," I said. And Jim passed me on as saved. This led to my being baptized on Christmas Eve and Mom was very happy; but as I left the tank, dripping water onto the carpet and shivering desperately, I remember I kept thinking: "How do I know? I don't know. I don't know anything about being a Christian."

But to Charlie I said, "Sure, I been baptized. Can't recall much about it."

"Well, you were probably too little to remember, I guess. But the important thing is you been saved. I see these Kansas City bums on the street all the time. They'll hit you up for a dime anytime. I always wonder where those guys would be now if they'd done things different. Had a faith. Been baptized. I keep a little Bible right here in my pocket all the time, so I'll never forget that I been saved. And I have to watch myself, too. All the time. It ain't easy when I face temptation, I'll tell you that. But I have made myself strong. You remember that, friend."

"Sure, I will."

It was getting dark when we came upon a small city. There was a sign that said: "Pratt, Kan. Pop. 3,000." Charlie said Pratt was one of the bigger towns in that part of Kansas, and I could sure tell that it was right in the middle of the wheat harvest. The fields came up to the edge of town. I suddenly made up my mind that I would get out. I didn't have a real reason, except that I was feeling miserable and hot and my head hurt. Charlie had been nice to me—we had stopped at a restaurant a piece back and he staked me to a sandwich and a glass of milk. I offered to pay him for the ride, but he said I could pay him by saying my prayers every night. I didn't tell him that I never had said any prayers, except in church, and I opened the Dodge's door and got out.

He was going to drive on through the night. I could have gone along with him; he asked me to, but I wanted to stay in the wheat. I felt, somehow, that I belonged there. He hollered goodbye and told me to be good and to come and see him in Kansas City where he had connections. I thought he looked kind of wise when he said "connections," but I didn't give that any thought. I was suddenly out there on the main street of Pratt, Kansas, and I didn't have any good idea where to go or what to do.

AN EVENING IN PRATT

PRATT, KANSAS WASN'T MUCH OF A CITY. IT WAS A LITTLE bigger than Iola, maybe, but nothing to write home about. A lot of the town's buildings needed painting and fixing up; the streets were wide and there were some cottonwood trees growing along the side streets and around a little park on one corner of the main street. There were a lot of cars, mostly Fords and Chevys parked along Main Street, and some of the stores were still open. A lot of the people on the street were men and boys, guys like myself, looking for a job in the wheat harvest. They were all dressed in work clothes, or in suit pants that'd seen better days. Most of the men wore hats, old felts or straw hats, some with the stiff brims and flat crowns same as those the city guys wore in Iola, but seedier looking. There were also a lot of people who looked like farmers, with very tanned faces, creased and furrowed. But all of them seemed real worried to me and there wasn't any laughter, the kind a crowd of men and boys would generate, standing around on street corners. The Depression was taking its toll all right.

I walked up and down Main Street, wondering what I should do and where I was going to spend the night. I didn't see how there would be enough sleeping room in the town for the crowd that was hanging around. I wondered where they'd all go when night really set in. I supposed they'd sleep out in the park, or maybe they had cars they'd crawl into. The large mess of men, and the uneasy feel of the town as dark came on, gave me a restless and uncomfortable feeling. I passed a line of guys squatting back against the front of a store which was still open. They were just squatting there, not saying much, and they looked ready and willing to go to work if anybody offered them a job. I got a feeling for hard times that I'd never before felt.

I guess I was too nervous and scared, possibly because all the troubles of the world seemed to me to be right there in Pratt, Kansas. The noise of the cars on Main Street, the call of a guy to somebody across the street, the desperate faces—it all added up to unhappiness and loneliness.

The crack across my head didn't bother me too much, but I wondered what would happen if I came across Zill and Harry in Pratt. They might be here, actually, because they were ahead of me when I was travelling in the Dodge. I really wasn't mad at them, I just didn't understand what was going on.

Counting the ten bucks that Zill had thrown down in the road, I still had fourteen dollars. Dad hadn't had but a dollar, he said, when he'd left Illinois, so I guess I should have felt rich. I went into a little counter place and had a bowl of soup and a piece of raspberry pie that only cost fifteen cents. I sat at the counter and had to hold my valise on my lap as there was a fellow squeezed on each side of me so close that I could hardly eat. I got out as soon as I could, and continued walking around. I passed two hotels. One was on the main street and was a very fancy-looking place, with a big lobby and nice chairs set out on a wide front porch. I could see men and women sitting in the lobby, looking as if they had the money to stay in such a fancy place. I didn't waste any time thinking about putting up there. What I really had in mind to do was go to the park and find a corner there to lie down.

But as I went down one of the side streets I came across a little hotel. It was sort of a square, old brick building, with no porch or anything, but flush to the sidewalk. There was a sign hanging in front of the place, faded-out mostly, "Corina Hotel" in mighty poor lettering. The evening wind was swinging the old sign a little bit, and it made small, rusty sounds.

The place didn't appeal to me. I could see inside and there were several men standing and sitting in the small lobby, not a dressed-up crowd like in the lobby of the bigger hotel. These guys looked really seedy, like harvest workers out of a job. I finally decided to go in and see what the place was like and what they wanted for a room. I was really bushed and desperate for a bed. The lobby was tighter and smaller than it looked, even from the outside. There was a counter at one side with a couple of bare, forty-watt bulbs hanging over it that let out a little flyspecked light. There was a bulb on the ceiling not much bigger with hundreds of flies buzzing around. The boys in the lobby weren't saying much, just sitting or talking low. The place smelled rancid, too, sour and moldy and sort of like urine. I was about ready to turn around and walk back to the street, thinking that I'd prefer the park or even a country road to what was there in the hotel. But then I saw this woman. She came out of a side door behind the desk and started to fuss around with some papers. I felt kind of silly, walking in there and standing around; some of the men were looking at me. So, I walked over to the counter and stood here while she fiddled with an old adding machine. She added up a few figures and pulled down the lever for the total. She never came right over to speak to me and acted like she didn't care anyhow.

She was a large woman with a bit of rouge and a sticky-looking green dress. I couldn't tell what kind of stuff the dress was made of, but it wasn't very clean. She had a short, fat neck and large shoulders and arms. There were little rivers of sweat running down her neck, out from under her black hair. In the yellow light the sweat glistened like rain on a dirty window. As I leaned against the counter I could smell her, too. She had a kind of worn and musty smell—perfume, maybe, and a lot of other things. Her odor was like a dog that gets wet and smells what my Mom used to say was a wet-dog smell. This woman's face, as far as I could see, never changed at all, as if she were wearing some kind of Halloween mask. And her lips never came quite together. I don't know how old she was. Maybe thirty, maybe older. She wasn't any high school girl. I knew that. I said, finally, "You got a place to sleep?"

"Maybe."

"You got a room?"

"What do you want it for?"

I had never thought much about such a question. Maybe I should have, but I didn't. I never thought much about anything. Her attitude made me kind of angry.

"A place to sleep."

"Ain't got no room. But I can let you sleep in the hall."

"Where?"

"Upstairs in the hall. Take it or leave it."

I didn't like her, and I sure thought she didn't like me. She was still sort of smiling. That never changed, but her mouth opened up a little wider.

"Give me a quarter. I'll let you use a blanket to sleep on."

I didn't want to sleep in any hall, but I felt the guys watching me and I didn't know what else to do. I gave her a quarter. She reached onto a shelf behind her and took off an old brown blanket. I didn't want the blanket either, but I took it.

"Upstairs," she said.

I went over to the stairway. It was pretty narrow and dark with a bulb hanging from the ceiling at the top. There was a little landing at the top of the stairs and then the hall turned and ran straight down the middle of the building. It wasn't wide enough to lie out straight across it; but there were guys lying up against the walls all the way down the hall. There was a little aisle down the center so you could get by without stepping on anybody. The air was very close. Stifling, in fact, and there was a smell of dirty feet and dried sweat. Back down the hall a kid cried as his father tried to dry him up. I figured the kid must have been pretty homesick.

"Shut up," the father said to the kid.

"I want to go back home."

"Now be still. Tomorrow we'll get us a job in the harvest. You'll feel better then. Some home-cooked grub will make you feel a lot better."

"No it won't."

"Where you from?" a guy lying next to the father asked.

"Kansas City. God damn, I stood all day last week out at the Armour packing plant. They only took on two guys all day. One was a Black guy."

"Well, they need them Negroes in the slaughter house."

"I'd even work there. It's that tough a time. Shut up, Walter. Go to sleep."

The kid sniffed and continued to cry. I really felt sick. I never had been much for mixing it close with a lot of guys, and I couldn't see any place to lie down either. I didn't want to touch anybody, and I didn't want anybody to touch me. I wanted to sleep outdoors, away from the odor and the feeling of fear and unhappiness. I turned around, went back down the stairs, walked to the counter, and shoved the blanket back to the woman.

"I won't sleep up there."

"What's the matter? Ain't it nice enough for you? A guy like you got to have a nice white little bed, huh?"

"Give me back my money."

"Nothing doing."

She stood there and laughed at me. I didn't know what to do. I should have turned around and walked out, but her laughing made me angry. I really wanted to reach across the counter and pull her over onto the floor, but it wasn't in me to do it.

"Give me my money. I'm not staying here."

"You ain't getting your quarter back, honey. But if you got some more money I might give you a place all to yourself."

"How much?"

"I got one nice room I been savin'. You can have it for a buck and a half. Give me a buck-twenty-five, I'll credit you with the quarter. How's that sound?"

I pulled out the ten dollar bill. I shouldn't have showed her I had a ten, but it was the first thing that came out of my pocket. She looked at the bill, as if she hadn't seen a ten all day. Maybe all week. Some of the guys standing nearby saw it too. She gave me change without saying anything. I put the money in my pocket.

"Number seven upstairs. The door ain't locked. Walk in and make like you was home, honey. And I just hope to God there ain't somebody already in that bed."

They were laughing at me, everyone within earshot and many of the fellows made remarks. I went fast up the stairs and found number seven back at the end of the hall, off by itself. I pushed the door open, and the smell was even closer and more raw than out in the hall. I found the light by leaving the door open and pulled down the broken chain. The wallpaper was dingy and full of dead flies. There were about a thousand more flies on the ceiling, and the old bed seemed to be suffering from a broken back. I put my valise on the floor and sat on the bed. Some roaches came out and scooted across the room.

I sat there for a long time, trying to make sense out of everything that had happened during that long, long day. All I could see was a whirling of land, of wheat, and of heat across the fields; of roads, straight and dusty. I was in the middle of a whirlpool. I hadn't ever seen a real big whirlpool, but I could imagine how the water would swirl around and around and suck at you and take you down. Sometimes there were little whirlpools in the Neosho river back home when it was in flood, and the brown water would start to go around, and if there were any little sticks or trash floating, they would turn around and around in the pool. It was like that there in the Corina Hotel. Colors, lots of them, dirty yellows, and browns and greens, and people too, wandering along, not going any place—they seemed to be caught up in the whirlpool. I couldn't get the spinning to stop. I guess it was partly the whack I had on the head or something. I took off my clothes, dumped them on the floor, and lay on the bed.

I knew I was awful tired. It had been a long, long day, the longest I could ever remember. I didn't like where I was, and I couldn't figure out why I was there. Last night I had been in my own bed at home, and it surprised me how fast things could change; whole habits of a lifetime altered so lightning fast. And now a foreign place, different, unfriendly. A dirty bed with dirty sheets. There was a special sour odor about the bed that was different from the smell of the room, sort of like a bed with a mattress that somebody has wet night after night. I hated it. I felt lonesome and sorry for myself. I finally fell asleep lying on my back because the lump on my head was on the right side, and I usually slept on my right side.

At first I thought I was having some kind of a nightmare: you're in a dream, fixed in there, and something heavy is holding you down. In the dream you are thinking about Dad, and he is telling about a nightmare he has over and over when a man without any face is sitting on his chest and he can't breathe. You don't have any strength to fight back. You want to fight and scream and get away, but you are being held right there.

I've had that same dream a number of times since, where you can't move or get loose or lift your arms or legs; but that first time it happened wasn't like the times since. I kept hearing far-off sounds and feeling the heat—that was the worst part of it, the heat that was burning me up. But it was the smell that woke me up, finally. I remembered instantly what the smell was, the musty room, and then I was able to move my arms. I still couldn't tell whether I was asleep or awake, but I could move. And I heard words, too, a guy saying, "Hold onto him. He's wakin' up."

Then hands grabbed me, and another hand was clamped hard over my mouth. I struggled, scared as could be, but they were strong, whoever they were. And they were silent too, I heard somebody say, real low, "You listen. You lay here and it'll be all right. If you yell or foller us we'll kill you, kid." At first I thought that the voice sounded like Zill, but then I knew it wasn't. "Come on," someone else said, and I heard them go out. I waited there on the bed for a long time. I was breathing fast, really scared. It struck me that I might have come close to being murdered. And one thing I was sure—I'd been robbed. I finally got up, felt for my pants, and eventually found them over at the other side of the room. Every cent I had was gone.

Trembling hard, I tried to wash up a little at the dirty basin that stood in the corner. Washing didn't seem to do much good; I couldn't get off the foul smell. But I quickly got dressed and out of there, passing several guys still lying asleep in the hall.

I guess it all had happened right before dawn, because the light was coming up as I went outside. I walked to the Pratt railroad station and hung around there until it got light, then I walked back over to the little park. My stomach felt queasy; I knew I better have something to eat. Although I had no money, there was still a sandwich left in the valise from the lunch Mom had fixed only yesterday. I ate the sandwich and felt better. An old guy who was up early, sitting on an adjacent park bench, told me that there was a Federal Government employment office up the street aways. He said I ought to go up there and ask for work. I thought maybe I would when it opened up. I plopped down on the grass and fell fast asleep.

INTO THE HARVEST

HE EMPLOYMENT OFFICES IN SMALL AMERICAN CITIES
and towns were sad places during the early Depres-
sion years. They could never stem the tide of un-
employment. I approached the office in Pratt with
great reluctance. I had never been inside a place like
that before, and as I walked toward it, I knew how
sheltered I had been.

The U.S.D.A. employment office at Pratt was very crowded when I
arrived. The office itself was inside a long, wooden building, and the
room too was long and narrow with a desk at one end and benches along
both sides. Today, the benches were filled with harvest workers looking
for a job. In fact, the desk was almost hidden by five or six guys hovering
around it, trying to find out, I guess, from the clerk or whomever, whether
there were going to be any jobs that day. I could barely see the fellow
behind the desk. He looked heavy, with several folds of skin hanging

down from his neck, gray-haired, and he wore a white shirt. He was sitting there with a cold cigar in his mouth, trying to answer questions.

The racket in the room was deafening until a young farmer came in and walked quickly toward the desk. He looked a lot fresher and cleaner than anybody in the room. The workers must have realized that the farmer was looking for help, because they all stopped talking. Even the guys at the desk turned around to look. The farmer, meanwhile, elbowed his way up to the desk, and I heard him say that he was looking for three good men. Immediately everyone in the room thought that he was a good man and could qualify. I know I did, even if I was beat; I still knew I was a good hard worker. I figured I didn't have a chance, though, with forty or more guys in the room all needing work, some worse than I did maybe. But I didn't have any money and didn't know how I was going to eat, so I too was desperate. The guy at the desk talked a while with the farmer, then yelled, "He wants two tractor drivers and a combine man."

Well, you never saw a flock of old hens fly, push and scramble onto a scattering of shelled corn, more'n those harvest workers did on the farmer. They were onto him all at once, and the whole crowd was yelling and whirling around, trying to get him to hire them. Pretty soon though, the farmer busted out of the mob with three guys. I never could see how he chose them. Then it again got quiet in the room. The harvesters returned to the benches, looking more hopeless than I felt myself.

I didn't see how anything could happen in that employment office that was going to be any good for me. But I hung around for a while, watching and listening, standing up against the wall, even though I wanted to lie down somewhere. My head hurt bad, and I drew my fingers across the lump, feeling the edges of the place which had hardened and crusted. I wondered what Dad would have done to find a job here in the harvest fields. He claimed he worked his way across from Illinois to Kansas, and I knew some of what he did, but I bet he never was in a room with forty or fifty guys all out of work and desperate. Maybe it was this kind of hard times that Dad wanted me to experience for him, but I didn't really believe that any more than I believed that he thought I'd learn much about the prairie grass in a dirty bed with some thugs holding me down and stealing my money.

About eleven o'clock a tall, old farmer-woman came in. There is something about a woman who does farm work that gives her away. She walks rather free and easy, but firm, as if she owned the world, and was used to driving mules, or working alongside men. I had seen some women back home who were like that. There was little interest among the men in the room when she came in, nothing like there had been when the young farmer had come. I guess nobody thought that a woman would come into the employment office looking for harvest hands. Most city guys believed women stayed around the house all the time, and most of the men in the room were probably from cities. I know that Dad felt that women weren't supposed to do hard stuff like men, but he sure was glad to have Mom help him with the milking and other chores. Supposedly all the public stuff that women were supposed to do, Dad said, was to defend folks' morals and maybe help lead the WCTU. He never was really sure that Kansas women ought to have the right to vote, and he and Mom sure had some hot arguments over that. He never did go to church, but he had read the Bible and he said that there were plenty of places in the Bible where God told how to treat women, making them your handmaids and all. He said he didn't hold with that himself, but it was there in the Bible and he wanted Mom to think it over, since she was such a good churchgoer. She got riled up every time.

Well, this lady entered the employment office anyhow. I thought I hadn't ever seen such a big woman. Everything about her was big. Maybe she wasn't quite as tall as I was, but she came pretty near it. She had long arms and big hands, as heavy as a man's, and the sleeves or her shirtwaist were rolled up. Her forearms were burnt dark brown. She was wearing bib overalls. Her face was large and wrinkled and her eyes were crinkly, as if she was going to laugh any time. Her gray hair hung down on both sides of her face and was put up in a knot at the back of her head, about like Mom wore hers. She carried an old felt hat that reminded me of Dad's.

Her mouth was clamped shut, a straight line right across her face. She seemed like a strong woman, and she'd had some hard times, you could see that. But there was something about her, sort of daring the world to be as big as she was. I just stood there and looked at her; maybe she saw me as she walked past.

The guy at the desk knew her. He glanced at her, looked down again at his papers, and says, "Howdy, Mrs. Settles. And what can we do for you?"

"Why," she said in a loud, man's voice, "Why, I want a man to help me in the harvest. I want a man who'll work and not cheat me. I want somebody who'll do the chores and do what he's told. You got somebody?"

"We got plenty of men who want to work, Mrs. Settles. You can just about take your pick."

"I got six milk cows. He's have to do the milking. My regular hand is on the tractor, and I'm sitting on the binder. I need a strong worker and a general worker, one who can shock grain."

Maybe there weren't any workers who knew how to milk, I'm not sure why, but whatever the case nobody came running. I didn't move either, and I don't know why I didn't. I knew how to milk, and I'd shocked plenty of grain, oats mostly, back home where they didn't use combines much. I didn't move and didn't say anything, mostly because I was too bashful to speak out in front of the others. She turned and looked over the guys in the room; her eyes went past me but when she got to the end of the benches on my side, she looked back again and motioned for me to come up to the desk. Maybe it was because I was taller, or maybe because I was younger. Anyway, she motioned and called to me to come up. "You, tall one. Come up here."

She was even larger up close. She stared at me a little while, then she said to the guy at the desk, "I want this one."

"You sure, Mrs. Settles? He's maybe too young."

"He's old enough."

"Yeah, but maybe you'd better take an older man."

"I want *him*."

The guy sighed. I thought it was because there were so many older men wanting work, but I guess he knew she would have her own way.

"All right. Whatever you say, Mrs. Settles. What's your name, son?"

"Bob Gard."

"You got a terrible bump on your head," Mrs. Settles said. "How'd you get that?"

"Had an accident."

"Have to put some salve on it."

"You ain't even asked if he can milk cows," the desk guy said.

"I knowed he could," Mrs. Settles said. "I knowed it right off. He's a farm boy."

"Let us know if he don't work out."

"I'll do my own knitting."

"He might not be any good."

"I suppose you'll tell all the world that old Mrs. Settles hired a kid, when she could of had an older man."

"Oh, no. It's your business, Mrs. Settles."

She strode out of there, and I had to hurry up to keep alongside her. I sure was elated about getting any kind of a job. Mrs. Settles was driving an old Ford truck, about a 1920 model, that seemed to be barely hanging together. The springs in the seat were coming out, and she had two or three old gunny sacks spread out to keep the springs down. She wouldn't let me crank up the motor. She said it kicked once in a while, and she better do it herself. It turned right over, and we headed out of Pratt through what I discovered to be some of the greatest wheat country in the world. The wheat went on and on, without any breaks; up and over the little rises, yellow, yellow in the hot sunlight, with the wind stirring the wheat a little, making it swell against the shimmer. As we got further out, we passed less traffic, until finally it seemed we were all alone in the middle of a yellow world. Maybe it was like that for Dad in the middle of the prairie. I felt as if I was feeling something akin to what he had, and I began to get excited. It was all different, so different from anything I had ever felt before. I had spent a lot of time on narrow roads through high corn, and I had always felt excited by the atmosphere of loneliness which I got from that. But this was like I was completely alone, although in the wheat it was a loneliness with a lot of color, and you could see above it, out over the whole land. It was as if me and the land were brought close together and yet the edges of the world had been knocked out, someway, so it all belonged to me because I could feel it so deep.

The old Ford chugged along, the gravel hitting up at the fenders in back. Mrs. Settles didn't drive very fast, so there was plenty of time for me to say something to her about the way the wheat made me feel, but I couldn't. I couldn't say anything, and then I didn't need to because she started in to talk. Maybe she knew I was thinking about the wheat fields, I don't know. Anyhow she started right in talking as if she knew.

"I've seen 'em go into it, during the early years of this century, those first big wheat combines, with platforms and a cutting sickle thirty feet or more long, and no tractor, no big steamer to pull it, 'cause they wasn't practical and couldn't travel fast enough to run the cutting bar. But the horses pulled the first ones. Twenty-five or thirty horses hooked together with lines on the lead team. What a sight! Oh, how I wished I could show you something like that. Everything's smaller now, and there's not much of a show to it. But back then! Fields two or three sections big, and the wheat so yellow and ripe. Here comes the great machines biting into it, and the horses laboring on the sides of the hills. Oh, the men took to harvest those days; how they worked! And the threshing crews! When they cut the wheat with binders and stacked it up and then threshed it out. Those crews would eat everything in sight, and some stuff that

wasn't in sight, too. This country ain't the same, and the men don't seem
to be the same. Too small! Too small-thinking. They think everything
has to be little and niggling. You believe in God?"

She sprang the question on me so fast I didn't know how to answer
it.

"I guess."

"Well there is a lot of hollering about God around here, and how
He's got everything set up good for a lot of these folks. But I never pay
much attention myself. I got plenty to look at and plenty to think about,
and I do things for myself. I've seen so terrible much. . . . I saw it all
happen, me and my husband. You look somethin' like him, when he was
young. I guess that's why I picked you out. He was tall like you. But
we seen it all. Them early reapers, and binders. We seen them cut it with
the headers that just lopped off the tops of the wheat, loaded her up for
stacking and the threshers. And we saw the first combines come after
those horsedrawn ones, big outfits, big as a railroad engine. And the
threshers! That was the big thing here. Nicholson-Shepard engine with
wheels near as tall as you, and a Red River separator; down the roads
they come, you could see 'em comin' a mile away, black smoke belchin'
out of the tall smoke stack. And how they could get things up for the
threshin'! Dug in the wheels of the engine and the separator so they
couldn't move and spread out the belt. Such a belt you never seen! Eight-
twelve inches wide and thick, and over the flywheel and onto the pulleys!
How the wheels and gears did move when they set her going! And the
men and wagons and the dust and heat. You never seen anything like a
big threshin' rig in action! Excitin'! And the women in the kitchen making
grub for those hungry threshers, meat they had to get that day from
town, from a store that had a big icebox, because you couldn't keep big
hunks of meat like that at home, not for more'n a day. And potatoes
and gravy, a barrelful of it; and any vegetables you could get, and biscuits
by the wagonload, hot, right out of the oven; and jam and preserves, and

butter, and pies until hell would of run over with 'em. Always a lot of mulberry pies because them berries was plentiful. You hungry, Bob?"

"I sure am." How could I help being starved with her talking like that?

"You look it. When we get home I'll feed you. I ain't much of a cook but there's plenty of it! But I tell you they do it smaller now. Little combines and tractors. But I do what I can to keep the romance of the big, big, harvest. I ain't got a combine myself, but I bind wheat. Got an old McCormick binder and tractor to pull it. There's still a few threshers who will come around and I want to keep doing it the old way, even if it ain't big anymore. . . . The wheat to me is the meaning of it all. People and wheat. That's what we busted up the prairies for. For the wheat. Kansas can feed the whole world. And does. Now we got hard times; but them times will change. You can bet on that.

"You ever see wheat stubble after the crop is off? It's something that calls and calls to me. I can't wait to get a plow into the stubble. It keeps on calling, next year! Next year! You ever heard that call yet?"

And she kept on talking, and the more she talked about the wheat the more I wished that I could hear Dad and her talking together. I sure would have liked to hear them go at it; his talking about the prairie grass, tall and waving and all, and her talking about the hills and spaces of golden wheat.

We drove up the long lane to her farmhouse, a simple structure once painted white but faded bad now, with a little porch on one side. There was an old barn and sheds and a granary, and old wire fences around the place all kind of leaning over towards you. There was a mail-order house windmill still clanking in the yard, pumping water into a big cement tank. There wasn't much sign of life except for some milk cows standing along a fence inside a little pasture where the grass was turning brown.

Mrs. Settles took me into the house. It was badly cluttered with old furniture and pieces of machinery and magazines and newspapers. There wasn't any order at all, but it was kind of easy-going like she was. She made me sit in a chair in the kitchen while she rubbed some kind of salve into the bump on my head. It stung, then felt better, and she got me to tell what happened when I got hit by Harry. I told her about leaving home, and she said I had better send a card back home and that she would give me one later. She said she understood why Dad had sent me away, and that if she had a son, she would maybe send him away, too. She would have wanted him to taste the big, free harvesting days, because around here the old joys of the real harvest were about over.

"Some men nowadays don't want to work!" Mrs. Settles cried, "They don't want to get dirty, and feel the dust and smell the smoke, and they ain't hardly anybody who can build a good stack of wheat anymore. And most of the horses are gone. Engines! Tractors! We got to have 'em, but it ain't the same freedom. The bigness is gone. The joy is out of the hearts of the men; it's gone. But I'm fighting for freedom. It's all I have left. Freedom to do what I want, when I want."

After she fed me cold chicken and homemade bread and coffee, we went to the field for the afternoon. She sure wasn't one to waste time. The hired man was a thin-necked guy named Sam. I never did know his last name. He drove the Hart-Parr tractor, and Mrs. Settles rode on the binder. Her wheat didn't look as good as some we'd passed on the way out from town. Her land seemed thinner, somehow, and sandier. She said I didn't have to work very hard since I had a sore head, but it seemed all right, and after the good food, I felt pretty well. I worked hard, shocking the bundles, since I knew how to do that and how to work in the opposite direction that the grain was cut, so that the butt ends of the bundles would all be in the direction I was coming from. It made them easier to grab. I worked hard the rest of the afternoon, and I was glad to do it. I felt pretty lucky to have a job, as a matter of fact, though Mrs. Settles hadn't said a word about what she was paying.

Late that evening I got the cows into the barn and milked them. After I had finished the milking, I took the milk up to the farmhouse, and Mrs. Settles strained it and set it out to cool. We had a good supper. Sam came and washed up on the side porch and ate plenty, but he never said a word all through the meal, which was fried meat and potatoes, and a big raisin pie.

But all through supper Mrs. Settles kept talking about the old days and the big harvests, and how those old time harvesters could eat. After supper she fixed me a bed out on the porch. I never was more tired in my life. I heard the western Kansas wind soughing through the silver maple trees and through the black currant bushes, and I went right to sleep. I never thought about the Pratt hotel or the robbery or anything. All that seemed far away, somehow, real far away.

THE WINDMILL

I WORKED VERY HARD IN THE KANSAS HARVEST FOR SEVeral days. Better yet, I was feeling real comfortable at Mrs. Settles' place. I wasn't getting top money, she was going to pay me thirty cents an hour, but it was all right with me. I was sure earning it. And although I had quite a bit coming, somehow the money wasn't too important. I was really getting to know Mrs. Settles well, and she talked to me friendly and easy. By now I would have done just about anything for her.

Several times Mrs. Settles took me out to a far end of the big pasture to show me a windmill her husband had built. It was tall, made of wood, with a wooden ladder and a high platform. She said he had made the platform specially large so he could climb up there and look across the flat Kansas lands. He liked to do that at sunset, she said. There was something about the wooden windmill that really got me. I could stand

and look at it for a long time and see something different every time I shut my eyes and looked again. It had a huge wheel at the top which was different from any other windmill I'd ever seen. This one had many sections of blades, each turned at a different angle. She said he'd made the wheel himself and that it was better at catching wind than any of the commercial ones from the mail order houses, Montgomery-Ward or Sears-Roebuck. He'd never bothered to patent it or anything. But that was his way. He just liked to fool around and make stuff, and the neighbors hadn't understood him, especially since he had a little problem with whiskey. The old windmill hadn't been running for a long while, but I never did get tired of going out there, alone, in the evenings, to study it.

One evening after supper we were sitting in the kitchen, Sam was yawning and I was about ready to turn in too. We heard somebody drive up in a car, and Sam went to the door to look out. He never said anything, but he got his hat and went away. In a minute there was a knock, and when I opened the door there was a funny, dried-up little guy standing there, bald headed, with his straw hat in his hands, and a white shirt opened about half-way down his chest. He was getting on in years, there was some gray hair still around his ears, and his Adam's apple stuck out about as far as I ever saw one. When I opened the door he started to come in, then he stopped in the doorway and looked into the kitchen.

Mrs. Settles saw him standing there, and for a minute I thought she wasn't going to say anything, or ask him in at all. But pretty soon she cleared her throat loudly and says, "Come in, Reverend. Come in."

He came part way into the room and stood by the table, turning his straw hat around in his hands. I could tell that they knew each other all right, and I could see that they weren't very friendly. Mrs. Settles didn't do much to help ease things. She said finally, "Reverend Somers, this here is Bob. He's the young man who's helping me in the harvest."

"So I know," the Reverend said.

"Well, Reverend, you might as well sit down. Just take a chair. You come to chat with me, I suppose."

"Yes, ma'am. I came to have a talk."

"First time you ever been here, ain't it?"

"Once before. You recall that."

She cleared her throat again. "Yes, I recall. When Horace died, and I threw you out."

"I tried to reason with you."

"Nobody can reason with you, Reverend. You ain't the reasonin' kind. You got only one point-of-view."

"You oughtn't to say that, Mrs. Settles."

"I'll say whatever I please."

They sat a little while, and I sure didn't know what was going to happen. She was bigger than he was, and I knew well how strong she was—if it came to a pushing battle I was certain who would win. You could just feel them disliking each other.

"You got to let him go."

"Let who go?"

"This young man here."

"What in the hell for? He's a good worker. I like him."

"You're ruinin' his life."

"Ruinin' his what?"

"You'll be the ruin of him and all his kin and all that they done, and all that they will do."

She got up and walked around so she could stand over near him. She stood there looking down at him. "Now you tell me how I'm ruinin' his life."

Reverend Somers got up too, and they stared at each other.

"You're teaching him to disbelieve in God. Ain't that why you hired him out here? To get a young man to ruin, with your infidel's slobbering?"

"Slobbering?"

"You holler out that there ain't no God."

"I say what I want. And I ain't slobbering."

"You are a blasphemer. God will come to punish you with fire and tempest. You are the only one. The only one anywhere hereabouts who don't believe in God."

She grabbed him by the shirtfront. Maybe she got hold of some skin too; he gave out a loud holler. I figured she was going to slug the Reverend, and I didn't know what I should do. In a way I felt that he needed more help than she did. And I felt pretty funny about being talked over, too. I didn't know that anybody cared what I did except Mom and Dad, maybe. I never figured anybody would talk about me, or care where I was working or whether I believed in God. That sure seemed like my business.

"It's my right to do and say what I want," Mrs. Settles said holding onto him. "Ain't you never heard of the U.S.A. Constitution?"

He jerked around, trying to get loose. His shirt tore a little. "Yeah. You say what you want, even if it ruins a young life. Folks here ain't going to stand for that, Mrs. Settles, and neither is God."

She started to haul him toward the door.

"Git out!"

"You best come to church," he yelled, "and fall down to your knees and ask for God's forgiveness."

"When I come to church," cried Mrs. Settles, "I'll come because I got a good reason. I won't be there because you or anybody else told me to come. Now git! And don't you ever come back. I sure got a mind to lay a board to you. And if there is some others who sent you, tell 'em I don't need 'em. They ain't going to do my thinking for me. You look in the Constitution of the U.S.A.—it's right in there. Everybody's got a right to think what they sees fit."

"There ain't no constitution in heaven. God's law prevails."

Mrs. Settles shoved him roughly out the door. She came and sat back down at the table, breathing hard.

"You believe in God, Bob?"

"I sure try to."

"Well, whether you do or not, it's your business. Nobody else. You hear? Nobody!"

She looked so fierce, I figured maybe she would set in on me next. I got up slow, yawned, and said I was tired and had to go to bed. I would have liked to hear her talk some more, but I was afraid to set her going. It was like Dad when he got started; he would just keep going on and on. All you could do was get up and leave. And sometimes he went on talking even after you left.

Mrs. Settles just sat there at the table.

On Monday when we had about finished with her harvest, Mrs. Settles asked me if I would mind going to a neighbor to help him for a few days. She said the neighbor was one who didn't approve of her or of the way she thought, but his helper on the wheat truck was sick, and he couldn't afford to hire anybody else. She wanted me to go over and help him and even offered to pay me herself. I wasn't going to take her money, but I said I would go.

I got up early the next morning and she drove me over in the truck. The guy, name of Roy Ellefson, was out in the yard fooling with his Chevy truck motor when we drove up. Roy didn't seem too pleasant when he greeted Mrs. Settles, not even when she told him I had come to help. But he didn't refuse. He said something like thanks, and asked, finally, whether we'd had any breakfast. Afterwhile he got around to asking Mrs. Settles to come into the house, but she said she couldn't and finally drove away.

Roy didn't turn out to be such a bad guy either. After Mrs. Settles had gone, he warmed up and said he was grateful to me for coming over, and he'd make it up to me. He seemed to be embarrassed, or guilty about Mrs. Settles. He showed me around the place, and I met the tractor driver, a young fellow from Pratt. I was going to stay at Roy's place as long as he needed me. He took me up to the barn where the Pratt kid, whose name was Quinn, was finishing up the chores. They showed me where

I would sleep up in the barn loft, on a cot. My bed was already made up with clean sheets.

"I reckon Mrs. Settles told you I was so hard up I couldn't afford a wheat scooper," Roy said.

"That's about it."

"Well, everybody's hard up. But I ain't that bad off. I'll pay you myself. Mrs. Settles has always sort of looked after me and my wife."

He cleared his throat, and I got the idea that he was caught between what folks thought about Mrs. Settles and what he thought. The three of us walked down the road to a field that Roy was figuring to start cutting this morning after the dew was off. A couple of little kids, a boy and a girl, came running after us, puffing the dust with their bare feet. The kids came up to Roy, a tall and husky feller, and took hold of a hand on each side. We walked into the field a little ways, an he broke off some heads, rubbed the grain out of the hulls, and chewed them. He told us that he'd seeded his field late and that it was ready to cut now.

"We'd better go back to the barn and get ready to work."

I was hoping that he'd say more about Mrs. Settles and what folks were thinking about her, but he didn't talk about her at all. And he never did again, really, not while I was helping him.

The kids were now holding my hand and Quinn's. I hoisted the boy on my shoulders and we walked along laughing and having a big time, until we got back to the house.

"You better come in and meet my wife," Roy said.

The kitchen at Roy's place was low and cool. There was a large, round table covered with a white oilcloth. A tall woman came into the kitchen, and she was holding a baby on her breast. Her face was already wet with sweat, and she kept brushing the black hair away from her eyes. "What's your name?" Roy asked.

"Bob."

"Vera, meet Bob. He's goin' to help us with the scooping."

"I'm glad you got somebody so fast."

"Well, I wouldn't have it if hadn't been for Mrs. Settles."

Vera didn't answer at all. I figured they must really like Mrs. Settles but were afraid of what folks would say.

My job was the wheat truck, the unloading of the bin on Roy's Baldwin combine where the wheat was collected. Roy rode the combine, his hand on the big lever that raised or lowered the platform. Quinn drove the Allis Chalmers tractor. I waited the arrival of the combine when it rounded the field and stopped near the place where it entered. I backed in the large Chevy truck placing the end of the body under the spout on the bin, and, coming around, opened the sliding door at the end of the spout. The wealth of the pure grain spewed out in a glorious stream into the truck body, as I kept it scooped away. There had been enough rain earlier in the spring and moisture through the winter, so the harvest was good. But grain prices were extremely low, hardly fifty cents a bushel. One partial round of the large field had filled the truck box, and, once filled, I eased the loaded truck away from the combine. My job then was to haul the grain to the farm where I scooped it out into the granary, because Ray wasn't selling his wheat at the moment. He meant to keep most of it until winter, to see whether prices might rise. Some experts were saying the low prices would cease by winter, and then the country would get back on an easier track again.

Round after round, all day, everyday except Sunday, the combine roared through the wheat. I could throw off a hundred bushel-load of wheat in record time, and was always waiting for the machine when it rounded the field. I prided myself that the combine never had to wait for me.

When I was waiting for the machine, I sometimes walked around the field, curious about the many plants and weeds that grew in the field edge. I wondered how many of the plants along the fences had been there when the country was open plains. I recognized some of the plants that were the same as back home. I wished that I had as much knowledge of the land, the soil, and the ways of prairie plants that Dad had. He never went to a formal high school, but he knew a lot more. He knew about the insects that burrowed into the top layers of the earth for the winter, and then came out the next season, opening the earth to the air and helping it to grow better crops. This produced taller grass, and the prairie flowers bloomed wilder and more full. And Dad told how the buffalo, sharp-hooved, tramped down and broke the dead stalks, preparing the way for the growing of the new grass, while the places where their hooves had cut made a bed for the grass seeds.

Apricot trees were growing wild and plentiful, and the fruit was beginning to get ripe. Often I ate the apricots and wondered whether possibly Dad might see some change in me for I'd found at least something. But I didn't know where I'd go or what I'd do once the harvest ended.

The harvest at Roy's place went really well. We were ahead of schedule, and Roy's spirits were very high. He said he'd make enough on this harvest, even with the low prices, to pay the interest on his farm mortgage; things looked some better than they had the year before. He never said anything about Mrs. Settles, and the way he talked about himself I figured that he must be better fixed financially than she was, and I began to wonder whether she had sent me over to help Roy because she couldn't afford to pay me anymore. I guessed I wouldn't ever know. Roy told me he would pay me himself.

The food at Roy's was good, and the beds that Quinn and I had in the hayloft were great for sleeping. I kept thinking I'd go over to visit Mrs. Settles, but I didn't get around to it.

THE TWISTER

ONE MORNING WHEN WE GOT UP THERE WAS A STRANGE, dry look to the sky, as though the air had dust sprinkled through. The sun, by ten o'clock, became desert hot. Roy said he expected a storm before the day was out; he hoped it would hold off a while because we were getting along so good that we'd be finished long before the middle of July. As the day went on it was easy to tell that a storm was coming by the way the insects acted. The large sweat bees usually buzzed around real fierce, and the smaller insects moved fast as lightning when they were swatted, but this morning they hung and buzzed and dipped. And when they lighted it was as though they were drugged; you couldn't hardly knock them off.

When we went out to the field after dinner the sky had turned light yellow and the sun had disappeared behind the light, high, and very fast-moving clouds. There was no wind on the surface of the earth, and it was so still that I could hear the young chicks chirping under the black currant hedge nearby. The air was sultry. It was difficult to breathe.

I had hauled three loads of wheat after the noon meal and the combine was stopped on the near corner of the field. The motor hadn't been running well, and Roy was fiddling with it. I walked over to the machine to see what I could do to help. Roy was filing the points when the entire countryside suddenly turned dark. "What's the matter," Roy said from deep inside the machine.

"Somebody turned off the lights," I said, laughing, and my laugh sounded hollow to me and far, far away.

"I ain't never seen anything like this," Quinn cried.

We stopped working on the engine and stared up and around at the sky. In the southwest it was black as night except for a tiny edging of white frill above whipping clouds.

"Don't like the looks of this," Roy said, swinging down from the combine. "We better make for the house, boys."

"I'll bring the truck over," I said. I started to run toward the truck when a faint breeze whispered into the wheat. It was ice cold at first, then it turned hot. I whirled around, and then we heard it . . . a low roaring that shook the earth. For an instant there was just the low rumble and the faint chirping of chickens from the far-off farm house. Then Roy grabbed a shovel off the side of the combine and started to dig in the sand under the machine. "She's a twister, boys," Roy yelled. "We'll never make it home. Dig in!"

The roar was terrific now, and we could see the storm coming: a huge black and yellow thing with an evil, big body and a tail that was whipping around and whirling up everything it touched.

I dove in under the combine, and the three of us scrambled together in the shallow hole Roy had scraped out. We clung together, and I heard Roy praying that God would take care of his wife and kids. There was a sucking sensation and the air seemed completely drawn out of our lungs and our bodies felt light and poised like arrows on taut strings.

The Twister

Then there came a hell of a roar and a smash and a clatter. Buried in the sandy earth with the terrible noise concentrated all around us, I flashed on many things: a field of blue flowers somewhere . . . I couldn't recall just where, along a railroad; a tall haystack I had climbed one time as a child; a woodland where I crept away when I was troubled; Mom frying pancakes. I also remembered a story Dad had told about his walking on the prairie in the early days when a hurricane-like wind suddenly began to blow. Dad had laid down in the tall grass, and seized hold of it with strong hands. The wind, Dad said, had flopped him up and down like a woman shaking a tablecloth. But the grass saved him. The thought of Dad bouncing up and down like that in the grass made me want to laugh, even though I was plenty scared. I also wondered what Mrs. Settles was thinking, if she saw the storm, and I thought of what Reverend Somers had said about hell. What I saw of the storm looked like the mouth of hell.

Large and small objects began hitting the combine. I put my hands over my ears and shrieked to relieve the dreadful pressure. Suddenly, the combine wasn't there at all and the sucking stopped.

We three laid together afraid to move, but once the roaring was less we got up, fearful and stiff. The Baldwin combine was the first thing we saw. It was lying over on its side fifty feet away with the big platform sticking straight up in the air. The Allis Chalmers tractor was upended, too, and the gas was running out of the tank. All the wheat we could see was ruined and lay flat, or else there was just no wheat at all, the stems skinned completely clean.

Roy glanced around, like he wasn't seeing anything, really, and then we all started running for the truck, still intact. The twister was still roaring off in the distance. We got into the truck and headed toward the house. It had started to rain hard, but through the rain we could see that Roy's house and barn weren't damaged very much. The shingles were ripped off one side of the barn roof, that was about all.

Roy's wife and kids came running down the road to meet us. She grabbed Roy and pulled him out of the truck, crying and kissing him, and the two children whimpered and shivered up to them. Roy broke away and said that there'd be a lot of people needing help, and we had better go. Vera said we should go to Mrs. Settles' place first. The storm was heading in her direction and though they didn't say it, I sure knew that both Roy and Vera were thinking that the Lord's retribution had possibly struck.

I turned the truck around, and we headed up the muddy road. I was awed by the storm's mighty force. Quinn, too, sat quiet in the middle of the truck seat as if he couldn't believe what he was seeing. As we drove we saw telephone and electric lines down everywhere, and all the fields were stripped of wheat. A horse stood in a ditch with its shoulder torn out, a white bone sticking through the shreds of flesh. Lots of cattle lay in open crazy, twisted postures. As we continued the storm seemed to have increased in violence.

"She'll be dead," Roy said. I was also fearful of that, the way Mrs. Settles didn't hold with the ways of God.

And then, suddenly, we saw wheat shocks that I had made standing unharmed, dripping water from the rain. All intact. As we came within sight of Mrs. Settles' house, we could see that her buildings were untouched and that the horses and cattle were grazing easy in the pasture.

Roy told me to stop the truck. We sat silent in the entrance to the lane for a long while. It was plain enough that the twister had lifted before it reached Mrs. Settles' place. No damage had been done to her wheat. "I can't understand it," Roy muttered. "Everybody's wheat ruined but hers." I couldn't help but feel glad and happy; I was sorry for the folks who had lost their wheat, but I was sure glad it hadn't been Mrs. Settles'. I told Roy I would stay here tonight and see if I could help her. He and Quinn drove away. Roy was really confused by the strange ways of God, as he said.

I had an idea where Mrs. Settles was and trotted down the big pasture toward the wooden windmill. If God was going to destroy her, he would probably take the windmill first; it was what she really believed in, that windmill/temple her husband had made to have something to set against the wind and small-thinking folks. I kept on running, and when I came in sight of the windmill I saw her all right; she had climbed up on the platform and was standing there, looking across the cyclone-swept country. Maybe she was thinking the same as I was—that I would surely like to hear what Reverend Somers would have to say next Sunday. Because, according to him, Mrs. Settles ought to have been destroyed, not the good church people. I got an idea for the first time that it was really rough, like Roy said, to figure out the ways of God.

And there was something else. I began to have faint thoughts that the affairs of people were somehow played out on a huge stage which included the land, and the people working it, and the violences of nature. Mrs. Settles was like some character in a play that was too large for any theatre made by mere human beings. She was like a character on a stage made by God and nature. And maybe Dad was meant to be part of a play like that, with his love of the way things were; and even my own leaving home seemed as though it was part of a kind of play. I couldn't articulate what I felt, but there was a kind of plot and story that demanded that I move on to the next act.

VISION

II

DISCOVERING
THE ARTS

A TRANSITION

HAT SUMMER WAS MY INTELLIGENT ENTRY INTO MY LIFE. I drifted to numerous places, worked finally as a laborer with a construction outfit in Kansas City. I think that I was always probing myself for the meaning in what I was doing, had done. More than anything I wanted to please Dad. Whenever I thought about Dad now, I suddenly realized I was thinking deep. Dad and home and all his experiences were twisted up with the prairie grass where Dad liked to sit. That prairie acre was a landmark to me now, and when I thought about the tall patch of old grass I liked to believe it provided some kind of deep comfort to Dad. I remembered going into the yellow house in Kansas City outskirts where I had a room. The window shades were down and the room was half dark. A big fly was buzzing between the screen and the part-opened window. I lay down on the bed, my mind probing the past.

I sensed that in all the tall grasses across the country—graveyards, old fence corners, along old railroad lines—there would be relics, forgotten furrows of old trails you could hardly see anymore but that were once deep ruts with heavy, grunting oxen, mules, horses and heavy wagons pulling along people who were searching out, hoping to find their dreams. And I knew too that there were a lot of relics in musty rooms, barns, and attics across the whole continent that could tell stories through their rust and jagged edges: an old piece of wheel; a rusty old pistol or an old knife blade, stone arrowheads, a woman's dress with old stains on it; or maybe a cradle of whittled wood. Things like that had never meant very much to me before, but now, the wild, tall grasses of the prairie and the old relics made the whole past come alive. I guess I had been dwelling on thoughts like that for a long time, without really knowing it.

I still hadn't any idea where I'd go next. I only knew that I had to search on and on for what Dad had sent me to find. And now it all seemed to grow more urgent. There were so many men driven by the hard times, men who weren't drawn by the lure of any tall prairie, but by the fear of being poor. A whole generation of men just wandering around the streets and roads of America. Who could say what they were searching for? Or running from?

Looking back, I can see how these things helped to give me a taste for the flavorings of places, but a taste for theater came my way through the purest chance. Certainly, Dad gave me no leaning in that direction. He was a country lawyer-farmer, a Kansas pioneer who set great store by the economic development and welfare of the countryside, but he had little sympathy at all for cultural matters. To him the arts were participated in by women or the weaker members of society and had no real place in dynamic community development.

Though he was a self-made and almost completely self-educated man, he and Mom encouraged me to go to the University of Kansas where he hoped I would become interested in law or business. I disappointed him by floundering around for a couple of years with no noticeable inclination for a profession. The nearest I came to it was once during a visit to Kansas City, Missouri, when a handwriting expert at the YMCA told me that I had a modest amount of literary ability. I could attach no possible value to his judgment, and neither could Dad. So I wandered America for a while in the middle of my college career, just as many other Americans were wandering and seeking during the early depression years. I returned to Kansas University no nearer a career than I had been before but with a keen remembrance of people and places I had known and seen and a deep liking for a wandering life.

Now it happened that there was a professor of speech and drama at Kansas University named Allen Crafton. He was small physically, as men go, with bright blue eyes and a thin nose that looked as translucent as a mellow clarinet reed. But there was so much about him that was legendary—tales spun by students which grew with the telling—that my characterization of him can afford to be extravagant and perhaps sound a bit like a legend.

Crafton was a pagan-god figure whose lips were stained with the juices of barefoot-tramped grapes. He had steel in his hands and art at his fingertips. He could paint a magnificent landscape or write a poem of mighty tone or of aching, small joys. He was capable of turning out— and did turn out—a novel in a week or a play in ten days. It didn't really matter that they were not published. He seldom tried the publishers.

Women tended to follow him with adoration, and good men shoved for a place at his side. He was regarded as a wit, a philosopher, a roarer of bawdy ballads, but he could be as sensitive as harp strings in a soft wind. He was a staunch friend, and he would fight for friends like a demon. He savored the unusual, but tolerated the usual and found it useful. He loved and was a judge of good liquor and good smoke, but he was grateful for inferior stuff if a poor man offered it to him. He lived the life of Everyman; yet he kept a personal integrity and was at once malleable and impregnable. He seemed to live a man's full lifetime every day. He had a quick mind capable of whipping out at sensation and fact and gathering them into a child's wondrous pattern of imaginative grace.

Crafton had imbibed the goodness of places. He had traveled to the far cities of the earth, and he spoke of them in their own fashion. He turned back the landscapes he viewed like the pages of a book, seeking the sights and sounds of old generations.

I first met Allen Crafton when I was a junior at the University. That was 1933, a bad time for everybody. Students I knew were living in chicken houses or in the back seats of Model T Fords. They were tracking down cockroaches in the University buildings at night and selling these quick insects to biological companies. They were doing most of the manual work of the city of Lawrence, and they were endlessly pleading with suspicious merchants and heartless landladies for credit. The struggle was primitive, too, and the highlight of the week might be a hike on Sunday night along the Union Pacific railroad and the Kaw River with twenty cents worth of hamburger for five fellows and a few matches to light a fire.

It was a bad time and a sad time. A few times some sensitive spirit got too tired and leaped from the Kaw River bridge, or gagged and burned his throat and belly with poison. But it was a good time for militant ideas and pleasures of mind clashing with mind.

Allen Crafton opened his home and often his purse to the Kansas students, but his generosity alone was not the reason for his popularity. He was an extremely able teacher. Among his course offerings was a course in playwriting. This course interested me. I had never quite forgotten the thrill I'd felt when I wrote my first poem, and I had been experimenting and dabbling with writing during my early college years.

I wrote some short narratives for a good teacher named Margaret Lynn, who'd been a close friend of Willa Cather, and who knew and loved the prairies and had written books about them. My writings, I remember, were all brief episodes about people and places I had seen in my wanderings. Miss Lynn said the sketches were good but that they were merely impressions and had little central idea. She said I probably had some good materials but that until I developed a philosophy of writing the materials would not do me much good. Although I was completely ignorant of every aspect of dramatic writing and although I had seen only a few plays in my life, I thought that a course in playwriting might do me some good and help me learn the philosophy of writing Miss Lynn had said I needed.

In 1933 when I decided to take Professor Crafton's playwriting course the depression was at its peak. There were more breakdowns caused by malnutrition, and our Chancellor, E. H. Lindley, decided that something drastic must be done. He assembled a lot of the cases of what students were doing to keep alive and went off one day to Washington to see FDR about American college life. The result of Chancellor Lindley's visit was the CSEP—"College Student Employment Project"—which created jobs in American colleges and paid students a small sum per month. To most students the money was a profound godsend. It broke the tensions. It rippled away the drawn tightness on the faces. It started up new fires and creative hopes. The CSEP was certainly not the greatest thing that FDR did, but it saved many young hearts from breaking.

I was one of the first students to apply for and receive one of these jobs. When the committee asked me what kind of work I would like to do which would benefit me and still allow me to earn the money, I replied that I did not know. I would like a day or two to decide. And it was during this small decision period that I first attended Crafton's playwriting class. He talked about character, and he had the great dramatic characters of world drama waiting at his lips to illustrate what he said. I listened with fascination, for I knew that he was talking about life itself and that the characters he was using as illustration were within my own comprehension.

After class, I walked over to old Fraser Theater. The heavy oak double doors were closed, and when I pulled them creakingly open the dim theater seemed very silent and lonely. I stood a moment looking at the empty seats and the silent blue curtain and the frame of the stage opening with its scrolls. There was a cold unreality about the place that made me uneasy. When I opened a door at the side of the stage, a curious odor came from the stage itself. Ahead of me there were six steps going up to the level of the stage, and in a moment I moved up them. There was an even deeper silence on the platform. A bare bulb burning high up cast a hard little light down upon the stage boards, and the curtains hanging around the stage seemed to move as if in a tiny draft. Ahead of me against a wall was a stack of scenery with a flat, dusty, dry smell about it, and high overhead there was a small creaking and swaying sound as though a small breeze were swaying heavy burdens hanging on wooden pulleys.

I put my hand on one of the curtains, and a filter of dust fell in the dim light. I walked out on the stage and wondered what I was to do here. I wandered around. There was a steep flight of steps at the left side going up into a high dimness. The floor around the stairs and near the walls was littered with pieces of crumpled kleenex smeared with lipstick and make-up, some odds and ends of clothing, and a pile of boards. I turned and stood in the center of the stage. It was the first theater I had ever taken the trouble to examine from the stage side of the footlights, and as I stood looking out at the seats that rose gently in front of me I tried to imagine the stage peopled by the characters Crafton had told us about. I found the experience pleasant, and I stood on the stage for a long while. The next day I saw the University committee and told them that I wished to work in the theater. They assigned me to Crafton.

He was rightly dubious at first, but after he found that I was willing to do any kind of work from scrubbing the stage to building scenery and acting we became fast friends. I got fifteen dollars a month for working with this master of stage design, lighting, painting, and costume. He was an excellent carpenter and a good sculptor and carver. He could write a play, if he wished, or act with wondrous art. But he was most magnificent of all as director of the play.

A Transition

Every day of my last two years in college was a day of creative joy because of my association with Crafton. The mighty dramatic literature of the world came to life for me. I read everything, looked everywhere for ideas. Food and clothing did not matter. The theater at Kansas University was my playground and I worked and dreamed there day after day.

I enjoyed working for Crafton at least partly because of his deep love of Kansas people and places. I stayed on as his assistant for a couple of years after graduation, and we talked increasingly of a theater of the Kansas people based on the history and tradition that seemed to make Kansas unique. One morning after one of our talks I was working on the stage and a thick cloud of dust began to drift down from the heights of the stagehouse. I was building some flats, but I let them lie and climbed to the attic. I went to the windows, and as I looked westward out across the great valley it seemed to me that the valley was curtained with thick, black velours. The richness of the prairie country was blowing away, and the whole plains lay in a whirling, drifting torment. It was as though from the attic windows I could sense all America writhing and gasping as from a great wound.

My father had been a kind of Kansas pioneer, but the frontier that he knew was ended. It could probably never return or be relived; the depression with its floods and drought and hungers was the end, perhaps, of a scene that begun with the push West and ended in the spiritual and physical torment of the American people. If the power, the drive, the call that had sent my father forth from Clark County, Illinois, to Kansas was now somehow responsible for young and old wandering futilely through the depression, then, indeed, I thought, we must seek a new, inward expansiveness that would enrich us, not so much in silver and gold but in our whole soul and feeling.

Crafton had said many times that this inward growing must be of the art that was in us and of a recognition by all people of the goodness of the stuff of America re-created in terms of theater so that theater might be an accepted part of our lives. In his own way, in his own theater, Crafton was making his belief live magnificently and was probably finding his own salvation. But I wondered how his idea could spread—how it could come to everybody.

As I stood at the attic windows alone with the great dust curtain curling around Old Fraser, it did not seem strange to me that, somehow, somewhere, I might become a tiny part of the spreading of such an idea. Afterwards, I began to wonder whether the people of America might be drawn closer together in tolerance and in joy in one another through their stories and songs, their presents and pasts told and sung in a theater and in books whose stages were everywhere and whose actors were the folks in the cities and on the farms, in the crossroad places and in the back places where the American past lay quiet and undisturbed. I thought about it a great deal and talked it all over with Crafton.

Then, one day Crafton told me that if I were really interested in native American theater and folklife materials I should go to Cornell University to study with A. M. Drummond, who had made some big steps toward a New York State theater. I applied for a scholarship to Cornell, received one. I was standing with Crafton on the side of Mount Oread one afternoon in the spring of 1937.

There was a silence between us, and my thoughts were reaching out beyond the valley to encompass my experiences in American places. I had heard American voices from the deep South, from the West and the Northwest, from New England and Texas and the middle country. I had heard and felt an unspoken sensation that was Canada. Somehow I knew that these voices and feelings must relate themselves to a theater I earnestly desired to help create but could not really define. I hoped Cornell and Drummond would teach me American theater.

ALEXANDER DRUMMOND

FTER LABOR DAY, 1937, ARTHUR HUNNICUT AND I, HE from the hill country of Arkansas and I from the rolling lands of Eastern Kansas, closed up the Phidelah Rice Playhouse on Martha's Vineyard Island, and went our respective ways. He to New York where he found work soon in a William Saroyan play, "The Beautiful People." I a little later through New York enroute to Ithaca where I would enter the Cornell Graduate School.

Martha's Vineyard was not a new place to me. For three summers I had worked for expenses at the Rice Playhouse, learning theater crafts. In 1937 I applied to Rice who was the founder of the Phidelah Rice professional summer playhouse. I had to earn at least beginning expenses for my sojourn at Cornell. I soon received a letter from Rice offering me a job as assistant to Leslie Allen Jones, the Playhouse stage designer, and scenic artist. I accepted the offer and in June set out with the Burdicks for the East Coast.

At New Bedford we put the car on the *Naushon*, Island steamer, and after the Burdicks got settled on the Island, I reported for work at the Playhouse.

My labors with Leslie Allen Jones were a job. I had been given a good training in stage work by Allen Crafton, and I had no trouble fitting into a professional theater studio.

The problem, which developed soon was Jones's health. Within a week after we opened the studio he was informed that he had advanced tuberculosis, and must return to Providence to go to bed. I watched him depart with great sorrow and some apprehension, for Rice immediately asked me to take over for Jones. I did so, with little trouble.

That good summer passed quickly. Arthur Hunnicut set off for New York, and I traveled through Providence to visit Jones. I found him cheerful and getting along well. I arrived on the New Haven Railroad train at Grand Central, New York City, at about ten the next morning, and found that there was a Lehigh Valley Railroad train leaving Grand Central for Ithaca and Buffalo, in about three hours. I bought a ticket to Ithaca, and considered what I should do. I had had a couple of encouraging letters from Brock Pemberton regarding a play I had sent him. Pemberton was a fellow Kansan, long departed to the Big City where he had become a successful producer. I thought maybe I could get to Brock Pemberton's office, see him, if I were lucky, and get back to Grand Central in time to make the Ithaca train. I found I couldn't do it, and the lure of getting on to Ithaca was greater then, than the chancy urge to visit with Pemberton.

I spent the time walking the streets adjacent to Grand Central, got a sense of the overpowering hugeness of the City, and felt the thrill that I am sure all young people with theater ambitions feel on their first visit to New York. I wondered how Dad would feel if he had come to New York as a young man, instead of to Kansas and the tall prairie grass. I made up a fantasy about Dad in the City, as I wandered back to Grand

Central, through the great concourse, and through the waiting room which seemed filled with about as many people as we had, totally, in Iola, Kansas.

I wondered then whether I would ever come to live and work in New York City, which everybody knew was the theater capital of America and maybe of the world. I thought then that I would probably never come to New York to live. I knew that somehow I was a small community worker. I was awed by the restless motion of New York, and by its magnitude. I had been told by my theater friends on the Island, what the City had to offer if you were strong, and willing to wait. But when I had retrieved my suitcase, and was sitting on the "Black Diamond" train in a green plush seat on the Ithaca coach, I felt my excitement grow into a greater apprehension and anticipation, for I knew that my real goal was upstate New York.

For me it was a great adventure, and of change. I doubt that Professor Allen Crafton realized the changes I would be going through, moving from Kansas to New York State. I was, in those years, so conscious a product of the prairie way of thinking and doing, so steeped in the feeling for the prairie Dad and my Mom had instilled in me that the Finger Lake Country into which I rode on the train from New York City seemed strange indeed. I imagined that the people I observed around the Lehigh Valley station at Ithaca looked different from a group of Kansas folk. I had no way at the moment of judging, but I was determined to get into the hills and valleys, near at hand, as soon as I could. I wanted to meet people where they lived, in the country, especially.

Later, I was able to do this, mostly on foot, for I had little access to a car. Sometimes a friend who did have a car, offered to take me into the hills beyond Ithaca, and as I grew more familiar with Professor Alexander Drummond, I found him eager to drive out to country places.

When I finally did go out to talk to people, I found them surprisingly like my neighbors had been back in Kansas; for, to my shock, I found that the dust storms had driven many farm people from the plains of

Oklahoma, and the flatlands of Kansas to seek the coolness and shadow of the New York State hill land ... land offered to them at low prices by mean-minded real estate speculators, who told these poor people that they could grow fabulous crops on York State hill land. Of course, it was not so. The Depression was as real in York State as in Kansas or Oklahoma. I saw despair on the faces of farmers who had bought an old farmhouse from unscrupulous dealers. These farmers struggled hopelessly on land long ago worn out for grain growing. I found, however, that York State people were very homeplace minded, and were sympathetic to their new neighbors from the West. As time went forward, I became extremely fond of New York Staters, and of their homespun way of looking at things, and their ability to spin yarns and to joke about most anything.

But my immediate anxiety was to meet Professor Drummond.

I got set up in a room on Dryden Road, Ithaca, New York, in September, 1937. Crafton had told me that Professor Drummond, who was the Director of the Cornell University theater, had started an interesting country theater at the New York State Fair in 1919. Crafton had told me, too, that Professor Drummond was quite unique, but he did not enlarge on that statement. I did not comprehend when I arrived at Ithaca that late afternoon, that I was embarking on an experience that was to alter my whole life, and that I was to make the acquaintance of a man whose ideas and examples were to be the actual groundwork of experiments in which I was to engage later.

It was three weeks after I arrived in Ithaca before I encountered Professor Drummond. During that time I noticed that students spoke of him with awe, sometimes with downright fear. When I finally met him I could see why. He was an immense man with great shoulders and a proud head. He held his entire body more erect than any man I had ever seen. He usually wore a hat turned up a little at the brim and crushed down in an indescribable fashion on the crown. Behind his glasses were wonderfully alive eyes that could freeze you or warm you according to the mood of the man. I was surprised to see that he used crutches—a result of an early polio illness.

One day I was nervously waiting for him in his office when he entered slowly but with sure movements. He got his chair into exactly the position he wanted, sat down at his desk, and began straightening out some papers. Then he opened a drawer and looked for several moments among some files. He got up from his desk and went to his bookcase. He pondered over several volumes, finally took one down and laid it on the corner of his desk. He said, "Oh, dear!" in a sudden expulsion of all the breath in his lungs, and then he sat down. Finally he sighed, looked at me with a kind of glare that had a great deal of distaste in it, and said: "Well, what do you think I can do for you?"

I said timidly, but a little pompously: "I want to work with you and for you, Professor Drummond. I am interested in a theater that will grow from the hearts and the everyday lives of the American people. I want to learn from you how such a theater may be encouraged."

He glanced at me quickly, then began to fiddle with some more papers on his desk. He picked up a letter and read it through carefully. I could see the date on the letter; it was about six years old. I thought that his careful reading of this old letter was eccentric, but later he made me understand that a fine letter, with all the ideas clear and the prose sturdy, was something to keep on one's desk and refer to and reread many times just for the sheer tonic of it. That was probably why Professor Drummond was reading the letter. Anyway, he finally put the letter down and said, "Well, I dunno," and began drumming the top of the desk with his fingers.

I got up to leave, thinking that he wanted to get rid of me. He let me get as far as the door of his office, then he said, "Oh, Gard!"

I turned around and he was holding out the book he had taken from the shelf. "Have you read Carl Carmer's *Listen for a Lonesome Drum?*"

I said, "No, sir."

"Well, you might look it over. Pretty good."

I took the book, thanked him, and got to the door again. He called me back several times to chat about seemingly inconsequential matters. I was puzzled when I left his office; yet I had the feeling that I had met a great man; that he knew a great deal about me; that I did not know anything, really, about him.

At Kansas I had learned the fascination of ideas. At Cornell I learned, among other things, the rigors of discipline. This was an ordeal by fire under a most terrifying master.

The method of this amazing man was so complex and painful that the agonized student did not really know what was happening to him until things had happened. Little by little, with stinging rebuke, calculated irony, or with fabulous small whips of rhetoric he stripped the student of practically every bit of encumbering ambition, pride, eagerness, and initiative. With students who could take it, his method was directly brutal. He might provoke the student with the most amazing accusations, defamations, and deflations, and when the poor student rose at last in desperate self-defense he would never be able to get a defense under way. Little vanities and conceits were either tossed out of the window or the student, in endeavoring to keep them, submitted himself to the most horrible tortures. He was often stood up before his classmates and flayed until, hot with shame and futile anger, he was sent forth to study himself.

All this torment was of course hitched to learning. The man was so mature, so worldly wise, that he pushed no one beyond the absolute limits of endurance, and the whole result of the Drummond ordeal was not only a vast respect and affection for the man but was also an increased desire for the ferreting out of truth and a new and stimulating liking for scholarship. For, after stripping the student down to nothing, Professor Drummond, slowly, and with the upmost patience, began to build him up again. This was almost an unconscious process. It might begin with a single "Good!" scribbled on the front leaf of a paper over which the student had spent his blood; yet so meager had been the Drummond praise until this point and so vast the Drummond integrity that the student grabbed this tiny straw of praise and wandered about in an ecstatic daze showing the paper to his friends and truly believing that he must have written a minor masterpiece.

If the student were acting in one of the masterly theater productions that Professor Drummond directed in the Cornell University theater, a note written on a slip of cheap, yellow paper might be handed to the student by the stage manager. The note might say merely, "Smith, one percent improved!" and the student would strive with all his might to make the part two percent better the next night, just to get another one of those priceless scribbles. Professor Drummond could inspire superhuman feats of intellect and strength with a word or a gesture, simply because the student felt that a word or a gesture without ridicule or debasement meant that he considered the student worthy of some small respect. It was a kind of signal that a small part of the student's self-respect might be assumed again.

Professor Drummond was a man with a volcano burning inside. When the fire burned bright he was incomparable, wonderful, brilliant. I thought he could tell stories beyond any living master of story-craft, or he could hold a group of keen intellectuals spellbound. When the fire burned low, however, he was grumpy, full of cliches and apt to complain woefully of his ills. He was, in other words, extremely human, with most of the human frailties that beset all of us. Some of his frailties seemed rather larger than ordinary, perhaps, because he was rude on occasion when rudeness did not actually appear necessary. He made little attempt to pay back the ordinary social obligations in the conventional way, much to the distress of hostesses who complained that he should certainly know better or that he was ungrateful for the attention heaped upon him. He paid little heed to the complaints about his misbehavior, but he found his own way to return kindness.

With students he was training, however, he was completely generous. He almost always paid the check at restaurants or bars. If a fellow achieved any sort of respect in Professor Drummond's eyes, then suddenly that fellow might be left to pay the check. If a student came to him in real trouble, he would be taken behind a closed door where no one might hear or suspect and be given excellent advice or helped with money. God knows how many Cornell students survived through the opening of his pocketbook or how many men and girls told him their involved private troubles.

The general principles upon which he taught had great bearing on my feeling for places and for theater in relation to places. His principles were basic to the broad approach to theater I have tried to develop. This partial list of the Drummond principles is my list, not his. I am sure that he never drew up any such list as this:

A man must have within himself the seeds of self-improvement.

He must not fear introspection; he must have an abiding faith in what he believes.

He must bring forth the best that is in himself in order to rightly understand himself and his works in relation to other men and to the arts.

He must respect knowledge and be able to discern and use wisely the best sources of learning.

He must respect people and must carry always a learning attitude toward any man.

He must respect place and the flavor of the countryside and develop fearlessly and poetically his regard for a familiar scene and remembered event.

He must be broad in outlook; he must not be a man pedantically interested only in the narrow, dusty corners of knowledge but one who is willing to carry ideas to the people everywhere.

He must see theater as a reflection of man; he must see drama not as a toy, a bauble, a plaything, but as an instrument sensitive to all the sights and sounds of mankind.

He must have ideas but no rigid fixity of mind that might make him argumentative, impatient, and intolerant of other ideas or ideals.

He must savor and try the temper of America and acquire a thorough knowledge and understanding of her peoples, traditions, figures of speech, and historical trends.

Often the ideas that one discerned in Drummond's teachings of what a man ought to be and do were taught in the very awesome and wondrous presence of nature, on top of a New York State hill, perhaps after a dinner at the Taughannock House, the Dryden Hotel, or some other country inn when the August northern lights were softly rolling the skies and the great valleys and wide stretches of the New York State land were mystically and faintly discernible. Then he was at his best. He would stand on the hill, a landmark himself, and point out the interesting places and scenes. At these times he was a poet, and the forgotten roads, the wild places where few persons went, the hulk of an old steamboat sunk in Cayuga Lake were the substance and subject of his poetry. He loved central New York above anything on earth. From him I learned a love for this soft, mysterious country of hidden drums and slender, deep lakes and long valleys.

If Professor Drummond liked any of the things I was doing at Cornell he gave little sign. During the first months no little notes on yellow paper turned up, except the kind that made me wish to crawl into a hole somewhere and die. I wrote plays and passed them to him, and he passed them back with many suggestions, often, for revision, but with no indication whatever that the plays were good in idea.

Professor Drummond's famous course "66" was the place where students came face to face with dramatic theory. Wide reading was required. Searching questions addressed to the students brought them one by one to the front of the class to sit at the master's right hand where he demonstrated how feebly they grasped the meaning of Aristotle, Komisarjevsky, Gordon Craig, Evreinov, Jacques Copeau, Appia, Bakshy, and Jourdain. I did not comprehend then how I would someday rely on the ideas of some of these writers.

I made scenery in the theater and helped work it for all the plays. Because I always spoke in tones so very low and so indistinct that many persons had great trouble in hearing me, Professor Drummond called me "the whispering Mister Gard" and generally worked on my sensibilities until along in the Spring, without any warning whatever, he suddenly cast me in the character of Captain Shotover in Shaw's *Heartbreak House*.

This part calls for considerable skill in acting; the character is a complex one; and the part calls also for a voice fitting a retired sea captain. I was numb with terror. Yet such was the personality and influence of Drummond that he drew a voice out of me. Little by little, with the most infinite care, my voice grew in volume and projection, and little by little Professor Drummond moved his rehearsal chair back in the auditorium. I had no idea, really, what was happening until suddenly during a dress rehearsal my curiosity as to whether or not I could be heard grew too strong to be contained. "Professor Drummond," I bellowed, "can you hear me?"

There was a short pause while the sound bounced between the theater walls, and there was a longer pause during which Professor Drummond seemed to be lost in a kind of wonderful self-admiration. "Gad!" he said, "the whispering Mister Gard has spoken!" And this was the only comment I received. But in all the long years of our subsequent and comradely professional relationship I do not think anything I ever did pleased him half as much as my development of a voice. I developed a voice simply because Professor Drummond willed that I should.

Despite this small encouragement, I grew more and more despondent because it seemed to me that I was slipping backward, that the freshness of the idea about theater I thought I had when I left Kansas was no longer good or powerful. I was conscious only of needing to know so much and of so often seeming to find myself incapable of mastering the disciplines of graduate study that Professor Drummond insisted upon. So I sank lower and lower, developed a very nasty disposition, and was on the point of chucking the whole Cornell affair. The Cornell library chimes that had seemed so lovely to me early in the year now seemed to symbolize the University's apartness from life. I was tired of books. I wanted somehow to be merged into a more direct life stream. I hungered for open country, machines, men, animals. I believed that I had failed to find at Cornell any semblance of what I had come there to find, sympathetic and expert guidance toward the kind of theater of people that I had dedicated myself to work for.

Then, too, I had written a play that I liked, based on experiences I had had, and I was proud of this work. Professor Drummond had been holding it for nearly three months, and I felt that he must have thought it pretty bad stuff. All-in-all, I was down in the dumps. So one morning in May I went to Professor Drummond's office and told him I guessed I had better be leaving Cornell. There was silence for a while; then he said, "Who told you to go?"

"Nobody."

"Better think it over."

He obviously had more to say, and I sat and waited. "Better think it over," he repeated. "I've been working very hard for the past two months to get you a fellowship with the Rockefeller Foundation. I want you to stay and help me start a new theater project in New York State. Maybe we can learn something about stories and people and theater that will help the whole idea of American theater along."

I sat very still. The reversal was terrific. I felt like laughing; then I felt a great wave of affection for this big man who knew so exactly what to do. And I understood in that moment that everything I had experienced at Cornell, every debasement of soul, every moment of torment, every indication of faint praise, every book I had read had been calculated to make me a better worker, a more worthy worker for a larger scheme.

He said: "I have just this morning received a wire from Dr. David Stevens in New York. He would like to have you come down to the Foundation and see him."

I stood up. "I would like to stay at Cornell if you really think I could help."

He shoved the play I was so proud of across his desk to me. "I was going to send you back your play this morning. I'm sorry I kept it so long."

I took the play and saw that he had written on the cover: "This play has a real flavor of America that I like tremendously. Come and see me. I have some news for you."

That evening I dined with Professor Drummond at the Ithaca Hotel. The check lay between us on the table for a long time. Finally I picked it up.

RURAL NEW YORK

THERE IS GOOD LAND FOR FARMING IN NEW YORK STATE, but most of the hill land is poor. Its top soil has been spoiled by careless growing, and the wild growth is creeping back. In the hills I found people from Oklahoma, Dakota, and Kansas who had fled to the East, away from the sting and filter of the dust. I saw how the hope had faded from these Western faces and how thin the crops they grew looked against the futile soil. I knew many of these families, and in the time that I knew them they seemed to drift away, one by one, leaving the hills lonely and without laughter.

For two months I soaked up the sights and sounds and the lore of New York State. I walked among the grape harvesters working on the steep hillsides above the long, narrow lakes. I cherished the picture of the foliage greens and harvest purples and the bright kerchiefs of the pickers. I sat with old men and heard their stories of past days. I met a wonderful professor from Cornell—a jolly fat man with a bald head and thick glasses. He sang the ballads of the land in a beautiful tenor voice, and when he knew that I was not going to write a book and use his material he told me masterful stories of New York State people and places. This was Professor Harold Thompson.

I traveled all over the state. I met the people everywhere. I heard yarns about outlaws, bogeymen, farmers, pretty teachers, milk strikes, revival preachers, murderers, buried treasures, race horses, haunts, wondrous cures, and probably hundreds of other things. I sat in crossroads stores, bent over back fences, sat on front steps, milked cows, chewed the fat with the boys at the Spit and Whittle Club at Dryden, New York, and generally engaged in any occupation that allowed for yarn swapping. It was a happy time, and all through it Professor Drummond left me quite alone. Then one day he sent for me.

I went to his office with acute hesitation. Surveying my activities, I could not actually see that I had accomplished much. I felt that what I had seen and heard from the people had point in the sort of theater I imagined might spring from the land and the people, but I feared that he would ask me what books I had read, and I knew that I could not impress him. I expected the ax to fall.

I went into his office. He was writing, and he wrote for a while. Then he said, "Well, what have you been doing?"

I blushed and said, "Professor Drummond, I have been hearing stories and swapping lies."

"Where have you been?"

I named two or three dozen places I had visited. He said, "Well, there's plenty to do."

"Yes, sir."

"You think this floating around is worthwhile?"

"Yes, sir."

He said, "I was hoping you would think so. It's the only way you ever get the real flavor of the region." He stood up. "I have my car downstairs. Let's go!"

Touring the central New York countryside with Professor Drummond was like being blind and suddenly seeing the unbelievable beauty of sunlight and landscape. It was like that, yet something more, for he seemed to endow the land with a mystic poetry that sprang from his sensitiveness to present and past. There seemed no back road that Professor Drummond did not know.

There was no hilltop he had not seen and no valley to which he attached no mysterious significance. The land, the people, and winds and rains all added up to a complete and satisfying unity for Professor Drummond, and so perfectly were these things reflected in his observations that word pictures dropped from his lips like impressionistic paintings.

Sometimes at night we would stand on a high place called Butcher Hill from which all the land seemed to drop away to the North, to Lake Ontario, and then all the grumpiness, all worldly disillusion, the entire burden of life rolled away from him and he would speak for hours of the legend and of the folklore of places.

As such talk went on and on, broken occasionally by excursions to eat wonderful country food in corners of the land that only Professor Drummond seemed to know, I fell more and more under the spell of the country. It was a bewitchment that stimulated fantasies of imagination and sapped creative strength. I lived every day as a mad kind of excursion, breathing into a subconscious creativeness everything I saw and felt and heard. I had no inclination to work. I rebelled against writing. The whole state was my stage, but I could not formalize the product of my sense into the characters that were like life, nor could I merge the fantasy of ideas that rushed through me into the tight packets that were the plots and themes of plays.

There was a sudden stop to this madness. I visited a county fair one day at Morris, New York. In one tent a stage had been set up, and the tent was packed with people. They were old folks and young folks and farmers and city people. They were eager; they were in festival mood. They wanted theater, excitement. They wanted hearty humor, dramatic pictures, furious impact. They had a right to expect such things, for the plays they were there to see were billed as being from rural life. Rural life to these people meant kindness, neighborliness, strong appreciations of land and wind and color. Rural life meant the strength of outdoor bodies, the good simplicities of food and work and neighborhood fun. Rural life meant songs and games, stout problems in land economics, education for the kids, and a savor of the things that were essentially part of their own place. Rural life meant a tiny thread of loneliness, too, and maybe a very occasional breath of tragedy. Rural life meant the neighborhood arts of careful canning, weaving, quilting. Rural life meant everything these people knew and understood—the whole goodness of their lives.

The plays were billed as rural life plays, and they were played by local young people and adults. When they began, I, too, was eager, for I had seen the broad, free life of American country places. But when the plays were over, I looked at the faces around me. Anticipation had turned to a solemn disinterestedness. There was no laughter, no tears—only definite exodus that was filled with vague irritation. There was no festival here—only the departure of an initial eagerness that had seemed very precious and deep.

The reason seemed to me then quite clear. The plays were not rural plays. True, they were supposedly set in the country, but their characters had no relation to the kind of country life I and the folks around me knew. They had very little relation to life anywhere. They were dreary in tone; they were filled with bad jokes lifted from a collection read somewhere or heard on somebody's radio. The characters were stereotypes of real people. They maundered on and on about poor housewives who had no pianos or washing machines or they talked in cliches about cruel fathers who would not let sons or daughters have boy or girl friends or join 4-H clubs. They hinted at shotgun weddings, and they dusted off the old conflicts between the farm and the city. They sawed back and forth on the fringes of obscene jests about the farmer's daughter and the city slicker.

I remember thinking, as I walked out of the tent into the autumn sunlight, that this was the only real theater the people in this place knew, that there could be only failure and disillusionment in such plays, and that such plays were evil and would kill any art that might grow here. I paused as I thought of the rural life that I knew in Kansas, of the wheat fields, of the mighty machines biting through the yellow grain, of the harvest parties, and of the wild singing and dancing. I thought of New York State grape pickers singing on a steep hillside, of a farm mother holding a little child against her breast, of the terror of a violent storm, and of faces full of suffering from pain and lost crops. As I stood thinking, the great Butternut Valley that was all around Morris turned golden in the afternoon light. I looked at the hills, and suddenly my spirit was filled and lifted with a clear knowledge. I knew that that there must be plays of the people filled with the spirit of places, and my aimless activities assumed meaning. I felt the conviction then that I have maintained since— that the knowledge and love of place is a large part of the joy in people's lives. There must be plays that grow from all the countrysides of America, fabricated by the people themselves, born of their happiness and sorrow, born of toiling hands and free minds, born of music and love and reason. There must be many great voices singing out the lore and legend of America from a thousand hilltops, and there must be students to listen and to learn, and writers encouraged to use the materials.

The next day I went back to Ithaca and sought out Professor Drummond. When I told him what I had been thinking, he said, "I'm glad some of the ideas have been jelling for you." And we sat down at his table and made some plans for a playwriting project for the state of New York.

Professor Drummond said that there were probably a lot of people in New York State who wanted to write plays. He said that we would try to get in touch with these people and that the results of our efforts might be such a bloom of country-grown plays that the entire state would enjoy the aroma of up-country life. He said that outside of the University playwriting classes, there had been almost no attempt to get the people to think and write dramatically of themselves. When I asked him how many people might try writing a play, he refused to estimate, but his eyes warmed up, and I knew that he was dreaming of a large number and that both he and I were hoping for sensational results. I suppose that when we were alone and remembered the soul-tormenting rigors of playwriting, we had some serious doubts, but these doubts did not in the least deter us from trying. Indeed, so great was our faith in the people, so real was our dream of a people's theater, and so confident was our belief in the goodness of the folklore and life of the region that it was almost as though some old central New York Indian god had endowed us with this dream as a special mission.

With the help of many supporting articles in the NEW YORK TIMES this dream soon became a reality. Our first talk was the preparation of a letter which we circulated widely through the mails and got printed in papers and magazines. The letter pointed out that many persons, young and old, should be interested in writing a play about New York State, that as soon as good plays became available they would be circulated throughout the state, and that anyone might receive advice and perhaps assistance by writing to Professor Drummond or me at Cornell University. The letter stated also that we were eager to get in touch with folks who might have some good ideas for plays so that we might pass these ideas on to possible authors and that we wished people would get in touch with us who might like to present some of these plays in their own communities.

Perhaps Professor Drummond knew what we were letting ourselves in for, but I did not. All I had was enthusiasm and a capacity for work.

I needed both, for immediately our mail overflowed the boxes. There were letters scattered everywhere. Such a good thing as a secretary to help handle this spate of potential culture was a part of our dream that we had not dealt with. But every letter was answered, and the ideas, the encouragement, the offers of free publicity, good will, even love, made us believe that maybe, just maybe, we had touched a popular chord. The letters were filled, some of them, with a sort of fresh hope, as though a farmer or a housewife or a grocer or a country doctor after years of working and thinking and dreaming suddenly saw a chance to speak of the things he lived by. Some of the letters were neatly typed. Others were written in illegible scrawls with soft lead pencils. A few were written in foreign languages—in French, German, and Finnish.

There were letters that I remember particularly well. One was from a farmer's wife in Cattaraugus County, New York, Mrs. D. H. Chambers. She wrote that she was much interested in writing a play about the Dutch Hill war, a rather comic incident on the land of troubles of the 1840's which took place on her farm. She wrote: "I have never expressed myself in the dramatic form, but I am willing to learn. I have a brother who has been fairly successful in dramatic writing and you may possibly have heard of him. His name is Maxwell Anderson."

There was a letter from a fellow up in the Adirondacks who caused me great concern. He wrote:

> Was reading this day of your playwriting announcement in the paper. I wish I had until July to submit my contribution. However, I plan, or want to send, or make a contribution. I know a lot of women folks will try writing plays, and I want to try just to spite the women. I don't like the idea of giving women more chance or call for action over men, as women are not only first in nearer all things but has the world with a fence around it.
>
> Now, has the story got to be submitted in play form, or will a story do the trick? Just what do you call a one-act play? I wish

I could get a specimen copy just in case I must submit full form. Will be glad to receive any assistance, and I am obliged to ask you to hurry.

There is not a preponderance of women characters in my stories, and only some have several characters. Do you require many characters, or will as few as several be enough? Please explain matters out to me. I want to find out what you want, if I can. Will a one-act play permit more than one continuous scene or scenery? How many or how few words would you say would suffice? Please tell me what constitutes a one-act play so that I can tell at a glance what it is like. A stamp is enclosed for reply. Such envelopes as I have are misfits. Don't see how I can send you the usual envelope, sorry.

P.S. What shall I write about?

This mountain man never wrote a play, though he sought and received plenty of information. But as the personal mail got less bulky, our boxes began to fill with larger envelopes, brown ones with first class postage, containing plays of every sort. These we read over and sorted out and mulled over, and soon again I was engaged in a tremendous correspondence, teaching playwriting by mail, offering encouragement, criticizing or praising what seemed hundreds of manuscripts. Overnight my job became almost completely office work, though I had no office and the manuscripts were apt to be spread over tables in any corner I might find temporarily vacant. Then people began to drift into Ithaca to see us about their work. A woman from Buffalo brought her play about Underground Railroad days at Niagara Falls. An old man with long gray hair came to see me with a jolly little play about antique collectors. A machinist from around Rochester brought two scripts about workmen. A girl from the western part of the state brought her play about grape pickers. A thin young man came with his play about a schoolhouse that was painted in big red and white checks. (One faction in the community

130

had once wanted the schoolhouse painted red, the rest of the community wanted it painted white. They had compromised.) Folks came from all points of the compass with plays that reflected many facets of regional life.

There was excitement in meeting these people and talking with them. They were new signs of an art expression that seemed to be springing up joyously everywhere, and so infectious was the spirit of this simple movement that Professor Drummond and I were caught up in it. We began to write, too, and several plays were our joint efforts. One of the plays I wrote grew out of an incident I had witnessed while wandering in the hill country of New York State. One evening I was on top of a high hill and I saw a thin old man sitting under a lone cedar tree strumming on a guitar. After a while he began to sing a slow song about a sad wind in a willow tree. I listened to him sing, and when he finished the song a wind came over the hill and brushed through the cedar. Then the old man stood up with, I thought, a dream on his face and made a speech to an old friend who was lying in a cemetery grave a piece down the hillside.

"Tom," the old man said, "I can see you over yonder astanding up beside your stone. I expect you recall like me when these hillsides was green with crops and the young fruit trees tender with spring blooms. You kin see them light yellow colors in April and smell the earth new turned.

"Looka, yonder, Tom, down the line of the hill there, see them timbers sticking up out of the long grass? That was the Ervay house and the Barnes house was down below it. Who's that beside ye, Tom? Lucy, I expect. And is that Lally over in the corner holding her baby?

"Everybody is gone off the hill but me, Tom. Young pine trees is growing everyplace now. Recall my place that was so fine set against the far side of the hill? Them white columns on the front porch was good to see. Could see them from a mile away, and my fields back the house spread with new wheat.

"The state's went and bought my farm, Tom, and they're making a woods out of it. The land's wore out, they say. Yesterday the mail stopped comin'.

"Nothin' but the wind left. There's wind ablowing through the old cedar, and it's the night wind over the graves."

The old man put his guitar under his arm and walked down the hill. He lay down with his head up against one of the stones. The old man took his place, with his lyric speech and guitar, in a play that symbolized the New York wild country.

From the famous frontier preacher the Rev. Lorenzo Dow we fabricated a play in which the Reverend raised the devil from a flour barrel in a settler's cabin, and thereby converted the entire settlement of Schoharie, New York. We wrote radio scripts about the old 999, the New York Central engine that set a world's speed record, and about Colonel Tom Meachem of Oswego and his big cheese—biggest ever made. We fixed the frontier propensity for tall yarn spinning into a play called "Bill Greenfield's Legend."

The main action of *THE CARDIFF GIANT* evolves from a conflict between George Hull, a tobacco salesman and an evangelist preacher. The preacher claimed loudly that there "were giants in those days" and Hull maintained there were not. The preacher did George down in the debate, and George went out and hired men to cut a great block of gypsum out of the river bank at Ford Dodge. Then George shipped this block of stone to Chicago where he got a tombstone cutter to carve the block into the form of a giant. George got the giant to Binghamton, then shipped it by wagon to Cardiff, the wagon traveling at night for secrecy.

George was first cousin to "Stubby" Newell, Stubby let George bury the giant on his farm. In the dead of night the deed was done. The giant lay buried for a year. Grass grew over the spot secluded under the shadow of a great hill. One day Stubby hired a couple of men to dig a well right on the spot where the giant lay buried. When the men encountered a great stone foot and dug a little more to see what manner of creature lay buried there, they both tossed their shovels and ran to the village to spread the news.

In a few days Newell's farm was tramped over by seething humanity. A tent was erected above the giant's grave, and Hull, Newell, and company, which included by this time the famous Homer, New York banker, David Hannum (later known fictionally as Harum), were coining money at the weekly rate of five percent on $3,000,000!

Everybody wanted to see the giant. Certain ladies viewing the sculptured wonder fainted dead away, for Hull's tombstone carver had left nothing to the imagination. A dentist, Dr. Boynton, pronounced the work to be of Caucasian, not Indian, origin and called it the noblest work of art that had come down to us. The Board of Regents of the state of New York came to view the colossus, bearing with them insurance in the words of the state geologist, Dr. Hall, who called the giant the "most remarkable object brought to light in this country deserving of the attention of archeologists."

And so it went. Preachers basing sermons on the giant gleaned converts like falling chaff. One fool from the Yale Divinity School identified the giant as a Phoenician idol brought to this country several hundred years before Christ. P. T. Barnum, recognizing the giant as a magnificent showpiece, offered to buy it for sixty thousand dollars, and when he was refused, went off to New York to make a duplicate. He displayed it as the only authentic Cardiff Giant.

Professor Marsh of Yale at last exposed the hoax for what it was—a crude and recently carved block of gypsum, something which President Andrew D. White of Cornell had maintained from the first.

While Professor Drummond and I were speculating about the Cardiff Giant as a potential dramatic subject, a dreamer from the south came to visit us at Ithaca. This was Paul Green, who long before had caught a vision of a people's theater, and who had been ever since working toward that end with Professor Koch of North Carolina University.

This tall man with the sensitive face and deep eyes made a profound impression on me. His plays were pointed out as the foremost regional dramatic expression in America. He spoke simply, yet like a poet, and everything in the earth and sky and of men had a philosophic meaning for him. He spent long hours talking with me. When he heard the story of the giant he began to grin and get excited and walk up and down. He said the yarn demonstrated the universality of human folly, and he insisted that Professor Drummond and I start writing the play immediately.

So one day in the early Spring we drove up to Cardiff, up Highway 11 that runs north from Cortland to Syracuse, and we paused a little while on a great hill that the glaciers left across the Onondaga Valley like a high wall. We looked down the valley flats, across the salt well derricks, toward the little town of Cardiff near which the giant once lay. The valley was quiet and mysterious, with the hill they call Bear Mountain shadowing it from the west. It was a scene to inspire awe. Several years later, Professor Drummond wrote the introduction to the published version of the drama, *The Cardiff Giant*:

> "The traveler south of Syracuse along Route 11 at close of day will sense mystery rising with the mile-long shadows from the great valley at Cardiff and with night coming down the dark slope of Bear mountain to the west, or off the star-crowned hills of Pompey to the east—mystery which could cause him to think some wonder might come upon us there, and he would, maybe, believe, as did Onondagans of the sixties.
>
> "For the Indians well knew this valley and these hills as places of old mystery: stone giants clanking through the underground; great men of old striding across the hills; gigantic Indian prophets of centuries gone who had foretold the coming of the white men, and who had prophesied that they themselves, after death, would again be seen by their peoples.
>
> "The early whites actually exhumed bones of huge, prehistoric men along the hills of Pompey, and later where the first

roads and the railways edged into the rocks on their routes into Canastota or Cazenovia! Mystery in the old days had possessed this land of solemn and rugged beauty; and so now from our "joy in believing" in a wonder, even the "American Goliath" is not perhaps so remote from some of us."

We found an old man in Cardiff, Mr. Nichols, who lived alone in a shack. He was the son of one of the fellows who had dug the well and uncovered the giant's foot. Mr. Nichols had seen the giant lying in its grave, and he had some yellowed photographs of the scene and the wonder. He took us to the exact spot where the hoax had taken place. From him we got the atmosphere and the flavor of the event. We found other oldtimers who remembered songs that were sung at the revival meetings or who had poems that had been written to commemorate the find. We discovered relatives of Stubby Newell, and little by little we assembled a fine body of working materials.

Such materials included, in addition to the items described, notes made from the newspapers of the period, the *Syracuse Journal* and the *Ithaca Journal*, especially, from articles in magazines describing the wonder, and from actual statements gleaned from published lectures by various personalities involved. We also dug a bit into the backgrounds of Stubby Newell and George Hull, and we did extensive reading relating to the topics of the times and to the state of New York crops and climate in 1869. In other words, we assembled a fairly complete body of information pertaining generally to the region in the particular year we wished to set the drama.

During our work collecting materials, we discussed the form of the play. We believed that the play must be flexible in form to allow for the inclusion of many scenes and numerous characters. We wanted to draw a merry picture of country life in New York State with its color and variety—including the social "bees," the rural school, the church picnics, the political argufiers, and all the rest. To do this, we knew that we must think more in terms of a "show" than of a strictly plotted play. Therefore, with the excellent models of the ancient Chinese theater, the "living newspaper" dramas of the Federal Theater, and the newly produced *Our Town* before us we conceived a New York State show.

I got up a first draft of the play which seemed pretty good to me, but Professor Drummond said: "Gard, this is too long. We'll have to cut it." And then he began to work on the play. He proved that he was a true lover of New York State and her stories for he lengthened the play, added characters, scenes, and generally filled the whole thing with his intimate understanding of the people, their language, their music and poetry. The final draft of *The Cardiff Giant* had ninety-eight speaking parts. In the first production in the Cornell University theater I played nine parts myself.

When the curtain rose to an enthusiastic crowd of New York Staters and the Narrator was on the stage saying, "You gotta imagine yer back in 1869; that's when the hoax jelled—in October, '69." It was as if the spirit of central New York State had come alive.

I can still feel the central New York State land calling me. When I close my eyes, the patchwork hillsides across the keep valleys are as vivid to me as though I stood on the Cornell campus on a May morning and looked west toward Mecklinburg. I might have lived and dreamed forever in the Finger Lakes country if it had not been for the war. But suddenly one day, there it was, and the course of our creative project in New York State was instantly altered. There was writing, yes, but it was frenzied writing on wartime themes, and when we looked about the land, there were no longer home-grown plays on country stages. Sadly we admitted that the dream must wait, and for me, indeed, the York State project is only a green memory. After that summer I never lived in New York State.

There were many ideas that I took away from Cornell. Most of these ideas were simply a part of the maturing of other, larger ideas and not definable in themselves. But the large ideas about regional theater that I took away were definable. Reduced to general terms they are these: A concept of theater must be broad enough to include many things. The traditional materials of the region, at least those having possible literary significance, must be assembled. Writers must be encouraged throughout the region. The people of the region must be "let in" on what the regional drama project is trying to do and a friendly public attitude toward the project must be established. The university should take the role of leadership in the theater arts not only on the campus but throughout the region.

VISION
III

CANADIAN
EXPERIENCES

SETTLING IN

I T WAS IN 1942 THAT PROFESSOR FREDERICK KOCH OF the University of North Carolina decided not to return to the Banff, Alberta, School of Fine Arts where he had been offering a course in playwriting, and I was invited to take his place. I well knew that I could never really fill Koch's position, but the opportunity to carry on his good work in native playmaking in Canada was challenging. I went to Banff, therefore, in the Summer of 1942, and was greatly impressed by the sincere desire of the founders and organizers of the School to establish the arts and crafts as a necessary part of regional life.

The Banff school gave me an opportunity for the first time to see the arts integrated in an educational program having wide regional significance. The art instructors, for example, were westerners eager to make their students and the public more sensitive to the western landscape. Walter

Phillips, internationally famous wood engraver and water colorist, and George Glyde, a young, British-born painter of remarkable power, did most of the art teaching. These men loved the West and were able to transmit to me through their personal approaches to painting a new feeling and regard for western places.

I walked with Phillips in the mountains and on the prairies, and from him I learned to appreciate landscape through an artist's eyes. He gave me an expressive understanding of the sharp beauty of grain elevators seen against the varied prairie backdrops, of washes and coulees, and of the stark fronts of stories and dwellings in the western towns. Through Phillips I developed a concept of painting and theater working together toward fine regional interpretation.

I consider, looking back, that this idea of combining the art expressiveness of a region was one of the most valuable ideas I gained in this period. It is an idea that I have never lost sight of.

And from the Banff students, too, I learned much about the West. Many of the students were westerners, and there was no false sophistication, no awkward self-consciousness in their use of familiar materials. They dramatized their own experiences—such as, for instance, the experience of a country schoolteacher faced by all the problems that a young, and sometimes extremely pretty, schoolm'am faces in the Alberta countryside.

The students wrote colorful plays about rodeos, prairie storms and mangled crops, drought and dust, or about aspects of the life of the many nationality groups or religious beliefs. (There were then 417 faiths in Alberta.) The plays were sincere and often quite playable. The students approached their subjects with a theatrical point of view. The traits of their characters seemed intensely real because, usually, the characters were drawn from life, boldly and without undue restraint.

At the end of the Summer of 1942 I found myself with a deep desire to remain in the Canadian West. I proposed to University of Alberta officials that a project devoted to the collection of the folklore of Alberta might have worth as a preservative measure before many old-timers who had actually settled the Province passed out of the picture, carrying their valuable recollections with them. I thought that such a project might do something to help playwrights, too, for I sensed that there was a great mass of uncollected regional lore which might, if it were assembled, be a value to writers.

In 1943 the Rockefeller Foundation and the University of Alberta set up machinery to make my wish possible. I taught the Banff course again in the Summer of 1943, and then stayed on in Alberta with headquarters at the University in Edmonton. My title was Director of the Alberta Folklore and Local History Project. "Local history" was tacked on to satisfy certain antiquarians to whom folklore meant total disregard for fact. There were no public archives in Alberta, either, and the University authorities thought that an emphasis on local history might do something to hasten an archives building.

The title of the project worried me deeply. I had no illusions whatever about myself as an authority on folklore or local history. I was interested primarily in creative aspects of the work and in the opportunity to test some of the ideas I had taken away from New York. It is needless to say that what I dreaded might happen did happen. The publicity the project received was too good to pass by. My role was cast for me. I was to be a leader, a missionary, a preacher in a kind of great revival meeting built on the argument that Alberta was God's own country, had the best yarns, the biggest liars, and the most glamorous history and the strongest winds that God ever created.

I had made one public address at Banff in which I spoke about the folklore of New York State. Immediately I was called by the press an authority on folklore. The Director of the Banff School—who was also the Director of the University Extension Division—soon bore me off, wildly protesting, on a round of public addresses about the folklore of Alberta. I was terrified, for I had hardly had time to read more than a book or two about the province. But I scrabbled around, did a month's work in a couple of days, and clinging desperately to a small sheaf of notes, was hurried off in a cloud of thick Alberta dust to begin my recitals of places and people about whom I knew so little.

It was my first experience with the bitter truth that a wide popular interest in native literature may be stimulated by a leader of a project such as mine only through playing a rôle—in my case the role of a kind of missionary with the sole aim of working up public interest in a region. In a way, I did not realize what I was doing. I went from town to town, mouthing the same stories because I knew no others, asking people desperately for yarns, materials about themselves and their places, shaking hands, uttering absurd platitudes.

It was a false role. I desired quiet, time to think, time to write, time to savor the countryside, time to appreciate the great prairies, smell the clean air, climb the hills, and time to look for the forgotten trails and search for bits of rubble where the old frontier forts had stood.

But these times seldom came. As I accustomed myself to my role I developed techniques that must have made me more palatable to my audiences. I picked up a wide repertory of Alberta wit, sayings, tall tales, weather lore, and assorted local history. I spread these far and wide. The laughter in the places where I spoke became more genuine, and my presentations became less desperate, but inwardly I was no less self-conscious, no less rigid, for I felt ashamed that I could not offer the people a warmth that could only come with greater intimacy with the region.

But even the shame left, little by little. I developed mannerisms in keeping with the materials I used in my lectures. I was able to stand on a platform and will an audience into a liking for its local traditions, and I became able to shake the hundreds of stretching hands, utter proper words, and to escape at the right moment.

It was all a great act applauded by the press and approved to a certain extent by the people. Not all of them by any means, of course. There were the native Albertans and the transplanted Albertans, the ones transported from down east or from the old country, who muttered that everything I was doing could be done better by a Canadian. And they were right. Absolutely. But I was an authority by this time, and their remarks could not touch me. I was riding high. Sometimes the press called me the Mark Twain of Alberta, and my ego fattened. I was invited to all the service clubs—a terrific honor. I attended banquets of hardware merchants and stock dealers. I fraternized with brewery executives, ranching magnates, and political personalities. Once I rode to one of my engagements in a private railroad car on the Canadian Pacific Railroad and drank expensive liquor.

It was ballyhoo, a capitalization on a people's desire to know themselves and to understand themselves. They looked on me as an authority who was to lead them. At first I tried to say that I was no authority on anything, that I was a simple guy, really, and that I only wanted to do simple things such as appreciate the region simply and honestly and be accepted by the people as one of them, but I was always on the outside because the people were trying to see themselves through me. And I was a false window, a glass that gave back only a dim, shallow image.

However, I had never been so respectable, nor so respected. I had the magic words. The prettiest girls smiled at me, and the strongest men were eager to shake my hand. In my work in New York State it more often had been the women that crowded around me. But in Alberta it was the men. For it was a man's land, and the stuff I had to say concerned men in their battles against nature. For a while I forgot the creative ideas I had developed with Drummond. I was caught in a kind of holy regard for tall tales and yarns that had little relationship to art. The role I was playing was the great thing. And my role was effective. It was a tremendous weapon, really, which I did not quite know how to wield.

I suppose that every man or woman who sets out to do a piece of regional work requiring a wide variety of public contacts must play a role. He becomes a leader for a certain idea, and he develops techniques which he thinks work. Sometimes the role becomes a mask, as it did for me, but sometimes, if one waits long enough, the mask wears away, and one finds, curiously, that the mask and one's own face are the same thing. The outward qualms, the shames are gone then, but inward scars remain. With some people it is the scars on a nervous belly, and with others it is the removal of a spiritual part that will never grow again.

I have found that I have always had to play a role to get the best results in my work. The Alberta experiment was the first brush at it but not the last by any means. When one attempts to be champion of a cause or a region he has to become a kind of symbol, like a statue almost, of the thing he believes, the single idea he is striving to put over. A symbol, blessedly, is often an unfeeling thing, just as a statue is, and one does not really mind. The people themselves will endow the symbol with spirit and the statue with warmth and life in terms of their own concepts of such things. And the statue may stride (full of the life people have given him) along his way, knowing that everyone loves role-playing and that crowds of women, especially, will follow after and idolize the best role player, just so long as he does not enter their private lives.

I do not mean to sound bitter, I am not bitter at all. For of late years I have grown into my role and will never again struggle against it. My role changed, modified, and perhaps flattened out my creative skills and swept away my nostalgia for a homeland, a place in which I could become an old-timer like the ones I heaped with laurels for their frontier manliness. I know that such nostalgia is not for me and will never haunt me again.

But between speeches and hand shaking in Alberta some solid work was going ahead. Looking back, I know that my tests of ideas in Alberta were extremely valuable to me later. And the things we tried to do to encourage a home-grown Alberta literature were satisfying to me. I confirmed, too, the idea that public relations is an essential part of regional work in the cultural arts. We had known that, vaguely, in New York State.

Settling In

In 1938, when I chanced to enter the picture in New York it had become apparent to Drummond that to be successful the whole regional concept of drama must encompass objectives other than mere playmaking. First and most essential was a study of the region and of the native source-materials of the region with an eye toward the collection of an authentic body of material that might be wisely and creatively applied to the dramatic form.

In New York we found it extremely difficult to reach the state as a whole. New York can never be considered as a closely-knit cultural unit. It is broken into many regions, each containing what might be considered a basic culture or tradition. We attempted a haphazard New York State radio series of plays, but the war halted our efforts.

In Alberta the job looked easier. The people, I soon discovered, were familiar with a sort of common lore of the region and were sensitive to the literary materials of the region. In other words, the stories the Alberta folks liked to tell best were distinctly regional in that they dealt with rains, hails, droughts, chinook winds, dust, various industries like ranching, dry-farming, oil, or with the whole memory of the frontier, which is quite a force still.

In Alberta, for instance, in the earlier days it was fairly easy to accumulate a lot of money in one year. There were oil booms and land booms and large ranching and wheat ventures, some of which paid off. One of my favorite stories is of a rancher who rushed into a Calgary store one day to buy a fur coat for his wife. He was dressed in an old green bowler, ragged trousers, and boots with soles flapping loose. The clerk who waited on this strange individual hesitantly took a fifty-dollar coat from the rack, stated its price, and had the garment thrown instantly back at him. The clerk brought out a five-hundred-dollar coat, and the rancher threw it on the floor and wiped his feet on it. The clerk then timidly offered the best coat they had in the store—a thousand-dollar one—and this the rancher said he would take. He asked whether the store would take his personal check. When the store said "No," the rancher whipped a check for $100,000 out of his pocket. The check was made out to the rancher and was signed by Pat Burns, the biggest meat packer in the province. The rancher had sold Pat Burns some cattle that day. He asked the store to take the thousand out of the check.

But if the frontier can produce such happenings, the Alberta climate can produce others no less wonderful. In the heart of winter the mighty chinook arch may form in the west and a soft spring-like wind may come puffing over the prairies, melting the snow with temperature rises of as much as sixty or seventy degrees in an hour's time. And usually there is plenty of snow to melt. Take the year of the Big Snow, for instance, when the snow was so deep it covered all of Morley Church except the tip of the steeple. Morley is over on the Indian Reservation west of Calgary. The old-timers tell me that the Indians would ride to church on top of the crusted snow, tie their ponies to the tip of the steeple, and go down into the church through a tunnel. One Sunday the Indians were terribly surprised when they emerged from the church to find that a chinook wind had come, melted the snow, and had left their ponies dangling from the steeple. That was the year, the old-timers continue, that a character named Dave McDougall traveled to Calgary by sleigh. A chinook slipped up behind Dave, but by whipping his horses he was able to keep the front runners on snow. The back runners, according to legend, raised a tremendous dust storm.

In southern Alberta, where the really strong winds blow, folks are said to walk around permanently bent over at forty-five-degree angles from facing into it. A rancher friend of mine from Macleod told me that he kept a heavy log chain tied to a post in his yard. This was his wind gauge. When the chain blew out at an angle of about thirty degrees there was a breeze. When the chain stood out at right angles the rancher figured he better tell his wife to get the clothes in before a gale hit. When there was a good steady wind the rancher's three boys practiced chinning themselves on the chain.

Such imagination, surely (or so say the Alberta newspapers), can flourish only in a section where the frontier "feel" is still strong.

Perhaps the painters do not paint on the street corners of Canadian towns as they do in Paris. And, it is probably true that there are not nearly so many pictures by native artists hanging on the walls of homes in western Canada as there may be in Norway. But the fact of the matter is that a movement is under way right now in Canada and in the United States that may well overcome the best-seller complex.

It is easy to point out that the frontier has left a hangover of the success complex to dull Canadian and American interest in homegrown literary and art products, and the results of the drive of the frontier are easy to see. Observe the mess of tanks, stacks, furnaces, and stinks that lie along the Turnpike as it runs into Chicago from the east. Or drive along the Mississippi as she curves south from Galena toward Davenport and witness the factories on the shore and the barges in the river. Go across western Kansas in wheat harvest time and see the combines with twenty-foot platforms biting into the grain. See the herds of purebred cattle and the infinite lacings of wires and derricks in Oklahoma. Or go to Alberta and watch a great new oil development.

These are easy to see. What is not so easy to see or to comprehend is the change that has come upon us of late years. It is a change so subtle that the farmer or the farmer's wife cannot tell you exactly how or when it came. All he or she knows is that if he or she wishes to sit in the front yard and paint a picture, no one will think it unusual. Or if he or she wishes to write poetry it is not necessary to keep it a secret any longer because many of the neighbors are doing it. The native artist has been accepted in many communities in North America, and no accusation of nonvirility is put upon a man for expressing himself in any of the arts and crafts. This has happened partly, perhaps, because we have paused from our frontier success story and have begun to look inward for creative things. This inward looking has happened most successfully where there has been a leader of vision to interpret, to stimulate, to encourage, or to help the development of a native arts movement naturally from the materials at hand—the legend, folklore, tall tales, and the feeling of the people about their own places.

It could perhaps happen everyplace, for even as the people of North America have made the chief end of frontier struggle the success of an industrialized or mechanized society, so they may be capable of becoming an art-conscious people in a short time. We do things in a hurry, once we get the idea.

The seed somehow must grow from ourselves. And the way to make it grow is to create an attitude, a friendly attitude, in which the native things may flourish. I must go on to say, of course, that the surest way to create such a friendly attitude in the communities of North America is to see that the product of the native artists is good—preferably superb. I am not speaking now of the arts that are purely recreative. These have their place, and where the frontier hangover is strongest the recreative arts may be the farthest development we can hope for. I am speaking now of the native artists who will create a product that is well above the mediocre, that is outstandingly interpretative of the artist and the region. This, of course, brings up the point of how such native artists are to be developed. In the instance of the creation of a good home-grown literature, what are the writers to write about? Or what is the painter to paint? The obviously good advice is to write and paint what you see and know best. To most people this is the event and association of community life or the landscape seen in a twenty- or thirty-mile radius of the home doorstep. Such advice cannot be gainsaid; yet in its very goodness—to write and paint what you know—lies the often bitter controversy of regionalism. For it is certainly true that the scholars and writers of the past seem to have divided the subject into battlefields and thus have greatly limited the scope of regional creation.

There were the "folk" specialists who held that good regional creative work must be related to the homely customs, sayings, and ways of the people who were vaguely classed as "the folk" of a particular region.

From this interpretation grew many stage and literary stereotypes: the mountaineer with his cud of tobacco and his whiskey jug, the shotgun wedding, and the elaborate dialogue so often a poor attempt at phonetic rendition of the actual speech patterns of a certain type of character.

There were those who argued back and forth in foolish arguments that nothing regional could exist in a city. There were those who shouted that nothing of any literary worth could come out of a rural area. Some authorities maintained that regionalism could be only state- or, even, county-wide. Others said that geography was the true factor.

In light of a calm estimate of contemporary conditions most of these points of view seem slightly awry. Anybody can guess that "the folk" no longer exist as they once did. Communications have so broken the older patterns of society that only in the broadest and most general terms can the people of any region be called "the folk." Folklorists who make a science of the collection of indigenous materials still desperately seek and classify such items, but as a creative force "the folk" idea is dead. Thus, "folk drama," as it was once defined, may be dead. And anybody can say with truth nowadays that rural and urban are so mixed and mingled that the edge of that old controversy has worn off.

How, then, is the writer or artist, looking at the things about him, to approach his creative work? Perhaps with the argumentative statements no longer present to hinder and plague and classify creative talent, the author or the artist may strive for a sincere creative grasp of the things he knows and understands and which he may now interpret with universality. For in universality lies the soul of great regionalism. Our authors must show us our familiar landscapes; yet their characters must be so created in true patterns of human life that those characters may be recognized and understood anywhere in the world.

Somehow we must find in North American regions the few persons capable of achieving such creations, and we must give them every opportunity to create; for in such universal interpretation lies understanding of our own place and our region, and understanding of us in other places, other regions, and other nations of the earth.

As I look at it now I can see that regionalism becomes terribly important to a project.

Regionalism, from my point of view, seems to become the development of a popular art movement drawing its vital force from the cultural streams of the region but transcending the smaller limitations of subject matter and method. Within the popular art movement, of course, must be the few native artists of great worth.

Radio or television drama may be an inadequate substitute for living theater, but the fact is that Canadians living away from the larger centers see few stage plays. There is an increasing movement in countryside theater in Canada nowadays I am told, but when I was in Alberta in the early 1940s the war had greatly reduced community play production, and the farmer or rancher found his greatest dramatic pleasure by simply turning his radio on in the evening and letting his imagination become his stage. For the great theater of Canada is a theater that comes out of the sky. Fine plays, both classics and contemporary original plays, wing out from the producing centers of the Canadian Broadcasting Corporation at Montreal, Toronto, Winnipeg, and Vancouver, directed by the finest radio producing artists in North America.

The CBC has shown an eagerness to let its writers experiment as they please, to try the unusual story, to break codes or taboos, and the result has been some of the most exciting radio drama heard in North America. The stir and discussion generated throughout the Canadian countryside when a radio play is produced which hits hard with idea and force of unusual treatment is comparable to the excitement that follows the *première* of a successfully serious play.

In 1944 Andrew Allen, in Toronto, and Esse Ljungh, then in Winnipeg, both had a deep sense of responsibility for the faithful dramatic interpretation of Canada. Allen's famous "Stage" series carried then a fair amount of dramatic material highly pertinent to the Canadian scene, and Esse Ljungh was forever seeking new, poetic talent to interpret the Canadian West. The production studios of the CBC were opened, therefore, to the plays of many new writers.

When the Alberta Folklore and Local History Project right from the start was flooded by yarns about Alberta told by a rich variety of persons, I began, in the Fall of 1943, to utilize many of these Alberta yarns in the form of weekly radio broadcasts over station CKUA in Edmonton, done always at a certain, specified time when the greatest number of listeners could be assured. I had had no time to shape these yarns into radio dramas; so I narrated them straight, and through these yarn broadcasts I built up a large following of people who, from their many letters, seemed to have an intense regional interest.

The Prairie Regional network of the CBC became interested, too, and, recognizing that the Alberta stories were fairly typical of the entire Canadian West, made time available to me. I was then able to cover most of Canada with my broadcasts. I consider that the two years of continuous broadcasting in Canada made a deep and lasting impression and established an attitude that helped in the development of a native drama of Alberta and the West. For in my radio talks and in public lectures I made it a point to tell the stories which might be most readily adapted to dramatic form. I talked a great deal about the countryside heroes such as Twelve-Foot Davis, the Peace River Country hero of generosity and kindness to travelers, Dave McDougall, hero of the tall tale, and Bob Edwards, the great Calgary humorist and editor of the *Calgary Eyeopener*. And as stories about these and other dramatic figures were told and retold on the air and their dramatic potentialities emphasized, it began to be more apparent to the people of Alberta that they had a wonderful set of dramatic traditions ready to be turned into fine plays that they would like to see or hear.

My own attempts at playwriting, when I finally found the time, were largely in radio. To gather material for my broadcasts I frequented local gathering places. During the war years, beer flowed only during certain hours in the western Canadian beer parlors. Usually the hours were between three and six, with servings of beer at three o'clock, four o'clock, and five o'clock. The practice was for the men to gather in the parlors, wait impatiently for the trays of glasses to come around, and to collect as many glasses of the good Canadian beer as possible. Then the yarn spinning would begin. It was certainly not my chief purpose to haunt the beer parlors of Alberta, but from the parlors flowed, along with the beer, a virile brand of lore that I delighted to hear.

There was a shabby man with bright, small eyes and chin whiskers, for instance, who came each afternoon to the beer parlor in the MacDonald Hotel in Edmonton. His yarns of curious doings throughout Alberta, always with himself as a participant, were examples of the most masterful exaggeration I have ever heard. Yet his tales were fretted and scrolled with authentic flavor of the West. His friends quite frankly said that "Johnny" was 1 percent man and 99 percent straight liar. He narrated how he spent hours frozen into the carcass of a steer in which he had sought shelter from a plain's blizzard. His time inside the steer was phony, but his descriptions of the blizzard were brilliant. He told of the year when there was no Fall or Winter, when Alberta bloomed the year around under the soft fingers of the ceaseless chinooks. He told of the year when there was no Summer and of how the Big Ice crept within a stone's throw of Calgary.

His yarns I managed to frame into a radio play that I called *Johnny Dunn*. Esse Ljungh produced the script from the Winnipeg CBC studios, and the heroic Johnny of the play enjoyed a wide reputation for a time as the type of all Alberta tall tale spinners. I eventually turned the radio play into a stage piece which had its *première* at the Banff School of Fine Arts in 1945.

There were other radio plays, too. One afternoon it was quiet in the MacDonald Hotel beer parlor between the five o'clock and the six o'clock ration. Johnny Dunn had drunk all the beer he could hold and had stopped telling tall stories for a while. It was during this small lull that another man at our table, a neat, elderly gentleman, told me the dramatic story of the great Frank slide.

This slide was a mighty avalanche that swept away a small mining town called Frank in the Crow's Nest Pass in April, 1903. The yarn was told so quietly, yet with so much feeling—my old acquaintance had lived near Frank when the slide occurred—that I was quite carried away. A few days later when I was remembering the old man's tale of how the side of the old Turtle Mountain had slid away in the early morning hours and of how they had afterwards found an unidentified baby lying on a huge stone after the slide had passed and had named her "Frankie Slide," the words and music of a song came to my lips. When I had set the song down I called it "The Ballad of the Frank Slide." Later the song turned into a Canadian Broadcasting Corporation play. Andrew Allen produced it first in Toronto in 1945, and it has since been repeated on the CBC networks many times.

A little while after the play was produced on the Trans-Canada Network I received a letter from a lady who lived somewhere in British Columbia. She said that she was the baby girl who had been found on the rock.

Looking back, I can see that the chief value of the small series of Alberta plays that I did for the CBC lay in the conviction that dramatizing native materials for radio would always be an important part of my regional program. The success of the CBC plays certainly led me later to try the same idea in Wisconsin, where I created a weekly half-hour dramatic series called Wisconsin Yarns.

The Alberta Folklore and Local History project confirmed for me the theory I had formed in New York State that a collection of native materials can be of immense value in stimulating creative writing. The project confirmed, also, my belief that a public relations program using mass media could greatly enhance the appreciation of native literary works. These ideas and beliefs which I had tried out in New York and Alberta formed the basis of the work I was to attempt within the framework of the Wisconsin Idea.

In Alberta I deepened my feeling for place and, I think, became more sensitive to elements in regional life—elements which can make any region unique, a place of distinctive flavor. Association with such persons as noted Canadian playwright Gwen Pharis helped me to develop these sensitivities. I became, in Alberta, aware of role-playing in my work and became conscious of a drive which stimulated and made possible my adventures in promoting regional arts and in gathering native materials.

HIGH RIVER AND
THE LOST LEMON MINE

I PUBLISHED MY FIRST REAL COMMERCIAL BOOK AS A RESULT of my work in Alberta. *JOHNNY CHINOOK* was a book filled with stories of the Canadian West, chiefly yarns from the wide expanses of Alberta. I was fortunate in being able to travel to many places throughout the seven-hundred-fifty mile length of the Province, and back and forth across its three-hundred-fifty mile width. I grew extremely fond of the Alberta people, and worked hard on the book, but didn't know exactly what to do with it. The matter was taken care of for me.

A lady arrived at my office one July afternoon. She was writing publicity for the Canadian Pacific Railroad, and she asked the golden question: Did I happen to know of anyone who was writing a book-length work on the Province of Alberta?

I kept my face as unemotional as I could and replied, "Why yes, ma'am. I do know of such a book." And I pulled the manuscript out of my desk drawer.

She asked whether she might take it that night to read. Eagerly, I gave my permission.

The next day she came back to say that she liked the book, and would I permit her to send it to a friend in New York, editor of Longmans Green and Company. Again, I gladly gave my permission, and within two weeks "Johnny Chinook" was accepted for publication. In my foreword to the book, I explained that the work was undertaken for the people of the Province of Alberta. Especially, it was undertaken to encourage other writers to use more freely the fine source material of the Canadian West. As a result of my year's work, there is at the University of Alberta, a fairly large collection of materials pertinent to Western backgrounds. I happened to be one of the last on the spot while some of the great pioneers of the West were still alive. I was able to collect many of their stories. The University of Alberta library now considers the collection one of their rarest.

It was part of my mission to go searching for tales, for the essences of places, reflecting in the stories of the people. One day my wandering took me south from Edmonton to Red Deer, to Calgary and beyond Calgary, south through the little foothill places, Okotoks, Aldreyde, High River. These places were at the eastern edge of the great ranching country that lay to the west, toward the foothills. High River of course, had the railroad running down the very center of the little town, and the front street buildings seemed lonely and stark as I swung down from the Canadian Pacific coach. I was headed for the office of the High River Times where, I had been told by Bob Needham, columnist for the *Calgary Daily Herald*, I would hear many good tales.

At the *HIGH RIVER TIMES*, I found Helen McCorquodale and Charles Clark busy with copy for the next day's paper. They both graciously stopped their work for a moment and considered my question about old-timers who might tell me tales about the old Alberta West.

"Stories!" mused Mrs. McCorquodale. "You must go to see Senator Riley. He's our grand old man here in High River."

"Get him to tell you the tale of the lost Lemon Gold Mine," Mr. Clark said. "He knows that yarn better than any man now living. He ought to. Spent enough time looking for it himself."

"One thing I want to ask you, Mr. Clark," I said, "I understand that the *HIGH RIVER TIMES* succeeded another paper here: the *EYE OPENER*, edited by Bob Edwards."

"Oh," exclaimed Mrs. McCorquodale, "now you've really asked for a story!"

"The story of Bob Edwards," said Mr. Clark with a twinkle in his eye, "is undoubtedly the greatest tale in Southern Alberta, or maybe in all the West for that matter. Tell you what you do. You go over to see Senator Riley and get the story of the Lemon Mine. Then come back and we'll let you see our file of the *EYE OPENER*, and maybe we can tell you a tale or two about old Bob."

"Senator Riley lives straight down this street," said Mrs. McCorquodale. "You can't miss his place. You'll have to make a detour around the C.P.R. station."

Mr. Clark was already on the way to his desk with a handful of copy. When I got my hat on and the door opened, Mrs. McCorquodale was making her pencil fly across a sheet of copy paper. As I went out the door, she muttered, "What in the world will I do about Women's Activities?"

"Yes, sir," said Senator Dan Riley as I stretched comfortably in a chair in front of his fire, and he sat down in his favorite chair where he could watch the people passing on the sidewalk, "yes, sir, this is a good country, and some wonderful things have happened out here. You wouldn't believe it, but a friend of mine, Buckskin Williams, had the narrowest escape from rattlesnakes I ever heard of. One time Buckskin was pulling out of Milk River with a freight wagon and noticed that every horse on the near side was crowding the chain. When the near wheel horse reared, Buckskin saw what the trouble was: a big rattler had struck, missed the horse, and hit the wagon tongue. The tongue started to swell, and Buckskin had to saw it off mighty quick to save the wagon."

The Senator glanced at me, his blue Irish eyes twinkling. When I looked at him, I could understand why he typified the fine traditions of courage, hospitality, and good humor of the ranching country. He has lived in the High River District since 1883. His hospitality is famous throughout Southern Alberta, and you are likely to find a variety of people at his house. The Stoney Indians consider him their great friend and adviser. The old-timers like to come to swap yarns; townspeople are always dropping in; and many travelers going through High River stop off to visit the Senator. He is very proud of his Celtic origin, and in characterizing some individual whom he admires he is fond of saying, "He is a fine man. An Irishman."

"You should have come around here ten-fifteen years ago," continued Senator Riley. "So many of the real colorful figures of the region are gone now. A lot of folks call themselves old-timers nowadays that have no right to the name. Old-timer used to mean something in this country. You might pass a man on the street and say, 'Good morning, old gentleman,' and he'd pass you right up; but if you said, 'Good morning, old-timer', he'd stop and know right away that you were one of the right sort.

"Time does slip by." The Senator was silent a moment, his eyes fixed on some point outside that I couldn't see.

"That's my son, George," the Senator said. "Just coming back from town. He and I batch here. I want you to meet him."

The front door opened and George Riley came into the room. He is a big man like his father and has the same twinkle in his eyes.

"George," said the Senator, "this fellow is collecting stories about Alberta."

"Read about you in the paper," said George Riley. "Say, you ought to tell him about Wild Bill," he said to his father.

"Don't remember much about Bill," said the Senator. "He was a queer customer. That's about all I do recall."

"Queer is no name for it," George said. "Nobody knew where the old cuss was from, and nobody in the world could have kept track of all the crazy things he did. He was likely to pop up anywhere, especially at dinner time. Wouldn't say a word, just come into a ranch house, sit down at the table and begin to stow it away. After a while, he'd get up and disappear."

George Riley laughed suddenly. "I know one time when he pretty near scared some women to death. Like I said, he was a strange customer. Well, God knows why, but one evening he went out to a fellow's cow shed and dug a hole in the manure just deep enough to bury all of him except his head. His hair was about two feet long, and he had a big beard, too. When he got himself buried in the manure, there was this God-awful head, just sticking out of the top of the pile.

"This rancher's wife and a friend of hers were out gathering the eggs when suddenly they saw this disembodied head sticking out. They dropped their eggs and ran a mile, I guess."

"Wild Bill had a way with horses," said Senator Riley. "It was a funny thing: somebody would have a mean horse that nobody could ride, and if Wild Bill happened along, he'd take that horse and ride him. Just throw a saddle on and ride away."

"That's right," George Riley said, "And he'd pop up in the most unusual places." He looked at me, "Don't know whether you know about range fires or not, but they're bad things in this country. Especially bad in the old days when the grass was longer than it is now. One way they had of fighting range fires was to kill a calf, split it open, fix a rope to the head and one to the hind feet, tie off each rope to a saddle, and drag the animal right over the edge of the fire.

"Well, one day a fire got started, and some of the boys set off after a calf some little distance away. They'd just about come up to it, when suddenly Wild Bill stepped out of a ditch, shot the animal, had it split open, and had disappeared again before the boys got there."

"Yes," said the Senator, "but Wild Bill was kind of crazy. We really had some great figures out here."

"Nigger John Ware was one," said George Riley.

"Yes, Nigger John Ware, Fred Stimson, Johnny Franklin, George Land—Howell Harris was another."

"Who was Howell Harris?" I asked.

"Harris was an Indian trader, buffalo hunter, and sort of all-round superman. In his later years he was a cattleman and manager of the Circle Ranch, one of the largest outfits in Western Canada. He built the first building of which we have any reliable record in High River, about 1865. The place was called Fort Spitze, about five miles from the present town of High River.

"Not long after Harris arrived at Spitze he made an enemy. A young brave, who had arrived only a few days before from some distant tribe, wished to avenge the death of his brother who had been killed by a white man. The brave decided that, as Harris was a big man, his brother's death would be avenged if he killed this white trader. This was the Indian custom: not necessarily the man who did the killing, but any white man's death would even up the score.

"This brave planned the manner of Harris' passing in the following way: before daylight the Indian would crawl to the roof of the low, log house immediately over the only door leading from Harris' room, and when Harris stepped out in the morning, he would shoot him in the back. It looked like a cinch, but you know how it goes—'the best laid plans of mice and men,' etc. You see, a certain woman to whom the Indian had confided his plans came to Howell in the night and gave him warning; and so instead of going out the door, as was his usual habit, Harris opened a small window in the rear, took his rifle, and slipping quietly around the corner, got a bead on the brave, and the Indian was soon on his way to the Happy Hunting Ground."

Senator Riley laughed silently. "I remember I asked Harris if the Indians didn't resent this. He said they did, but he squared it with a half gallon of whisky."

"Nigger John used to work for Harris, didn't he?" asked George Riley.

"He did," said Senator Riley, "and if there was ever a dead shot with rifle or revolver, Nigger John was that man. One time Nigger John aroused the enmity of a young Blackfoot brave named Lightning Streak. A woman was the cause of the fracas, as usual. The brave issued a challenge to mortal combat which was accepted by Nigger John.

"The agreement was: Winchesters at eighty yards. The combatants were to stand back to back. Harris, as referee, was to count: one, two, three. At the word three, they were to turn, begin shooting, and walk toward each other till one or the other went down, or their guns were emptied.

"It was unlikely that John would have far to walk as he was a dead shot. Sure enough, John killed his man at the first shot, losing, however, the lobe of an ear by the Indian's bullet. Immediately another young brave volunteered to take his brother's place, and after the preliminaries were all settled, the fatal words again rang out: 'One, two, three!' Again John whirled and killed his man—hitting him directly between the eyes. But the crown of John's Stetson was punctured by the Indian's bullet. That was that."

"Is that all that happened?" I asked.

"Oh," said the Senator, "the women mourned, and the tom-toms beat to celebrate the passing of the two braves, and probably their heroism furnished the subject of tales told round the campfires for years to come, by those who witnessed the duel and by their descendants."

"Mr. Clark said you might tell me the tale of the lost Lemon Gold Mine, Senator," I said. "I have heard."

"The Lemon Mine," said the Senator, and he laughed all down inside him. "I ought to know the story of that. Enough of my time went into looking for it. And enough of my money, too.

"Are you comfortable? Have a cigar."

The History of the Lost Lemon Mine was told me bit by bit, year by year, around many a campfire, by that old frontiersman, Lafayette French, as we traveled, prospected, and camped in the vastness of the Rocky Mountains in the years that are past.

For a better understanding of this story, I will tell you who Lafayette French was. French was born in Pennsylvania in 1840 and came to the western states as a very young man. There he spent several years on the American frontier. He appeared in the Northwest Territory as an Indian trader and buffalo hunter in the pre-Mounted Police days. He came after the Lemon Mine had been found and lost by two prospectors he had previously staked in Montana. One, Blackjack, was dead—murdered on the eve of discovery by the other, Lemon, who was driven insane by his deed. Lafayette French came to this country to rediscover the Lemon Mine.

Sometime about the spring of 1870, a party of miners left Tobacco Plains in Montana to prospect the North Saskatchewan River, known even at that time to contain showings of fine gold. In the party were two men known as Blackjack and Lemon. The former had the reputation of being the best prospector in the West, having found some of the richest placer camps in the western states, and was the real discoverer of the famous Cariboo diggings in British Columbia. These two experienced prospectors were staked by French and traveled with the party to the Saskatchewan River. They found gold, but not in paying quantities, so in the fall they decided to leave the rest of the party and return to Tobacco Plains to winter.

They gladly availed themselves of the opportunity to travel south with a large half-breed party, headed by one La Nouse whom I knew well. This escort offered protection against the hostile Blackfeet and Blood

Indians. They traveled south by the old trail which lay along the foothills. La Nouse and his party were bound for Fort Stand Off; Blackjack and Lemon headed for Tobacco Plains (a large Roman Catholic Mission in Montana); so they separated.

The two prospectors were supposed to have gone up High River and over the mountains by an old and plain trail used by the Indians from Tobacco Plains who drove large bands of horses in to what is now Alberta every fall, and drove them back again loaded with pemmican. Blackjack and Lemon were passing the river as they proceeded. They followed showings of gold to the head of a mountain stream. There they found rich diggings from grass roots to bed rock, about five feet. They sank two pits, and in bringing their horses in from picket, accidentally found the ledge from which the gold came—a ledge of decomposed quartz.

French, who saw samples of this rock at Fort Benton, described it as resembling a body of gold with a little rock shot into it. The sample of this placer was coarser than anything ever found in the placer gulches of the western states. Is it any wonder that many men, then young and in their prime, spent the rest of their lives in a useless search for this Eldorado?

In the camp that night, the two adventurers had a disagreement as to whether or not they should stake the find and return in the spring. One favored this, the other opposed it. The argument finally terminated with Lemon killing his partner with an ax as he lay in his blankets. However much he might have wished to flee from the scene of the tragedy, he could not do so until daylight; so he built a huge fire and with his gun under his arm marched back and forth all night.

Little did he think two pairs of human eyes watched him and had witnessed the entire tragedy. Two young Stoney braves, William and Daniel Bendow, had followed the pair, watched them sink the holes, and saw them panning the gravel. They were waiting for what those strange white men might do on the morrow.

As the night wore on, Lemon was half crazed with the thought of the terrible deed he had done in his passion; and with a dim sense of humor the Indians whistled occasionally to further distress the unfortunate prospector. With the first streak of dawn, he mounted the big roan horse that French had given him and took the trail across the mountains. The Indians packed up what was left: camp outfit, grub, rifle, etc. Taking the two remaining horses, they started to Morleyville to report to their chief, Bearpaw. He must have been much interested as he made the young braves swear never to reveal to any person the location of what they had witnessed. It is not uncommon for whites to commit perjury, but no Indian was ever known to do so.

Many of those in late years who endeavored to locate the Lemon Mine know how religiously those two sons of the mountains kept their oath. Many bands of horses and herds of cattle—fortunes in themselves to those people—have time and time again been offered, but that strange fear of the penalties prescribed by that terrible oath rose up before them, and they both died with the secret locket in their breasts.

I knew them both well and traveled and camped with them in the mountains. They were splendid types of the old Indian chieftains, heads of a large following of their own progeny, ruling their little kingdom with kindness and with wisdom. How I admired this type of Indian: their dignity, their independence, their kindliness to their own people, their deep knowledge of nature. That book which is closed to so many contained valuable and interesting secrets.

But to go on with the story! Lemon arrived at the Mission at Tobacco Plains and at once confessed his crime to the priest whom he had known the preceding winter. He had with him the gold they had saved on the day of the killing, also a sample of the rock which they had found. He seemed half-crazed, and his crime weighed heavily upon him. There was at the Mission a half-breed named John McDougald, a man versed in the mountain travel. The priest dispatched McDougald to the scene of the tragedy on instructions given by Lemon as to the location of it.

McDougald found the place, buried Blackjack, built a mound of stones over the grave to keep the wild animals from digging up the body, and returned to Tobacco Plains. Later the Indians reported to Bearpaw the finding of this mound of rocks. He at once dispatched William and Daniel with orders to tear down the mound and to scatter the stones. This they did, and the last trace of a bloody murder was removed from the face of mother earth. How well she has hidden her secret ever since in spite of all efforts to uncover it! The Indians were ordered to hunt no more in this locality nor to use the trail. Mountain trails that are not used soon become impassable and so this trail is not used today—unless it may be one of those opened up in later years by forest rangers.

Lemon spent the winter with his spiritual friend and, although he acted strangely at times, was for the most part sane enough. So during the long winter a party was formed and equipped to start in the spring to work the prospect. As soon as the snow made it possible to travel, a start was made. But they were not alone. All the miners who had wintered in that part of the country had heard of the rich find and were filled with hope of much gold to be found. They formed a large party—about seventy-five men—and followed Lemon and his men.

They stopped at Crow's Nest Lake, proceeded north from there where Lemon camped the party, somewhere about six miles from the original find. This was necessary in order to get grass for their large bunch of horses. Lemon and his party had camped some little distance from the main body, and early next morning, leaving two men in camp to look after it and to kill deer, they started, followed, of course, by the other party.

Lemon was unable to locate the place and, after a fruitless search, concluded he had taken the wrong gulch. This would not go down with those who had followed him, and they accused him of trying to throw them off and threatened to lynch him. Lemon mounted his horse and rode back to camp where he became violently insane. His own party stood guard over him all night and in the morning started back over the mountains. They reached Tobacco Plains, and Lemon, although he had lucid intervals, never fully recovered his reason. He lived for many years with his brother who was a cattle rancher in Texas.

So ended the first expedition and so have ended many more. Every one has been unsuccessful and many of them tragic.

Next year the priest outfitted another party from Tobacco Plains. This was to have as its leader, McDougald, the man who buried Blackjack. McDougald, who was at Fort Benton, was to meet the rest of the party at Crow's Nest Lake; they were to proceed north from there. McDougald left Benton to keep the appointment, but at Fort Kipp—a whisky trading post—he drank so much booze it killed him. The party at Crow's Nest Lake waited a week before hearing of the death of their leader. And so they turned back.

Next year another large party was equipped and got as far as the lake when mountain fires burned all the timber and grass, so they were forced to abandon the enterprise.

The year following, the priest sent a small party under the guidance of Lemon, but on nearing the place Lemon went mad again, and they were forced to take him back.

It would appear that the priest now gave up the quest, but it was taken up by others. One of these was a member of the first Lemon party, a man named Nelson; but after a summer's useless search, the party disbanded, and each man continued an independent search. Finally Lafayette French followed a lone trail. Once sickness overtook him back in the vastness of the hills, and he was barely alive when he finally reached my ranch on the head of Willow Creek. There he was nursed back to health, and the next spring saw him again ready and eager to renew the search.

It was about this time that my curiosity was aroused as to what French was looking for; slowly and gradually he told me the story. He began by showing me a rough pen and ink sketch of rivers and mountain ranges, and at the head of a stream with three forks was an X. He told me that the map was made by Lemon and that the mark was the Lemon

Mine, the richest thing ever found in the Rocky Mountains. He told me that that was the reason he had come to Alberta and said he would continue the search as long as he lived. From that time until his death fifteen years later, I was associated either directly or indirectly with French in his prospecting.

From him I learned the Indian trails, the passes, and the camping grounds; learned to pack, to travel, and to love the silent mountains. And so, though I found no gold, I can truthfully say now that I have found something that gold cannot buy.

French went about his work methodically—he was, in fact, the most methodical man I have ever known. He spent some months in the '90s with the two survivors of the several expeditions that had come into the country. He even had one of them come by pack train to Crow's Nest Lake and then north in an endeavor to have this man identify some of the landmarks of the district traveled by the first expedition headed by Lemon. He kept La Nouse and his band of half-breeds through the winter of '83, so as to check in the spring and to discover where Lemon and Blackjack parted company with him—La Nouse having gone to Fort Kipp and the two prospectors to Tobacco Plains.

French fed William Bendow, the Stoney Indian, and his retinue one winter at Lee's ranch on Pincher Creek and, in the spring, put twenty-five horses and twenty-five cattle in a pasture which would become Stoney William's, when he showed them the location of the killing. On the second day of the expedition William said he could go no farther—the terror of that oath came over him—and the expedition was abandoned.

Only a few years before French's death he made a bargain with the same William to show him the place he had looked for so long. William and his band were on their way to Morley and agreed to camp at the old George Sage place—an abandoned ranch on the middle fork of High River—until French could get George Emerson and myself to join them. That night William died suddenly. His people secured a Red River Cart and proceeded with his body to Morleyville. The night of their arrival,

William's son-in-law also died without warning. Is it any wonder that the Indians believe there is a hoodoo on everyone who tries to locate that place? In fact, old Indians refuse to talk about it and literally freeze up when the name is mentioned.

French was terribly burned in a fire that destroyed the Emerson house on the night of his return from his last prospecting trip. On the evening of his return, he wrote me a letter and posted it at the Bar U Ranch. In it he said that he had at last located IT and was coming to High River the following day to tell me everything. On his arrival he was unable to talk to me before he died; so if he had really solved the problem which had occupied so many years of his life, the secret died with him.

Many attempts have been made since that time, the most notable in 1929. Many there are who say "nothing will be found on this side of the mountains," but geologists designate a tract of country between Crow's Nest Lake and Mist Mountain on the head waters of the Highwood River as the disturbed area in which precious metals might be found. In my opinion, if the Lemon Mine is ever found, it will be in this territory which is really a trough of the Cretaceous Sea bounded on the west by the Paleozoic limestone of the main range of the Rockies and on the east by the Livingstone range, also of limestone. This trough is now a north and south valley, transversely cut by three watersheds of the Sheep Creek, Highwood, and Old Man rivers. The area is rich in coal, some low grade phosphate rock, and low grade deposits of iron. There are interrelated beds of conglomerate ash, a hard green rock occurring chiefly in the south and known as the Crow's Nest Volcanics. It is called the disturbed area because the beds of sandstone and shale, cradled between the ranges, are often found pitched on edge. The most remarkable feature, both within and without the mountains, is that both main streams occupying wide valleys flow on transverse strike lines rather than north and south. Yet nowhere on these streams have colors of gold ever been found, though it is safe to say every one has been prospected by someone at some time or other since the finding of the Lemon Mine.

If one were to give credence to stories that drifted down from the early days, the search for this Eldorado has claimed more than Blackjack's life. There is the story of a white man's skeleton found in the gap of the Old Man River and with it a bag of gold. There is the story of two men badly wounded stopping over night in the '90s at the ranch in the foothills. They carried gold dust and were fleeing from the West. They rode away next morning for Fort Macleod, but never arrived. Had they rediscovered the lost Lemon Mine and then been followed and killed by the Indians?

From time to time old mounds are found; the remains of cabins, old rusted muzzle-loading guns, and I. G. Baker tin containers date these. But a man in the mountains does not abandon his outfit.

For me the Province of Alberta was fascinating because of the character of the land, and the almost larger-than-life aspects of its folk heroes.

When I returned to the office of the *HIGH RIVER TIMES*, Mrs. McCorquodale was still writing copy. On being reminded that I wanted to hear a story about Bob Edwards, Mrs. McCorquodale took off her glasses and said with a twinkle in her eyes, "You know, Bob Edwards is a tradition here in High River."

"Then he published the *EYE OPENER* here before he went to Calgary?"

"He most certainly did. In fact, he tried publishing a paper in several Alberta towns none of which really seemed to appreciate the honor. As it was, he was educated in France and Belgium, and eventually drifted out to the Western States.

"He started out to be a farmer, but farm life apparently didn't agree with Bob. The farmer he worked for was pretty unreasonable about working long hours, and Bob argued with him about it. Eventually Bob persuaded his brother to purchase the farmer's place, and as soon as the deal went through, Bob took great delight in booting the farmer off.

"When he finally came to Canada he wanted to start a newspaper out here in the West, so he began to tell all his friends that he was going to start a paper in Wetaskiwin and that he would call the paper THE *WETASKIWIN BOTTLING WORKS*."

"Why in the world did he choose that title?" I asked.

"Well," said Mrs. McCorquodale, "Bob explained it by saying that his paper was going to be a corker. And it certainly was! He tried publishing in Wetaskiwin, Strathcona, Leduc, and finally in High River."

"Why did he leave High River?"

"Well," said Mrs. McCorquodale, "old-timers of High River maintain that what put the finishing touches on Bob Edward's journalistic career in High River was not so much what he said, as what he *did*—or was blamed for doing. They gleefully refer to the final outrage as 'The Incident of the Mixed Gramophone Records.' "

It seems that a traveling salesman came to town with something very enticing in the way of gramophone records, choral music designed to take the place of choirs at church services. The salesman won the consent of the church management to try out his sacred music at the Sunday service next day. Flushed with success, the salesman shared the story of his almost-certain sale with the boys round the hotel. They were all hospitality and enthusiasm.

But, as a matter of fact, the salesman had two suitcases of records on hand, one strictly sacred and the other of a most dubious nature. While he was enjoying social diversions which kept him fully engaged till church time, busy hands were at work switching records from one suitcase to the other. You can have one guess as to whose were the busiest hands of all.

However, there is no admission of guilt, no hint of shame, in the bland report of developments which appeared in the next issue of the High River *EYE OPENER*. Bob Edwards describes the catastrophe of the mechanical choir as follows:

> On being told that there was just one Methodist Church in town, the stranger explained his business. He was a gramophone choir promoter. Having long realized the difficulties which small town churches experience with their choirs, he had devised a

scheme which solved the whole cheese. All church troubles are traceable to the choir. If the minister eloped, it was sure to be with a member of the choir, and so on. His gramophone choir would put a stop to all the nonsense.

Through the kindliness of Dr. Stanley (the main pillar of the church), this rather scrubby-looking person obtained the promise of a fair trial for his gramophone choir on Sunday. Needless to say, the man kept going full blast all Saturday night in the room adjoining the bar, and when Sunday dawned the professor was in horrible shape from lack of sleep and too much of Jerry's fine old Glenhorrors. Anyhow, when Sunday evening came with the fateful hour of his church appointment, he was not himself at all.

All High River was at church to hear the new gramophone choir, and the back pews were filled with the tougher classes. Sure enough, the machine was perched on a little table, with the professor capering round fussing with the records.

"Hymn Number 471," announced the preacher. "*Hark the Herald Angels Sing!* omitting stanza three."

"See here," protested the professor, "this here automatic choir omits nothing. I can't hop and skip in the middle."

The people were evidently charmed with the music of the Edison quartet, and even the preacher looked gratified.

The next hymn announced was *Nearer My God to Thee*, and the congregation looked forward expectantly. Preliminary coughing and settling drowned out the gramophone announcement, but the machine had not taken many turns till it was realized that the heavenly choir was singing *Just Because She Made Them Goo-Goo Eyes..*

The professor hastily stopped the machine and started another record, but the minister stopped him. "The resignation of the gramophone choir is accepted," he said. "Let us pray."

Next morning the scrubby-looking professor might have been seen ambling to the depot on his way to Macleod. His records must have got mixed on Saturday night. He was a failure at church, but a brilliant success at the bar.

So that was what happened. Suspicion, not too surprisingly, centered on Bob Edwards as being a foremost promoter of the dirty work. And present survivors of that dark hour in town history are generous enough to admit that the plan of switching records was Bob's. They merely plied the professor with red-eye.

At any rate, Bob's doom was sealed as an instrument of evil, and in an issue immediately following comes the stark announcement:

> The Presbyterian Church has asked us to remove the notice of services from its cozy corner abaft the locals. And they got it for nothing, too! Feeling must be strong.

And an exasperated tone can be detected in the same issue:

> These small towns are awful. Westaskiwin threw us down. Leduc threw us down. Strathcona, being dead anyway, shook its shriveled finger at us. High River is passing us up. Ye gods! That we should have lived in such places and whooped them up free of expense.

So with this parting shot, Bob departed for the tolerant and generous atmosphere of Calgary.

after Midnight who had once again rejoined his friends in the pasture, and said, "Boys, that black will be the greatest horse in all Canada. Just drive him back in here."

This time, before mounting Midnight again, Jim sat with the other men and discussed the young horse's technique. Midnight resorted only to straight bucking. He didn't sun-fish or fence-row as so many bucking horses do in order to get rid of their riders.

Jim was thrown a third time, and now the boys expected the boss to resort to unfair tactics in order to break the spirit of the black, but Jim refused to do this. If the horse played fair, Jim would also play fair. On his third attempt, Jim lasted a few more jumps, and he believed that eventually he could ride that black devil.

At the end of the day both Jim and Midnight were worn out, but Jim had ridden Midnight without breaking the spirit of the big black horse.

Midnight learned fast after that. He became one of the best cutting horses in Jim's outfit. But only Jim could ride him. If any other cowboy tried it, he was promptly bucked off and with such force that he didn't care to attempt the job again.

Between Jim McNab and Midnight grew a strong friendship, but even Jim had to be careful. If the black fancied himself mistreated or his natural love of freedom threatened in any way, he would buck, and when he bucked even McNab was not able to ride him.

The horse had never been extended nor his bottom tested, so when Jim had to make a trip to a ranch some ninety miles away, he rode Midnight. When the time came for them to leave, Midnight started out proudly, head high, and never stopped once for the whole ninety miles. Nor did Jim have to use spurs.

Jim McNab was very proud of Midnight. He was certain that no man except himself could ride the black. Many persons urged him to enter the horse in various stampedes, and finally Jim entered Midnight in the stampede at Macleod held to celebrate the fiftieth anniversary of the coming of the old Royal Canadian Northwest Mounted Police.

Jim led Midnight into the arena, and there are many who remember what a magnificent horse the big black was that day. He towered above the ordinary stampede horse and really "stole the show" though he gave the two riders who had drawn him very little satisfaction. He piled them both in short order.

As time went on, Jim entered Midnight in other stampedes at local points, and always he bucked off any rider who was brave enough to climb on him. Jim feared that punchers gouging Midnight with spurs would make him an outlaw, and that is what happened. But Jim could not resist seeing the big horse spill the arrogant riders of the Red Deer and Medicine Hat outfits who claimed they could ride Midnight.

Under repeated urging, and taunted by the boasts of would-be-conquerors of Midnight, Jim entered his horse in the big Calgary stampede of 1924. Interest ran high, and many excellent riders, drawn by the large purse and the fame that would come to them were they able to ride Midnight, entered the contest. The contest was to last three days, and McNab deeply regretted having consented to enter his beloved Midnight, well knowing the punishment the horse would receive. But Jim had given his word and took the horse. Midnight was plainly displeased with the whole proceedings. He showed the strain particularly when he was tightly cinched, placed in the narrow chute, and surrounded by strangers.

McNab stood by and watched the struggling throng as horses were liberated from the chute with riders up. He had been pleased when he had learned that one of the most boastful riders from the Red Deer outfit had drawn Midnight. Midnight was excited. He had been taken from the quiet Cottonwood, away from his friends, and placed here among strange men who prodded him through the bars of the chute.

Finally Midnight's turn came. It was plain that the horse was insulted and mad clean through. The Red Deer rider took his seat, touched Midnight with the spurs. The signal sounded, the gate flew open and Midnight leaped. On the third jump he spilled the boaster—almost busted him, for the man lay still and had to be helped out.

The other great riders were not so confident when they actually beheld Midnight in action. The horse was heroic. In the entire three days not a single rider was able to stay on his back. Midnight was acclaimed the champion bucking horse of Western Canada.

But Midnight played fair. Not once did he try to kick or jump on a fallen rider. He appeared satisfied when they were bounced off his back, and sometimes he even turned and placed his nose on the fallen man before he trotted back to the chute.

During the Calgary stampede, McNab had many offers to sell Midnight, but Jim loved the fearless black and refused them all. He took Midnight back to the Cottonwood and let him rest from the exciting struggle. But the relationship between them was changed. Midnight would still come to McNab's whistle or call and in other ways still showed affection for the boss; but he never forgot nor forgave the cruel treatment he had received at Calgary. When McNab tried to ride him, he was quickly bucked off.

McNab had feared this would be the case. He didn't blame Midnight but was deeply grieved that he had consented to the maltreatment of his great friend.

Possibly it was his grief that led Jim to sell Midnight; for the horse was now an outlaw and fit only for the arena. He was sold to Peter Welch, of Calgary, who toured Canada and the United States with his string of rodeo horses.

And now began Midnight's great career as a rodeo horse. His fame spread. He became one of the most renowned horses in America.

One of the best riders in the United States came to grief at the hands of the Canadian champion. Bobby Askins of Ismay, Montana, came halfway across the continent to ride Midnight at Toronto in 1926. For four successive days Askins watched Midnight buck his men off in the preliminary contests. On the night before the final day Askins expressed the hope that he would draw the big black in the finals. Askins drew Midnight, and 20,000 fans crammed the huge stadium at the Toronto Exhibition grounds to see the ride.

It was a good ride but a short one. When the chute gates opened up, Askins spurred Midnight right behind the ears. The black horse was so astonished that he stood stock still. The packed grandstand roared with laughter as the big horse walked out of the chute with short, mincing steps.

Pete Knight, who was perhaps the greatest rider in the world at the time, whispered to a friend, "I wouldn't want to be up there right now for all the money in the world!"

But Midnight was already in action. Down went his head, and on his first terrific leap he almost shot the Montana cowboy out of the saddle. He clawed his way back desperately, but to little avail. On the eighth jump Midnight tossed Askins high in the air, and then for another four jumps he pitched so high and so hard that one of the stirrups smashed in two as it hit its mate over the saddle.

"He's even better than they told me he was," said Askins as they helped him to the first aid tent.

Two weeks later at Montreal, Pete Knight and Midnight staged the greatest tussle in the memory of the cowboys of the period. Although Pete was still aboard at the conclusion of the ride, he stated that it was the most terrific ride he had ever experienced. This was one of the very few times Midnight was ridden in his thirteen years of rodeo competition.

Midnight was not the wild type of outlaw. By nature he was gentle. He would do anything for a few lumps of sugar. He grew to love the competition of the arena, but he never resorted to tricks to unseat his rider. He simply put his head down and bucked, higher and higher at every jump, until on the fifth or sixth jump he would give a little twist which seemed to catapult the rider out of the saddle as though shot from a gun.

He loved to travel, and when he was sold to Eliot and McCarty of Johnstown, Colorado, he got a chance to travel from Calgary to Fort Worth, from Cheyenne to Madison Square Garden, and finally to Europe.

Midnight died at Eliot and McCarty's ranch at Johnstown in 1936. He was twenty years old. His owners placed a gravestone over his resting place as a tribute to his courage and love of liberty, and on the stone, they inscribed this verse:

> *Under this sod lies a great bucking hoss,*
> *There never lived a cowboy he could not toss.*
> *His name was Midnight. His coat was black as coal.*
> *If there is a hoss heaven, please God, rest his soul.*

And Jim McNab, who was the only man Midnight really loved, is said to have stated:

> *I miss you Midnight, since you were away;*
> *The once blue skies have turned to ashen gray—*
> *Seemed to dim the sunshine from the range—*
> *But fond memories of you will never change.*

ROCKY MOUNTAIN HOUSE

I N THOSE EARLY 1940 YEARS THERE WAS A PART-FREIGHT-part-passenger Canadian Pacific Railroad train that operated daily between Red Deer, Alberta and Rocky Mountain House. I was especially eager to visit Rocky because I'd been told in Edmonton that the little foothill town was still about as primitive as they came. I sat, during the train ride through scrub timber and some muskeg, with a gentleman from Calgary. He regaled me with many stories. One I remember well.

"Yes sir," said the Calgary man, "the hotel in Rocky gets kinda cold on winter nights. Recall meeting a feller coming downstairs one frosty mornin', carryin' a wash basin . . . you know the old porcelain kind they used to put on a wash stand? Well, I says to him, 'Say, where you goin' with that wash basin? "

" 'Why,' he says, 'my upper plate's froze in here. I'm goin' outside to bust her loose.' "

I stayed in the little new-lumber hotel that night, and I didn't find it *that* cold. Maybe because I didn't wear an upper plate.

There is no doubt in my own mind: Rocky Mountain House leads Alberta in the export of curious news items, friendliness to strangers, and that special atmosphere that breeds adventure. Perhaps David Thompson, the explorer, touched that region with a magic wand when he wintered at the Fort on his way to the Pacific. Possibly the old Indians endowed the place with their magic; or perhaps the spell goes farther back, to the time when the Rocky Mountains were forming. Draw your own conclusions but take it from me, there's witchery at Rocky Mountain House.

I had heard so much about this fabulous spot that I almost hesitated about visiting it. Perhaps I had a fear that a mysterious portal would open, and like the fabled traveler of old, I would find myself shut within some mystic cavern.

I must confess that this romantic nonsense was mostly shaken out of me by the C. P. R. when I rode their thrice-weekly train from Red Deer to Rocky.

The spell came back, though, when I arrived. I was met at the train by the young school inspector, Finlay Barnes, who carried me off to a typical Rocky Mountain House dinner, and delicious fare it was—baked moose meat with dumplings and mountain blueberry pie. In the evening I made a little talk in the Legion Hall and was not at all surprised when a large dog, named Skipper, came gravely in and seated himself on the platform. The townsfolk also took Skipper's presence as a matter of course and I was informed that the dog was *especially* fond of music—Bach and Beethoven were his favorite composers—but that he attended every meeting of more than two persons and seemed to know beforehand when meetings and concerts were going to take place.

I was much impressed by Skipper, especially when he arose and offered to shake hands just before I began to speak. I told the audience,

"When the dog walks out, it will be time for me to stop speaking." I had spoken perhaps six words when Skipper gravely stalked off the platform and walked toward the door. I hurriedly said something about the excellence of a dog's standards of judgment and brought Skipper to a halt half way down the aisle. He thought the matter over, finally decided to stick it out, and even offered to shake hands again when the talk was over. *Some* dog! But not unusual for Rocky. They accept Skipper just as they accept the Ogopogo.

For my less well-informed reader perhaps I should explain that the Ogopogo is a horrible monster which lives beneath the waters of the North Saskatchewan River and has special headquarters at Rocky Mountain House. He or she—they've never been able to determine which—is much larger than the *Okanagan Lake* Ogopogo in British Columbia and much more fierce and terrifying than those rather meek Ogopogos occasionally seen in Ontario.

A hint as to the great serpent's sex I found in one account which tells of the Ogopogo having been seen shortly before freeze-up last fall, swimming toward Edmonton with six little Ogopogos happily trailing along in the wake. This, I would suppose, seems to imply that the Ogopogo is a female. I mentioned this tale to a citizen of Rocky who immediately began to suspect the presence of a second Ogopogo—a male.

The Rocky Ogopogo was, apparently, first viewed by an Indian named Chief Walking Eagle who, staggering into town one day in 1939, gasped that a "fish fifty feet long, and as big around as an elephant" had pursued him across the river!

When asked where he got the "fire water," Walking Eagle became most indignant and recited numerous of his Christain virtues, which settled the matter as far as Rocky was concerned. Folks knew that Chief Walking Eagle was telling the truth.

Unfortunately, the river was frozen over when I visited Rocky, and I was not able to catch a glimpse of the monster. I have promised, however, to return during the month of May when the Rocky folks have promised to have a special showing of the Ogopogo for my benefit. I haven't a doubt in the world that they'll really produce a monster. They do such things at Rocky.

One time—back in 1927 to be exact—the gods of the plain and mountain became angry with Rocky. Why this should be so I have not been able to discover. Possibly it was because the region hadn't furnished its usual tribute of mystic events that year. Whatever it was, it was enough to cause the gods to loose a terrific cyclone on the village. Cyclones were usual in Kansas where I grew up, but at Rocky a cyclone seems to me to be the deliberate act of an outraged deity.

The cyclone stuck in July after a long spell of oppressive hot weather. The storm swooped down about three o'clock in the afternoon and caught the town entirely unprepared. Folks simply didn't know what was happening. One fellow ran into the open vault of the bank, while another hopped into a big icebox and slammed it shut. Another man grabbed at the nearest object, the knob of a door. The wind blew the door away and left him holding the knob. A schoolboy was out in the woodshed when the storm hit. The cyclone blew the building away, leaving the boy standing there with his arms full of kindling wood. The wooden sidewalks along the main street actually changed sides! Down at Ross's garage, an envelope blew right into a plank—so far they had to dig it out with a jackknife. They didn't dig it out right away, of course. As a matter of fact, it stayed there quite a while and became one of the local wonders.

One lady, who knew about cyclones from living in South Dakota, was out in the yard. She took one look at the approaching storm, knew what to expect, grabbed her baby and dove for the cellar. She heard the storm hit, knew the house was shaking. Presently when it was over she climbed the cellar steps, only to find that the trapdoor was no longer there. The house had moved six feet! Her husband had to cut a hole in the floor to get her out.

The children at Rocky were especially delighted to find the storm had carried away the curfew bell. The bell hasn't been found to this day, but the kids didn't know when they had a good thing, for now a whistle is blown for curfew.

One whole side of Main Street was demolished—with a single exception. One store was left undamaged. The Indians were so impressed by this obvious sign of the Great Spirit's favor that they took their trade to that store for years.

But the unusual applies to *individuals* as well as to Ogopogos and cyclones.

At Rocky I encountered what I believe to be the only "tree man" in Canada. His name is John Eagle. He doesn't live in the tree anymore, but he did until it blew down. You see, John Eagle used to be a sailor. He traveled around the world more than a dozen times, saw just about everything there is to see in the world, and came to settle down in a tree at Rocky Mountain House. He was tired of the ocean and the cities. He explained:

"You see too many strangers in the cities, and too much of too few strangers on a ship. The noise and crowds are worse than the wolves and bears."

He wanted solitude. At first he lived in a tent, but one night a high wind arose and blew the tent down on him. At the same time he fancied he heard the howling of wolves. He climbed a tree and spent the night there. The swaying of the tree reminded him of the swaying of the ocean. He got a wonderful idea! He would build a house in the tree.

He began the house the next day. First he built a platform, and on the platform he set a tidy little cabin. He insulated it with shavings from the planing mill, and finally, he had a warm, comfortable dwelling. Fuel was the biggest problem, but he solved it by leaning poles up against the platform, pulling them up, and sawing them on his own doorstep!

Sawing wood makes me remember the tale about a former inhabitant of Rocky who bore the impressive name, Silas K. Vandermark. Silas came from Oklahoma where he was said to have extensive oil holdings. This was evidenced by the rolls of money he occasionally had in his possession but not by his appearance; for Silas was a man who had a horror of washing. So great was his affinity for earth, in fact, that he lived in a dugout some little distance from Rocky. When that dugout fell in, Silas simply dug another and crawled into it.

It is generally thought that Vandermark's family wanted to get rid of him, so when buying him a railroad ticket, they just touched a spot on the map. To my mind, their selection of Rocky was not chance; it was simply magic.

The fuel problem was easily solved by Silas K. Vandermark. He would merely draw a pole up to the entrance of his dugout, stick it through the door and into the opening of his stove. Whenever the log burned off, he would just shove it in a little farther. This absolutely eliminated any wood cutting. His kitchen economy also showed ingenuity. Silas would kill a pig and hang it up in a tree. He never bothered to dress the pig at all; he'd merely walk out and cut off his morning bacon, ham, or whatever he was after, and let the rest hang. He never built any sort of shelter for his pigs and horses. He simply took the pigs into his cave with him and would have done the same thing for the horses had there been space.

In spite of his many eccentricities Silas was most kind-hearted and always insisted on offering a visitor something to eat. Not many cared to partake, but they appreciated the gesture just the same.

He would have certain Rocky businessmen write letters for him, but he never let the man who wrote a letter read the answer received; that he took to someone else.

Whenever Silas got a shipment of money from his Oklahoma oil fields, he would attend local auction sales. He bought large quantities of junk; though what he ever did with it, nobody knew!

One time his money was late in arriving, so Silas was forced to look for a job. He went to a lumber boss and applied, but the boss was not impressed with Silas' appearance. He handed Silas a bar of soap and said, "Here. Scrub. Shave. Get a haircut. Come back and I'll give you clean underwear, overalls, and maybe a job." Of course, Silas refused. He stated indignantly that no job was worth that much. He went back to his cave; soon afterward more money arrived from Oklahoma. Nevermore was Silas forced to humble himself in that manner.

When he finally died from pneumonia brought on by the general atmosphere and condition of his dugout, he had no money. What did he do with the sums which he received from Oklahoma? He certainly didn't spend them. It's a fact that he neither drank nor smoked. His only expense was auction goods, and all he bought was junk. Did he bury his money? Well, a lot of Rocky Mountain House citizens think he did. In fact, looking for Silas' money is a favorite summer sport!

Rocky Mountain House has two railroads. When I remarked that this was an interesting if not an astounding fact, I was told about the famous "Battle of Horburg" which once furnished excitement, not to mention comedy, on a battlefield sixteen miles long—from Rocky westward to Horburg.

The Canadian National Railway was on the job first and had some twenty miles of grade completed west of Red Deer before the Alberta Central awoke to the fact that a competitor was seriously threatening its territory. The Alberta Central at once began a railway of its own.

The old settlers were amazed! For a long time they had been dreaming of a railroad, but here, in the wink of an eye, were two railroads working day and night to beat the other out! The citizens lapsed into happy anticipation of two payrolls, two bridges across the Saskatchewan, two gangs of laborers to feed—in fact, double of everything! They didn't mind that the two railways would be easily within whistling distance of each other!

In 1911 the C. N. R. was far in the lead. They had, in fact, laid tracks to within a mile of Rocky Mountain House. Here, however, they encountered their first serious obstacle in the form of a new piece of grade that cut right across the C. N. R. location. To the C. N. R. boys the solution was simple and direct. At night they tore the barricade away. By day the Alberta Central boys built it up again.

All this was done with good humor. As T. C. Hargrave, writing in the *CALGARY HERALD*, says: "On the one side were Swedes, Norwegians, Austrians, Italians; on the other side were Italians, Austrians, Norwegians, and Swedes. The battle was on, according to our old-timers, until the ties had been turned four ways and were plumb wore out!"

The river, of course, had to be crossed before any train could run on to Horburg, but the Alberta Central didn't wait to build a bridge just then. They sent gangs across and built a couple more barricades on the other side of the river at right angles to the C. N. R. right-of-way.

This didn't stop the C. N. R. boys. They jumped the river, too; and both outfits began playing leapfrog with stretches of track clear on to Horburg.

The Alberta Central, however, was first to attempt bridging the river. This was an expensive undertaking, since their own rails did not yet run even to Rocky Mountain House. They'd been too busy checkmating the C. N. R.!

So the citizens of Rocky saw their pastures turn even greener. Cement must be hauled from Red Deer, Lacombe, Innisfail, and Bowden for the new bridge; and it must be hauled by teams, since nothing could be hauled on C. N. R. rails.

The cement was hauled, but it was not easy; the roads were nothing but bogs. The mules died off under the strain. Oxen were the only animals which could stand up under the heavy loads of cement. As Mr. Hargrave says: "Skinners left the Calgary and Edmonton Railway with sacks of cement and a fresh shave, and arrived in Rocky with long beards!"

However, they received $1.25 per sack for hauling, and the job looked like a long one; for as soon as the Alberta Central bridge was completed, the C. N. R. would certainly begin their own bridge. However, this dream of fortune was not to come true. The Railway Commission decided in 1912 that only one bridge was needed across the Saskatchewan; they also stated that the Alberta Central (now taken over by the C. P. R.) would stop at Rocky Mountain House, while the C. N. R. would continue on to Horburg and Nordegg.

So if you are interested in knowing—should you ride from Red Deer to Nordegg on the C. N. R.—why the train runs for three or four miles on C. P. R. track, and why it crosses the C. P. R. bridge, remember the "Battle of Horburg," possibly the longest battle in Canadian history—and maybe not yet entirely finished!

I think a great deal of the magic which I attach to Rocky Mountain House lies in its romantic name. It was explained to me that the name was given to the old fort by John MacDonald of Garth when in 1802 the Union Jack, together with the flag of the North West Trading Company, was raised above the main building. He named the place Rocky because of the rocky formation of the river bed, Mountain for the beautiful view of the Rocky Mountains from the point, House, of course, was the usual designation of a fur-trading post. Rocky Mountain House! a lengthy name but a good one, a name that one remembers. A much, much better name than the one the railroad wanted to change it to (but I shall tell more about that presently).

Only the chimneys of the old fort are standing now, and these are partial restorations made a few years ago by the Historic Sites and Monuments Board.

Romance hangs heavy over the spot, however, and it is not hard to recall that the first white man to reach the site was Peter Pangman, one of Mackenzie's partners, and that Pangman inscribed his name on a great pine tree near the river edge which for years was known as Pangman's Pine. Nor is it hard to recall that David Thompson wintered at the fort before his trip to the Pacific.

Stan Hooker, manager of the bank at Rocky, who drove me out to the Chimneys, told me that often a square nail or other relic of the past is picked up on the spot. A few years ago Mr. E. C. Brierly, who now owns the land on which the old fort was situated, was digging a well, and down about four feet he came onto a two-foot thick layer of ashes, which seems to imply that the ground level was once much lower.

Mrs. Grace Schierholtz, Rocky Mountain House correspondent for a number of western newspapers, gave me other interesting sidelights on the Chimneys. I had heard that a treasure of some sort had once been buried near the fort, and I asked Mrs. Schierholtz to tell me about the treasure.

"Oh," replied Mrs. Schierholtz, "that's a long story. Well, you asked for it, so here it is! You see, the country around here was known for years as Blackfoot country. The Blackfeet didn't seem to get along with the other tribes or with the white men. In the winter of 1819 the Indians decided they had some kind of grievance against the traders. They held a council of war and made plans to sneak over to the fort in the night, burn it down, and scalp the whites.

"Most fortunately for the traders, there was an Indian, half Cree and half Blackfoot, who had been doctored by the Factor, and chose this time to display the gratitude that is sometimes lacking in both white men and red. He had been one of a party at the fort with furs the year before; and after the dipper had been passed a few times, this young brave became so jovial that he danced too close to the steep river bank and tumbled over. The bank goes straight down for almost one hundred feet, and the fall might easily have killed the foolish young Indian. He got off with a broken leg. The Factor and his men, perhaps feeling a trifle guilty when they remembered the whisky barrel and the dipper, took the victim and set his leg. They cared for him until he was able to rejoin his tribe.

"When this young brave heard the murderous plan of his chief, he slipped away and warned the Factor. There had been peace for a number of years, and the white men had begun to think their troubles with the Indians were over.

"The fort was understaffed, without enough guns, and almost no ammunition. The only thing to do was to flee; but before going, the traders buried as much of the supplies and furnishings as they could, including three cannons and a keg of rum.

"The Hudson's Bay Company had a map showing the location of the three buried cannons, and a few years ago they sent a man out here to locate them. He hired a crew and they worked here for weeks, but they didn't find a trace. The Company reluctantly decided the measurements shown on the map must be inaccurate."

"What did the Rocky Mountain House people think about this digging?" I asked.

"Oh," said Mrs. Schierholtz, "they watched with great interest. But perhaps they were really more concerned about the keg of rum—rum aged for a hundred years! And would you believe it? The location of the rum is not shown on the map!

"After the trading post closed in 1875," continued Mrs. Schierholtz, "there were very few white men in the district until 1904 when the homesteaders began to trek in. Red Deer was well started by then. There were rumors that the railway was going west, and the pioneers were in a hurry to get in on the ground floor. By 1907 there was a fair-sized settlement of Ontario and Old Country homesteaders.

"These pioneers were over sixty miles from the railroad until the 'Battle of Horburg' brought the railroad scurrying through to Nordegg, sixty miles west, to tap the rich Brazeau coal fields.

"Some years ago, one of the railroads decided the name Rocky Mountain House was far too cumbersome to print in timetables or on tickets, so they quietly understood to change it to Lochearn.

"The howl that went up must have been heard as far as Ottawa; for every old-timer was justly indignant. Rocky Mountain House means something, but what is there to an insipid name like Lochearn? They admitted that the three words made considerable writing, but they liked them. The name links the modern town with the days of the fur-traders and explorers. It makes readers remember that this place, though it looks like a new town, is really over 200 years old!

"One of the few residents in favor of the change pointed out that the name is *odd*, to put it mildly. He cited an instance. His brother in New York went down one day to send him a telegram, and when the girl in the office read the address, she flatly refused to believe there was such a place. The customer insisted in vain that he had a brother living there; furthermore, he had many letters postmarked Rocky Mountain House.

"The clerk repeated that there simply couldn't be a town with such a name, and she stuck to her guns. The man had to call an official before he could have the wire dispatched.

"Our citizens retorted that they didn't care whether New Yorkers believed there could be such a place or not! They insisted on keeping their name which had a history. They protested so loud and so long that the railway company finally pretended that it was all good, clean fun, and they had never intended to make such a drastic change. But for some years the place was listed as Lochearn in the timetables—until that issue was out of print!"

Lumbering is Rocky's leading industry. At one time the place was one of the leading lumber centers on the continent. Lumber from the mountain slopes built homes and schools and churches the whole length and breadth of western Canada. Lumber went from Rocky as far as Chicago, Detroit, and New York. Rocky shipped out ties to build the railroads, corral posts for the ranchers, pit-props for the coal mines, telephone poles to string across the endless prairies. That was in the boom days. Today Rocky has settled down to steadier times, shipping out millions of feet every year, going farther and farther back into the woods to get it.

Some of the camps are far out. Nobody calls in, and lumberjacks are inclined to lose track of time. According to one story, a traveler showed up at one of the camps in the middle of January. The camp cook greeted him with great joy and asked him to stay for dinner. The traveler replied

194

that he was sorry but he couldn't stay. "Please stay!" urged the cook. "It's mighty cheerful to have a visitor for Christmas dinner!"

Every Wednesday at Rocky is Pig Day. Pig raising is one of the thriving businesses of the region. Pigs have always done well there. On Wednesday long lines of pigs converge on the town. Some come by truck and wagon, but many are simply driven. It is a common sight to see a pig-drive down Main Street, with the animals behaving just as contrary in town as they do on the farm.

One old farmer came to town one day and brought a few pigs to sell. He sold his pigs, bought half a dozen others, and started driving them right up Main Street to where he had his wagon. It was a boiling hot day in mid-summer, and he was dressed in just a shirt and bib overalls. He used nails—like all bachelors—in place of buttons, and this day because of his strenuous exercise the nails worked a little loose. He was racing down the middle of Main after his pigs when a couple of the essential nails gave way. He lost his overalls. Nobody knows where they went, but one thing is certain: their owner didn't show up in Rocky again for a long, long time!

Travelers leaving Rocky don't care to go on the train leaving Wednesday morning. All the trains are mixed, freight and passenger, but the pig-train on Wednesday is more mixed than usual. The odors are not entirely pleasant, and the train stops at every siding to pick up pigs and more pigs!

Furs are still shipped from Rocky, too. Not so many, of course, as in the old days, but this year at least, the trappers are doing well. When I was there I was told about two trappers who had come in a day or so before with over three thousand dollars worth of fur. This was only half through the fur season, at that.

There is coal, natural gas, and oil in the country around Rocky; and wild berries come out of the region in crates and carloads. The Indians gather lots of Seneca root which goes, or did go, to China to be made into cough medicine. One Indian lady—so they say—brought in enough Seneca root to get herself a permanent wave!

And there's gold, too. There has always been gold in the North Saskatchewan, not in large quantities, but an industrious man can still make four or five dollars a day panning if he chooses. Stan Hooker drove me down to the river bank to look at a curious boat built by a man named Frank James who had the idea that there must be lots of gold in the deep potholes of the river. He built the boat with a special pump to hoist out the deep river sand. His scheme has never been tried; the boat is standing idle on the river bank, but old-timers tell me that there *might*, there just *might*, mind you, be something in the James scheme.

You will find a variety of types of people at Rocky, and among them all the spirit of independence is strong. Some of the settlers have done well; anyone can do well just now if he chooses, there's such a shortage of help. Nature is kind to Rocky folk and provides meat and fruit, plenty of wood for building and fuel; one doesn't need much actual cash.

I am told that many a family around Rocky seldom sees more than fifty dollars in cash the year round. I was told the story of one settler who came to the municipal council for aid. He wanted enough road work to do him till spring. "How much money will you need?" asked the council. "It's three months till spring, how much money will you need each month?"

"Well," replied the settler, "I could get along fine on a dollar and a half."

They tell me of a woman who once worked in one of Europe's royal households. She came out with her husband, farmed with oxen, cleared brush, and pumped water by hand for eighty-five head of cattle. She's now one of the district's honored pioneers.

I heard also of a former officer of the Russian Imperial Army who fled his country at the time of the Revolution. When he came to Rocky he didn't have a nickel in the world. Today he and his wife own a 160 acre farm and are doing well.

One man came to Rocky only a few years ago with nothing except two dollars worth of groceries. He made a deal to cut cordwood that first winter in return for a team, some traps, and a gun. He got the equipment, but when spring came he needed a dollar's worth of garden seed, so he walked twelve miles in to Rocky and persuaded the Chinese laundryman to give him a dollar's worth of work. For a year or two he went on like that. Now he makes a fair living and has relied only on himself.

The Indians at Rocky also maintain their independent spirit. One of the very few remaining bands of Nontreaty Indians lives about thirty miles from Rocky Mountain House. Last summer the government tried once more to persuade them to accept treaty, but this proposal was flatly turned down by a vote of 177 to 23. In refusing the offer the Indians argued that this was their country and had been theirs long before the white men arrived. Since they had never taken treaty they had never given up their right to the land. They said that the white man was the intruder and should leave them in peace on the land that had been theirs since the world began.

An interesting legend exists among this little band of Nontreaty Chippewas. The legend concerns Chief Jim O'Chase, a famous Chippewa who died in 1932. When Chief O'Chase was a lad of seven, his band was camped in the hills along the Red Deer River. A scout suddenly reported that a larger band of hostile Indians was spying on the camp. Under cover of darkness the Chippewas moved out to safety, and in the early morning hours resumed their journey. It was not until the forenoon that they discovered Jim O'Chase was missing.

The boy had become separated from the band in the darkness, and later when he wakened under a clump of bushes, he was being nosed about by a big bull buffalo. This was in early spring, and the boy followed the buffalo herd about all summer, snuggled up to their shaggy bodies for warmth during the night and eating—nobody knows what!

Late the next fall his uncle, still searching for some trace of the missing nephew, heard him whimpering in a dense, scrubby coulee and there found the lad alive and well. The boy said that his buffalo friends had deserted him that morning—when human help was within reach.

Asked what he lived on, he replied that his God had fed him.

Most of the people at Rocky are convinced that their region is the best in the world and wouldn't want to live anywhere else. They hope that sometime a road will be put through from Nordegg, sixty miles west, to connect with the Banff-Jasper highway. They believe this will make Rocky one of the important tourist centers of Western Canada.

Two or three years ago some of the enterprising citizens of Rocky decided that they would take a car from Rocky to the Banff-Jasper road, just to show doubters that the idea was practical. They chopped down trees, forded rivers, and succeeded! A remarkable feat when one remembers that they went right through the mountains.

The foresters at Rocky told me that this road would almost certainly be put through, and when it is I hope Rocky has the boom the citizens anticipate; for I have a real fondness for this place of so much good humor and so much that is laughably mysterious.

I like Rocky just as I like High River. High River is the capital of the ranching tradition. Rocky Mountain House is a capital, too—a capital of courage, good humor, and independence. Long may they both live!

VISION

IV

HOME TO
WISCONSIN

MEETING THE STRANGER

**S**PIRITUALLY AT LEAST I WAS READY TO MOVE TO Wisconsin when the time arrived, even though the exact nature of my role there was not yet clear to me.

I must look backward now, before the Alberta experiences, to set the scene for my coming to Wisconsin.

It is a morning in May, 1938. Alexander Drummond of Cornell has just returned my play called *THE WILD HILLS* about dispossessed people in the hill country of Central New York. Drummond tells me I should take the play manuscript and go to New York City to the Rockefeller Foundation to see Dr. David Stevens, the director of humanities.

Stevens didn't ask about my play. In fact he never even saw it. But he had the Foundation pay my expenses out to Kansas where I visited my parents. Stevens was absolutely right to suggest that I go. I was able to think things through, see more clearly there, at my boyhood home which I had once left, that what I wanted to do was to work with people, help them realize their relationships to the land, to their heritage. I tried, excitedly, to explain all this to Dad one afternoon. But he seemed to grasp it only dimly. He was then too buried in the past. He was proud of me, I think, but I never knew whether he thought I had found the Grail of tall grass, the mysterious Stranger, or what. He never really asked me. I could not tell him that I had, perhaps, met several Strangers.

Many things then transpired. I returned to Cornell. Professor Dummond had in production a masterly interpretation of Chekhov's *Uncle Vanya*. It was a 1938 summer production in the Willard Straight Theatre, and for some of the key roles outside performers had been obtained. Performing the sensitive, beautiful part of Sonya was a young woman from Battle Creek, Michigan, also once a Drummond student, named Maryo Kimball. My own part in the production was tiny, the role of a serf, and at one time I brought onstage some needed props and whistled for the dog. But my role didn't make any difference. I watched every performance of *Uncle Vanya* through from beginning to end. As the summer closed Maryo Kimball and I were engaged. We were married in June of 1939 at her family home in Battle Creek.

Meanwhile Professor Drummond and I had accomplished or stimulated the writing of many New York State Plays. I was thoroughly steeped in the lore and legend of central New York, and would have been perfectly happy to remain there the remainder of my life. But at just this time I received a letter from Dr. Stevens saying that travel money (he mentioned $400) was available for an exploratory journey throughout the United States. The idea, I am sure, was to enable me to discover where I wanted to work and to live permanently.

David Stevens had a sure knowledge of men and women. He seemed to be able to tell always what a person wanted, what his essential dreams were. I had never articulated mine to him. He simply knew. Maybe it was because he himself had been raised in the crucible of the Middle

West, and had the life and lore of the people of the heartlands deep inside him. I don't know. But along in the spring of 1942, after I was deferred from Army service, I received a further letter from Dr. Stevens. "I am sure," he wrote, "that you have been giving some thought to where you are going finally to work. Things will straighten out. Right now the bottom has dropped out of the arts in America. But the war will end, and the arts will come back stronger than ever. We will have a new kind of federal support for the arts someday, mark my words. Where would you like to work?"

I really couldn't answer, but the question fascinated me. Sometimes I had thought about returning to Kansas where I lived as a boy, where I had obtained my first impressions of art, became tuned to nature, knew that I had some inclinations to become a writer, and from whence I had set forth on my first odyssey. But then there was the element of not knowing how to return. I feared to return to Kansas for of all journeys the return is the hardest, and the complexities of boyhood seemed too immense. So where?

I traveled again to New York to see Dr. Stevens. He mentioned Wisconsin among other places, and he ordered the financial officer of the Foundation to issue me the check for a special travel grant of $400. When I returned to Ithaca, Maryo and I packed our Pontiac car and, with saved wartime gasoline coupons, set forth. There was never a journey, I thought, that had so much of wanting, of need, and of the necessity of discovering an intuitive relationship of self to place. We went west and north and curved back through midcountry. Our money lasted remarkably. Each week I sent Dr. Stevens a letter describing what I had seen, and the potentials as I felt them in regions toward an acceptance of a people's art. I spoke with people when and where I could; formed my deep impressions that this or that place was where we belonged. We were looking for a spiritual home. We arrived at Madison, Wisconsin.

I am in Madison suddenly, in June, 1943. I have left Maryo and the car in Michigan at her home in Battle Creek. Everything is a wartime scene, the Northwestern train from Chicago is packed with service personnel and college students. I have never before visited Wisconsin. I can get no taxi from the station. I walk up through the city square, stare at the State Capitol, wander up State Street. At the moment I have no thought that Madison will be my home for the next fifty years. I am struck by the sight of the main building of the University of Wisconsin, Bascom Hall, as it rests on College Hill, visible from State Street; and I turn and see behind me the State Capitol, also visible. At the moment the jointure of state and university has no meaning. Later the meaning becomes clear.

Stevens has suggested that I visit at Madison with the Dean of the Agricultural College. I do not understand why. Shouldn't I proceed first to the University Theater? Or to the chairman of the Department of Art? If I am to work in the arts, why the College of Agriculture? But Stevens knows better.

At Agriculture Hall I am directed to the dean's office. The dean is in and will see me. I am ushered into a very large room with a huge desk at one end. At the desk is an immense figure who, I have been told, is Dean Chris Christensen. The huge man rises as I enter. He appears to tower to the ceiling. Behind him, on the wall, is a large oil painting of a farmer in the midst of a yellow field of wheat. The farmer figure also is monumental, much larger than life. I recognize the painting, and the artist as John Stuart Curry, also a Kansan, a leading American regional painter. Dean Chris invites me to sit down and then wastes no time. "Stevens wrote me you were coming. Perhaps someday you will want to work in Wisconsin." He pointed at the painting. "I brought Curry here to lead rural people in art. I want to do the same with literature and drama. I want poetry in Wisconsin to become as important to Wisconsin people as dairying. Come and join us at Wisconsin."

Golden words!

I spent most of that day listening while a noted rural sociologist, John Kolb, and Dean Christensen told me about the Wisconsin people:

the downtrodden peoples from Europe who sought freedom; the down-east Yankees and the wheat farmers and tradesmen from New York State who sailed on the packet boats of the old Erie Canal and then came through the lakes to Milwaukee where they spread out across the woodlands and the prairies like a wave. They told me of the Indians who left their names, their effigy mounds, and the mystery of their legends across the face of the Wisconsin earth, and of the lumbermen who hewed down the mighty forests of the north. Dean Chris spoke of the hunger of the people for education, of how they had opened the University in 1849, the year after Wisconsin reached statehood, and of how, little by little, the University had broadened its services until the whole state was, in effect, the University.

On the walls of Dan Chris' office were also several rather primitive paintings of rural Wisconsin, and he told me that an art movement was springing up among the farm folks. Every year there was a big exhibit of rural art in Madison. And there was a theater tradition, too. The great days of living professional theater were gone in Wisconsin, of course, but the State had had the earliest little theater movement, a group called the Wisconsin Dramatic Society, which was dedicated to the writing and production of plays about Middle Western life. Personalities such as Tom Dickinson in dramatic literature; Zona Gale, the young Portage author; and Laura Sherry from Milwaukee, were members.

Unfortunately the Wisconsin Dramatic Society was no more, but University Extension had, for fifteen years, kept workers in the field of drama, encouraging playwriting and play production in the cities and in the country. True, no great original plays of the people had yet sprung to life, but the public attitude toward theater was healthy; even the great Wisconsin Dairyman's Association was deeply engaged in theater.

That evening when I wrote to David Stevens I said that of all the places I had visited Wisconsin had seemingly done the most to establish a popular concept of drama and art. Somehow everything clicked. I knew that it was in Wisconsin where I wanted to live and work. There was an atmosphere upon the Wisconsin land that was different from other states—an atmosphere that seemed to proffer a deeper humanness; a distillation of a folk desire for a complete oneness of human struggle and earth.

And so it was in late May, 1945, as if preordained, I received an offer to join the faculty at the University of Wisconsin, and begin a new cultural program.

Alexander Drummond and David Stevens said it was what I must do. Stevens had been born at Berlin, Wisconsin, the son of a Methodist minister, and I think he was especially delighted that Wisconsin would be our new home. Maryo and I packed up to move to Madison. We wanted roots, a home. Wisconsin might be a good place to search for these prized things. Zona Gale, the famous author who lived in Portage, had said that Wisconsin was a land of good neighbors and friendly communities where deep, intensely human values of community life existed.

SIGHTS AND SOUNDS

So, ONE DAY LATE IN AUGUST, 1945, I, A STRANGER, was sitting on a bench on the campus of the University of Wisconsin at the top of the Hill in front of Bascom Hall. It was afternoon: long shadows fell across the grass and there was a feeling of quiet loneliness everywhere. The summer session had ended, professors had departed, students had vanished, and I was quite alone.

My loneliness I knew sprang from sources deeper than the quietness of the campus. On this hill I was alone spiritually, without the steadfast bulk of a Drummond to bolster and inspire me as his presence had on many a New York State eminence. In Alberta I had been alone, but it was quite a different loneliness there. It was wartime when everything seems speeded up, hectic. Also, I had been on a short-term project. But now I was to begin work as director of a new, long-term University regional cultural program. I had come to the top of Bascom Hill hoping to experience a first delicious feeling of curiosity, of belonging, of anticipation that a move to a new base had always held for me. I looked down across the slope to the foot of State Street, and at an angle between the trees I could see the top of the State Capitol. There was no breeze at all. A slow, faint sound of traffic wandered vaguely up the slope, but somehow that sound, too, seemed only a part of the general stillness.

Above me in front of the building sat a Lincoln statue. The quiet pose bothered me somehow, and I had a guilty sense that the figure was staring into me, seeking my reasons, my sensations, as I was myself.

I moved away from the statue to the front of the building and idly read a plaque that was fastened to the stone. It was a statement about academic freedom: "Whatever may be the limitations which trammel inquiry elsewhere, we believe that the great state University of Wisconsin should ever encourage that continual and fearless sifting and winnowing by which alone the truth can be found." It was taken from a report of the University of Wisconsin Board of Regents in 1894.

I thought about what the plaque said, and this too, bothered me. "Sifting and winnowing" was what I was doing a lot of within myself, and somehow this idealistic statement seemed to urge me on, to dare me to define my motives and my dreams. I moved uneasily away from the plaque onto the grass and sat down under a tree. What was to be my role here? I wondered. What was this Wisconsin experience to mean? The quiet, the peaceful campus, the contemplative mood of the place vanished. I was frightened, suddenly, for I sensed that quietness, solitude, moments of contemplation would soon be extremely rare for me. A tightness began in my belly.

Looking around, I realized for the first time how completely I was a stranger in this place. The realization was shocking, for I had been extremely conscious of one of the more superficial reasons for coming to Madison. This reason was twisted up with nostalgia. I had traveled constantly in Alberta; I had been on the move, in a way, since the depression days in Kansas; and I thought that I desired more than anything else a feeling of being at home, of soil where I could put down real roots, where I could live at peace and with an honest faith that the work I was doing had importance to the people about me.

I probably knew, too, that deep roots would not be easy for me to put down in any one soil, for the strange restless drive that had impelled my journeys would send me on a continuous search. My pleasure had been the changing colors on the land and the patterns of landscape. Perhaps my pleasure had been the few creative thrills I had received from seeing my own creative work used and from hearing the few utterances of public approval. I wondered whether much of the energy that had seemed so abundant in New York and Canada had not been motivated by fear—a hangover from my student days in the depression when often there was no job and little food.

I understood that I had a sincere liking for places and for people, but whether I could turn such liking into the kind of responsibility required to form an outstanding program in theater and allied arts in Wisconsin, I did not know. The Alberta experience, while it sharpened my appetite for the lore of places, had, perhaps, shown me my chief weakness, which was lack of an abiding faith in the worth and goodness of the work I had to do. As yet, my role-playing had not become a genuine thing, and the public aspects of my Alberta work were, I found, basically distasteful.

I had faith in my regional approaches; somehow I knew that I was on the right track, philosophically, for me, but a larger thing, a cause, a drive beyond restless seeking that might transcend all the weaknesses within me was vaguely felt but undefined.

I wished that I could experience a spiritual drive like the one that had carried Dad into the Kansas land in the '80s, determined, and without question, to see that a certain kind of human progress concerned with breaking, tilling, and building was carried forward. His problem of faith was easy, I believed. The rainbow was ever apparent to him and the gold was really waiting. There were irritations, delays, and obstacles, but these were regarded by Dad as romantic barriers to be swept aside with knightly charges and missions. Knighthood paid off for Dad in ways as simple and as definite as a wooden box six feet long or a bag of clanking pieces of money. The Grail was the land itself and the expanding nation.

Unhappily my problem was much more complex. I sensed that America must come to her maturity through cultural activities, and I sensed that I must be a part of that. But the things I must do were the things I feared. I had been brought to Wisconsin to do a certain job. There was concern at the University of Wisconsin over the state of the cultural arts and the relation of the arts to the folklife. Cohesive forces, I had been told, were lacking in society as a result of the war. A new and integrated pattern for the cultural arts was necessary if the University was to continue to meet its obligations in the realm of cultural service to the people of the state. The University authorities felt that it was time to extend the University's services more completely into the field of the cultural arts and that the arts should be related directly to community life and made a vital part of the everyday experience of the people of the state. A substantial challenge.

THE WISCONSIN IDEA THEATER

NDIVIDUAL RESPONSIBILITY AND INITIATIVE IS SO HIGHLY thought of at the University of Wisconsin that if I had gone out into the state and had not been heard from for several months, I doubt whether anyone would have questioned whether or not I was doing valuable work. It is wonderful to work in an atmosphere and in a tradition of that kind.

But I didn't go anywhere for a time. I sat in my corner and thought and made plans, or visited around the University with men who had been pioneers in many fields. It was stimulating, and for almost the first time I felt that I had stature and respect among men who had made remarkable achievements in fields outside my own. My status at the University I found, was rather unusual. Mine was one of the first appointments the University had made that cut across departmental lines. I was a member of the faculties of three University divisions, and this, I was told, had been done to give me support and backing of the entire University.

These early days at Wisconsin were good days, but they were worrisome, too. I was eager to get into the field, to meet the people of the state. But I held myself back. I believed that certain things must be done first. There must be a name for a great state-wide theater movement. There must be a state-wide office at Madison with roots of communication going into the state. There must be plans for a theater on the campus where new plays by the regional authors could be played in try-out productions. There must be a playwriting project set up. There must be liaison made with the arts of music and painting, so that the whole field of a person's art concept might progress. There must be a touring company organized to carry plays of the region to the people of the region, and there must be a banding together for purposes of education and philosophy of all the theater interests of the state; and there must be a folklife organization to preserve and collect state tradition. And although I had freedom and good will I was still, with the exception of a few, almost alone in understanding of the largeness of the thing I was going to attempt. I worried considerably.

The name was a first concern. I thought of such inept titles as the "Wisconsin Theater Program," the "Wisconsin People's Theater," the "Wisconsin State Theater Project." I discussed possible names with many persons, but nothing materialized. Then one day I was reading a book by a man named Charles McCarthy. This book was called THE WISCONSIN IDEA and it seemed to mean a wonderful sort of expression of good will that arose in the state after 1900–a peaceful means used with intelligence to accomplish reforms and general good for all the people. Later, after the political meaning of the Wisconsin Idea had slipped into disuse, the University became the symbol of its meaning in the undiscouragable quality that has come to mean broad and untiring service, and a giving out of the fruits of knowledge by those that have knowledge, to those who have a need of it.

The term itself seemed to have no very general usage when I first went to Wisconsin. Indeed, many persons I talked with about the Wisconsin Idea had heard the term but had only the most vague idea of its meaning. I was greatly intrigued by it, however, and it suddenly occurred to me that here was the perfect name for the new Wisconsin experiment in theater, especially since the name reflected so strongly the University's idea of service.

We therefore had some letterheads printed up with the name The Wisconsin Idea Theater along the top of the sheet and it seemed to me that I had found a very unique and original name for our state-wide work. It was a week or so later that I made an interesting discovery. I learned that in 1913, in the very heyday of the original concept of the Wisconsin Idea, there appeared the first issue of a small magazine called THE PLAY BOOK published by the Dramatic Society of Milwaukee and Madison. Leading figures in this organization, which was really the first "little theater" movement in the nation, were Zona Gale of Portage, Thomas Dickinson of Madison, who later became a leading writer on the American Theater, William Ellery Leonard who later achieved a national reputation as a poet and Thomas Wood Stevens who became a greatly loved teacher of drama, and play producer. And in this first issue of THE PLAY BOOK there was an article, entitled of all things, "The Wisconsin Idea in Theater!"

The article was written by Percy MacKaye who also became well known for his plays and his poetry. He wrote, THE WISCONSIN IDEA which today [1913] is stirring our nation so deeply in government, science, civics, agriculture and the progress of the people's self rule, is big with a promise even greater, perhaps, than that which President Van Hise of the University has suggested so admirably in his work.

"The part played by the University of Wisconsin in the development of its idea appears likely to strike even more deeply into untilled fields of man's spiritual nature than the plowshares of the state into nature's loam . . . and the seed being sown in the former is being selected, nurtured with the same scientific spirit as the latter. I refer to the work being done for the art of the theater by the Wisconsin Dramatic Society.

"The policy of the Society is to produce plays of Middle-Western life, written and acted by Americans of the Middle West. Wisely purused it should achieve a notable success. The Society deserves the interest of all Americans solicitous for the growth of the theater as a social institution. The Society desires . . . to quicken the art of the theater in the soil of society itself, through technical training of the imaginations, dramatic instincts and latent art-impulses of the people in all their natural and local variety. I would take occasion only to note the tremendous vitality and importance of this movement as a necessary and inevitable extension of THE Wisconsin Idea."

So in 1913, 33 years before our version of a Wisconsin Idea Theater was conceived, there had been this statement which at least approximated one theory on which Frederic Koch of North Carolina and Professor Drummond and a lot of other people had been working: that fine playwriting could be nurtured in the regions of America, and that the result would greatly contribute to theater art. I was particularly eager, therefore, to see what had become of this first movement in Wisconsin, which apparently had had such an excellent start.

An examination of the remaining issue of THE PLAY BOOK show that the idea of an indigenous theater slowly sank from view. The writers and the editor of THE PLAY BOOK turned to a pedantic approach to theatre, and though a few of the plays that had been written as part of the philosophy of the movement like THE NEIGHBORS, by Zona Gale, remained popular, the basic principle of the encouragement of plays of middle western life seemed forgotten. Perhaps it was the First World War that was responsible. In its deeper sense, however, it was probably the social unrest that lead to the unstable 1920s and that bred a literary trend that emphasized the expatriate type of writer, removed from his homeland and looking back with dissympathy upon the scenes with which he was most familiar.

When I thought about it, it seemed to me that probably it took the great depression to awaken sincere regard for the American scene and its interpretation through authentic materials, and an awareness of the tempers and themes of the American regions. The dust storms of the 1930s, as I well knew from my Kansas days, focused attention on those troubled areas and the people. The wonderful myth of American individualism: every man's ability to pull himself up by his own bootstraps and to make himself an independent part of American commercial life, was at least partly undermined. Sham and unreality suddenly dropped away, and somehow, out of the crying trouble, a new love for the American scene was born.

Thinking about it like this I was very proud that I had unconsciously chosen a name for a new Wisconsin theater movement that had such tradition. The gap had been bridged, and it seemed to me that now we were ready to begin on a permanent project, for certainly a great trend in literature was toward sympathetic American portrayals of scene and character. Folklorists were having a field day, and great treasuries of American folklore were actually best sellers in American bookstores— something that had certainly never happened before. The American drama, too, sometimes behind the other arts in the reflection of trend, was trying desperately to catch up, with some musicals and dramatic shows carrying strong native themes.

The drawback, of course, to a mature theater and interpretation of the state was the lack of new writers, capable of writing good serious and comic plays. I determined to do what I could about this lack, and to provide as many stages as I could that would be the workshops of the new writers. I envisioned a plan somewhat like Alexander Drummond's in New York or along the lines of the one I had directed in Alberta, where the materials of the region, the stories and the songs might be collected and made available to writers. I determined that a playwriting project would be among the first of the many phases of The Wisconsin

Idea Theater and then subjects of Wisconsin folklife. I hoped to write myself, and to discover major themes and subjects of the region.

Cogitating about such responsibilities, I began to look, to listen, and to learn. I heard of the pioneers who swept into Wisconsin in the 1830s and '50s and '60s and '70s from many nations, with a deep hope of homeland. I saw the results of their long, hard effort in the transformation of the land, and I wanted to know more about what they did, and what their motivation was. Suddenly the first thoughtful phases of the beginning Wisconsin Idea Theater were over and I was plunged into the active process of creation.

I was, of course, intensely interested in the Wisconsin land and the lore of the people. I had learned to turn my imagination almost at will into a theater where the dramatic highlights of the past and present were rolling across the stages of my mind in a sort of panorama that seemed to roll on and on without end. Sometimes, in the middle of a Wisconsin woods, I would stop for a moment to listen to the wind rising in the pines, and the wind would make me remember how it must have sounded in those greater forests before the lumbering days, or how the wind carried the great flocks of passenger pigeons across the sky, darkening the sky, rippling the water, scurrying the clouds, driving the rains, hurling the sleet and snow, casting the storms upon the Wisconsin pioneers. And as the wind would die to a whisper I could hear voices in the wind. Lonely voices. The pioneer women were lonely sometimes. Perhaps I was hearing their voices. Or perhaps the faint wind was the symbol of a memory of the freedom people sought in Wisconsin, and found. The wind remembers.

Sometimes in the night, thinking about my new weekly dramatic radio program, "Wisconsin Yarns," I would hear the wind and it would seem filled with fear. In my mind I could see a boat wrecked on Lake Michigan; the old *Lady Elgin*, maybe, that proud ship that carried three hundred Milwaukee citizens to their deaths on the evening of September 7, 1860. Or the fear in the wind might be a great storm sweeping up the

Mississippi Valley to strike suddenly at the quiet towns along the river's banks in Wisconsin or Minnesota.

Or the rivers themselves stimulated me to wondrous imaginings: Often I would stand on the stoned banks of the old canal lock at Portage, Wisconsin, and I would remember the dream of those men who had joined with this canal the Fox River to the Wisconsin. And I would remember that the dream was about laden ships coming through the Great Lakes to Green Bay and through the Fox River system and so to Portage where, through this mile of canal, they would enter the Wisconsin and steam down to the Mississippi and so on down to New Orleans and the Gulf of Mexico. Or I would remember the lumber rafts that floated down river on the St. Croix, the Chippewa, the Black, the Eau Claire and Wisconsin, and how the proud side-wheelers churned up the Mississippi.

And sometimes as I went through the Wisconsin countrysides it was as though I heard imaginary cries of joy. The pioneers shouting for joy at this new land to break and clear. Or it was the crying of thanks to God of the mingled European peoples: the '48 men from Germany trudging into Wisconsin, fled from their revolution-torn nation; or the Norwegians, the Danes, the Swedes, the Poles, the Finns, the Lithuanians, the Hungarians, the Yugoslavs, the Welsh, the Cornish folk with their mining picks and their pasties, the Scotch folk and the English folk. These cries my mind was hearing were from the Swiss people coming to settle at New Glarus, or they were the cries of Kentucky and Virginia men coming to settle the Southwest part of the state. Those cries were the cries of settlement. New land! Rich land! Free land! New life in heavy hearts! Yes, the pioneers, the new settlers, the blood and bone of Wisconsin.

And I was hearing laughter, too, the laughter at tall frontier tales spun by the people about this land to which they had come. And with the laughter is the cheering for the local heroes. Cap'n Scott of old Forts Howard and Crawford who was the best shot with rifle or pistol living man ever saw. Never touched liquor, Cap'n Scott didn't. If he had he sure couldn'ta bored two potatoes tossed into the air, firing as he would from the hip. Was a remarkable man, was Cap'n Scott, just like Davy Crockett, for when coons saw the Cap'n a-coming they would come down off'n their perch and surrender, just like they did for Davy. And when a reckless fellow one time challenged Cap'n Scott to a duel, the Cap'n calm as could be, shot off a piece of the feller's liver and restored him to the best health he ever had!

Or did you ever hear of the Scotch Giant? Seven feet and six inches tall he stood. Lived over to Belmont. Weighed four hundred and fifty pounds, he did. Could swing a plow over his head with one hand, or lift a bar'l of whiskey by his fingers. Could hold a dozen eggs in the palm of each hand and not break one! Or did you hear of Pierre Paquette that worked up to Portage who was so strong that when one of his oxen gave out Pierre just yoked himself into the team and pulled along with 'em? Or did you hear o' Allen Bradley of Rock Island that measured four feet around the chest and wore moccasins because no shoes would fit him? His hands were broad as shovels and he could cut seven cords of body maple in a day. Could lift a thousand pounds. Easy.

Or maybe those cheers are for Whiskey Jack who was hero of the raftsmen, and fought and drank his rowdy way all up and down the lumbering rivers! Or maybe they're for Ernie Hausen, who lived right over in Fort Atkinson, Wisconsin, and was the world's champion chicken picker. Can pick a chicken blindfolded, or handcuffed, or wearing mittens, or with his bare feet, and his world record is picking a chicken clean in three and one half seconds. He can make eighteen or twenty-four dollars an hour picking chickens. Easy.

There's a drumming sound in the air sometimes in Wisconsin. There's a strange drum that sounds from Lake Michigan, too, whenever a ship is lost. And there was a sound that I'd fancy I'd hear sometimes that was like the sound of a breaking heart. Maybe it's old Chief Black Hawk's heart breaking when, after the Black Hawk War, most of his people had been killed, and he'd been taken prisoner. Or I was hearing the breaking heart of Eleazer Williams, of Green Bay, Indian missionary, victim of grand delusions. Perhaps it was his heart breaking when at his death, he must have realized that he simply couldn't make the world believe that he was the Lost Dauphin of France, rightful heir to the French throne.

And along with the imaginary things heard, my eyes were seeing the lore of raw theater, and transmitting the feeling of theater to my creative self. I noted the rising land of the Baraboo Range of purple hills, and knew an inner theater that the mystery of their color brought to life. I was seeing the pea vineries in canning time, where Mexican laborers wearing bright handkerchiefs were working side by side with the Wisconsin farmers. Their movements, as they pitched the green vines into the shelling machines, was the movement of living drama.

One time I stopped to watch a country auction, and I saw the personal belongings of the last member of an old Wisconsin family being auctioned off. The auctioneer lifted from a trunk a yellowed wedding dress, and when he asked for bids there was a titter of nerved-up laughter that brushed across the audience. And then the laughter was still as a very old lady made her way from the back of the crowd and offered her small bid for the dress. It was undisputed and she took the dress and tottered away with it. At a local gathering that night I heard the story, and it was like a play, for the dress had been worn fifty years before by *one* lady, but it *should* have been worn by the old lady who finally bought it.

A feeling for places, and at least an instinctive understanding of the lore of the people seem basic to the creative processes of anyone wishing to make sincere and honest dramatic interpretations of regional scene.

UNIVERSITY AND STATE

HE UNIVERSITY OF WISCONSIN IS ATTACHED TO ALMOST all aspects of state tradition, personality and life. For example, in Dane County, in Primrose Township, there is the birthplace farm of Robert M. LaFollette Sr.—Fighting Bob—certainly the most famous son of the state, and doubtless its greatest public speaker. He learned the art of oratory at the University. In his early days of political barnstorming he used to speak from the back of a wagon; sometimes the crowds numbered upwards of five thousand, yet no one ever said that Bob LaFollette could not be clearly heard. He had the gift of projection, just as Abe Lincoln did when he spoke on a windy and dusty 1859 day in Milwaukee to thirty thousand, and was, apparently, understood by everyone. The noted speakers of that generation like LaFollette—Robert Ingersoll, Stephen A. Douglas, Edward Everett—did not swallow their words. They spoke deep down, from the abdomen, casting words from the front of the palate, throat and mouth relaxed and moist, spitting it out to the furthest edge of the audience. They never dreamed of amplification.

I have strong feelings about LaFollette. From his earliest boyhood he had an inclination to self-expression. When one of his teachers requested that Bob address the little country school, LaFollette, unwilling to do anything so usual as stand in front of the class, climbed to the top of the belfrey and spoke to them from there. He had a natural gift for language, and particularly loved the words of Shakespeare. It was not an accident that he chose the subject of Iago for his most famous collegiate oration. He chose it because he understood that there was a gulf between good and evil that required exposition. He learned, from his early oratorical experiments, a method of swaying audiences which he was able to use throughout his life. He wanted at one point to be an actor, but from humble beginnings became a symbol of a richer life for all.

His neighbors in Primrose Township were Yankees from Ohio and Indiana, along with Norwegians, Swiss, and some Germans. In 1856, in February, Bob's father, Josiah LaFollette, passed away, killed by diabetes and pneumonia. The services for him were very simple . . . just a prayer by Deacon Thomas and some hymns. He was buried on Green's Prairie near Postville. Young Bob was scarcely ten years old when his father died.

LaFollette never did get over the loss of his father. When his mother died in 1894, LaFollette, Dr. C. A. Harper, and his brother William drove to Postville, taking with them a coffin half-filled with cotton batting. LaFollette himself then went into his father's opened grave and collected what remained. Somehow, the father remained an ideal with him and symbolized the strong ethical values which Robert LaFollette later came to represent.

LaFollette first learned to speak and project at the University from Professor Frankenburger, the most heralded speech teacher and master of rhetoric Wisconsin has ever had on its faculty. After his most glorious oratorical triumph, the Middle Western Oratorical Championship at Iowa

City in 1879, LaFollette returned to Madison and was met at the North-western depot by a hoard of students, stirred in those simpler days by an oratorical championship. It was a great day for Bob and for Wisconsin because soon thereafter he cast his lot with those attempting to create a better society.

Out of the crucible of the University as it was in those days came LaFollette, well grounded in ethics and moral point-of-view by no other than the University president, John Bascom, who personally taught ethics to every senior. Bascom was slightly unhappy with LaFollette because the country boy from Primrose had been entertaining some very liberal religious views. On the day Bob returned from Iowa City, Bascom, out of displeasure over an essay Bob had written that seemed to doubt the power of faith, did not attend the arrival of the young conqueror at the station. Reluctantly, he later allowed Bob to graduate. Bascom believed that man should extend his mental threshold far into the realm of faith. But LaFollette was, apparently, somewhat more practical. In any case, after his entrance into the practices of law and politics, LaFollette de-veloped deep social concerns. No doubt these were results of his obser-vation of the needs of farmers and farmer's wives, and of the whole mood of reform in government, economics, and culture. He developed basic ideas which led finally to the creation of the magnificent "Wisconsin Idea," so all-powerful through the early years of this century in setting the thread and temper of the University and its relationship to the State.

As I grew more interested in the State and learned more about LaFollette and his personal life, I developed a strange sympathy for him, and a personal bond that, I suppose, must have come partly from his father-son relationship. LaFollette's father did die when Bob was a very young lad, and as he grew up, through the stories his mother told and the antagonistic comments of his stepfather, his concern about his real father, long dead, became a vital force. From the illusory life he built around a dead parent grew strong idealisms that eventually made La-Follette a state leader in political and economic reform.

As I mentioned, the "Wisconsin Idea" was a term coined by Dr. Charles McCarthy, Professor of Political Science and head of the Reference Library in the Legislature, to describe the socio-political ferment in Wisconsin in the early 1900s. Wisconsin was, at that time, extending political democracy by passing and administering laws, such as workmen's compensation, that eventually were accepted throughout the country. But the "Wisconsin Idea" was complex: it meant the drafting of experts, such as Dr. McCarthy, in framing and administering legislation for the benefit of the people. The University, naturally, played an important role in the innovations. In education the "Wisconsin Idea" meant extending the educational and cultural opportunities of the University to all the people of the state. It meant, according to the pronouncements of University President Van Hise, a classmate of LaFollette, "service to the state" by the University. Dr. McCarthy was one of a small band of enlightened men who worked for the development of University Extension. In 1907, the Legislature approved a budget which greatly expanded Extension (which actually had been started as early as 1885) and brought Extension within Van Hise's definition of service to the state.

Charles R. Van Hise will long be remembered for the part he played in bringing the University of Wisconsin to the people. He was famed for his knowledge of rocks and minerals; he had acquired a national reputation as an authority on political economy; he was high in the councils of the nation in matters of national and international importance. But it was in the field of educational democracy that he will be best remembered by the people of this country.

During the fourteen years of President Van Hise's administration of the University, Wisconsin blazed the way in smashing American university traditions. Wisconsin led the way in the idea of a new university dedicated to the principle of service. Insofar as the University of Wisconsin could be made an instrument for the advancement of the welfare of the people, to that extent would it meet the ideals and principles which were being formulated by those leading it. The University went out into the state. The University of Wisconsin no longer was a thing of mortar and stone, of books and courses of study, of declensions and formulas centered around a campus.

The University of Wisconsin went out into the fields and made two ears of corn grow where one grew before; it went into the barns of the state and made cleaner and healthier livestock; it went into the crossroads school houses and put fire and ambition into the young people of the state; it went into the communities and brought better sanitation, better ventilation, better municipal government, purer water, set up preventives for sickness and disease; it brought about cleaner milk, better cheese, kept hogs healthy; it elevated the people into higher regard for educational values, and responsible citizenship.

I also believe that the entire state is interlinked through its traditions with the University in real and perhaps even mystical ways. It could be that the ancient Indian gods had something to with the creation of this original university on the hill above Lake Mendota. For if the old Indian shamans conducted councils and ceremonies seated around the effigy mounds still on these heights, how logical that the wisdom which has since derived from College Hill in the humanities, arts and the sciences should follow the track of the ancient wise men.

There is a great Burr Oak tree that still stands on the University of Wisconsin campus on Observatory Hill, not far from the old astronomer's house. This dwelling was formerly the residence of the president of the University; in the 1890s they moved the president to the lower campus to an old Victorian dwelling.

But before all that happened, the president's house was there on top of the hill, and the old oak tree nearby became known as the "President's Tree." It has been there for at least 400 years, my friends in botany tell me, and it was there when some of the Indian mounds were created. The tree has seen a fearsome number of events and persons come and go. Some years ago, then President E. B. Fred had the old tree cabled together, fearful that a heavy wind might destroy it. He left clear instructions that if anything ever happened to the tree it was to be taken down and carefully examined.

Events the tree has witnessed in its interesting life include: its use as a target by the sharp shooters at Camp Randall, then the state induction camp for Civil War soldiers (supposedly the tree once had a great hole in its trunk where a cannonball had struck—the hole apparently healed, and whether there is a cannonball inside no one knows for certain): Blackhawk, the Sauk chief, retreating in 1832 with his band, crossed the UW campus near the old tree; likewise, there is a myth that Abe Lincoln, who got as far as Fort Atkinson with the Illinois militia, supposedly arrived at the future University setting and climbed "College Hill." Whether true or not, the stories and myths are fascinating.

The land on which the University of Wisconsin-Madison now stands they say, was once owned by a mysterious half-French, half-Indian, named Pierre Pacquette. He is one of my favorite Wisconsin characters, a big man who could lift huge objects with great ease, variously heaving to his shoulders a live horse, a keg of lead weighing upward of eight hundred pounds, and it is said, once lifted an iron object weighing two thousand pounds. Perhaps the tales are exaggerated, but Pacquette was apparently an extremely strong man, one of the giants of pioneer times, capable of drawing his fair share with a full-grown ox.

For the most part Pacquette was a gentle soul, very trusted by the Winnebago Indians. He may have been the victim of one of the first "contract murderers" in pioneer Wisconsin. He was shot in the breast by Man-zi-mon-ika (Iron Walker), an Indian who, Pacquette's great grandson Joe Kerwin told me, was sent up from southwest Wisconsin to murder the strong man. Reason? Pacquette was too influential with the Winnebago, and thus many good land deals might be sidetracked. It certainly is true that folks were after Indian lands in those days, and Pacquette well may have been an obstacle. His feeling of sympathy for the Indians was great. All of Pacquette's land, and other possessions, vanished in the settlement of his estate.

How curiously the University is interlinked in all these matters: about one hundred and thirty years after Pacquette's death, in the early 1960s, when the great University had spread unbelievably over the whole hill and surroundings, I heard Pacquette's story from his great grandson, a retired Madison fireman. I conceived then the notion that Pacquette should be the leading character in a massive regional drama which would celebrate many of the historical and mythical happenings at Portage. I had plans, with the City of Portage, to build a "revolving amphitheater*" on a huge turntable and produce the drama around the circumference turning the whole audience to the stages: the various scenes of settlement, of Indian war, perhaps even exploration, certainly the military presence of Fort Winnebago. Pacquette was to be a leading figure; so were Zachary Taylor and Jefferson Davis, once soldiers at the Fort; so was Juliette Kinzie, wife of the Indian agent, a cultivated, lively and deeply sympathetic woman from Connecticut who brought a flavor of civilization to the frontier.

I wanted very much to see the project come to reality. How thrilling to the thousands of Wisconsin citizens to have seen the great events of the Portage unfold, scene by scene. But the theater was never built nor was there ever any play. An anti-trust suit filed by the United States against a large corporation, which was on the point of funding the project, killed it.

But the University is and was a catalyst, and can bring interrelationships into play, cause ideas to be born, dreams to float, and surprisingly often something does really happen.

Anyway, I am virtually certain that at some time, Pacquette stood on the land that was later to become the UW campus beneath the "President's Tree." I would have liked to see them together, a mighty man and a mighty oak tree.

Yes, there are many ways in which the University is attached to Wisconsin's most colorful personalities. The John Muir story is yet an-

*The noted architect, Buckminster Fuller, actually drew plans.

other example. Muir, a Scotch lad, came with his family to Wisconsin, to the little lake then called Fountain Lake, where he learned his early ecology. I have never forgotten the story of how the raw farm boy set forth from the homestead when he was about nineteen, laden with his inventions, including a couple of curious homemade wooden clocks. He exhibited his ingenious treasures at the Wisconsin State Fair, then held in Madison, and eventually found his way to the University seeking knowledge, thirsty for it, and the University admitted him, though he had no academic background. His room at the northeast corner of North Hall was filled with laboratory apparatus, books, and clocks.

Muir got his first lesson in botany under the "Muir Locust," a black locust tree that stood on the slope above Lake Mendota (Muir Knoll, now), and there Muir and a kindly fellow student, Griswold, talked about the locust blossoms. The old locust tree died in 1953; some of the wood was made into paper knives and gavels by Walter Rowlands, a noted agricultural specialist, and President Fred presented these objects to many friends of the University.

Part of my affinity for the State certainly comes from the spirit of the University which offers help to any citizen desiring it. I believe this is the source of our greatest strength as an institution; that the faculty of the University of Wisconsin has been willing to share knowledge and to help people. In the folklore of the University this is the great truth that emerges again and again.

Wisconsin folks have always been enterprising and have always risen to challenges, possibly following the example set by a noted state citizen, Hercules Dousman of Prairie du Chien. In order to repay Dousman for some valuable services which he performed in the early days, the Federal government told him that he could have title to all the land he could ride around in a single day. I suppose they pictured Hercules leisurely riding around a few acres in a buggy. Not so. Dousman stationed a swift horse every five miles and did a solid day of Pony Express-type riding. He covered so much land that the Government backed off a little, but according to the folktales he eventually owned a large chunk of southwest Wisconsin.

In a sense it is this delightful type of enterprising spirit that makes Wisconsin so attractive to me. I come down the Wisconsin River canoeing, these days, and remember the great rafts of sawn lumber with steering oars fifty feet long, and the strong raftsmen who brought them through the narrows at the Dells and around the "Devil's Elbow." And although the rafts have vanished and the mighty timber has long been cut, I still think of the blind bard of the lumber camps, Emery DeNoyer, and the songs he often sang.

And I think of all the folklore that has made up our early industry, and the people who sang and told stories that reflected their work and needs . . . thinking about the way the timber was cut and what happened then; and the new necessities that arose in agriculture and science as the patterns of life inevitably changed.

It isn't hard to recall how naturally the University responded to the changeover from timber to agriculture in the north, and how the University suggested new methods that helped folks on the farms overcome the stubborn cutover, to farm in new ways, and to look ahead to an overwhelming tourist industry.

Or when I am traveling around the state and see the big barns and fine herds, I can't help thinking of Professor Stephen Babcock and how, without his butterfat milk test, dairying might never have attained the stature it did. Babcock lived in a yellow house on Lake Street in Madison. I didn't know him, of course, but I knew the house well, and the Hollyhock garden behind it. Most fittingly, seed from the Babcock Hollyhocks has been given out and scattered over the entire state by 4H Club kids.

I like that. Throughout the State the springs of lore nourish something or somebody at the University, and the University brings back to the State some expansion of a stimulus or idea and spreads it for the good of all. If the State has its own kind of lore and heritage, so does the

University, and one is related and often made out of the other. It's a fine feeling to have been a part of the Wisconsin tradition, and of the University where all of my later-life work has been done.

In spite of the unique relationships between the State and the University, some important work was being done at the grassroots in the cultural arts. I was crisscrossing the state in many directions, helping to encourage a community theatre here, an exhibit of rural art there. Many people were writing plays and sending them to me, and some were produced. I had to keep my main eye on such things for in native arts lay the purpose of my being in Wisconsin. But I found equally fascinating the exploration and life of the Wisconsin people. I viewed the arts and native stories, customs, fairs and festivals as all part of the same cloth, and I wanted to learn as much as possible about Wisconsin places and to distill an atmosphere of place and of people who lived in the Wisconsin places.

OUT STATE

NE JANUARY I STARTED OUT TO COLLECT THE MATE-
rials for a book. We had been having some unpleas-
ant weather in southern Wisconsin, not very cold,
but wet and clammy. I had a new pair of overshoes
purchased at Cubby Cosper's General Clothing Store
in Spring Green, a new pair of long winter underwear, and a new bag that my niece had given me
for Christmas. It was a particularly fine bag for my purpose, for it was
a combination of brief and overnight case, and in it I stowed my small
tape recorder, many rolls of recording tape, ballpoint pens, and spare
batteries. I was all set to sample the flavors of Wisconsin!

On the Monday morning I started we were having a spell of bad fog
in the Madison area. As I had breakfast I heard the Dane County Sheriff's
Department report urging all travelers to forge abroad only if essential.
My wife wondered whether I should go, but I have always responded to

fog—it stirs me creatively—and anyway, having waited for twenty-five years to begin the book I had in mind, I considered my travel extremely essential. So I did pack up that morning and set forth in a Ford out Highway 14 toward Cross Plains, Black Earth, Mazomanie, Arena, and Spring Green, hoping to glean on that day some interesting views of past and present Wisconsin in those places. Whenever possible, I would press further afield to Richland Center, Muscoda, Boscobel, Mineral Point, Dodgeville, maybe down to Monroe, and even out to Cassville.

Before I left Madison I had called up Robert Graves, who lives near Spring Green behind Frank Lloyd Wright's Taliesin, and Bob said he would be at his farm around noon. If I dropped by we could have a little drive around the country.

It was a bad day to see the country. Fog in the Wisconsin River Valley behaves in queer ways. It can shut you in completely—impenetrable walls—but then it may open up suddenly, especially in winter. In the clear places you can see the dark etching of the land perfectly, almost intensely; then the fog drops in again and is thicker than ever.

On the January day when I went out to see Bob Graves, the fog descended like a heavy set of gray theater drapes and held the car and me in our own world. There was only the slushy sound of tires hitting the pockets the melty weather had left in the pressed-snow road.

But I don't really need to see the countryside this morning. A sharpened memory reveals the hills and the valleys to me, and I recall the many summertime trips I have made along Highway 14 and the back roads adjacent; the way the hills looked then: the different shadings of the grasses; the prairie vegetation that still exists on the slopes and along the highways, or along the railroad right-of-way. In summer there are masses of wild flowers, switch grass, and prairie Indian grass, big and little bluestems mixed with the invading cedars. The birds have planted many cedars on the hills—the tall red cedar on the uplands and the creeping juniper on some of the sandstone outcrops. Not so many years ago the hills were almost bare. Now, in places they are nearly covered again with evergreen, for the cedar waxwings, fond of the fruits of the cedar, have carried seeds far and near.

The hills in southwestern Wisconsin are in a period of change. I doubt that this change is anything new. These hills have been covered with vegetation, then bare, then covered again many times. The north-facing bluffs have birch and red and white oaks and basswood; on the south-facing slopes are prairie grasses and bur oak.

In the early spring wild flowers begin to cover the partially balded hills. A succession of flowers will appear in a definite order, until fall.

First come the pasqueflowers in March, followed by buttercups, purple aven, birdfood violets, catspaw, sheep sorrel, and puccoon. The yellow flower of the early spring is the buttercup, and the waxy petals are like small, hot suns in the prairie grass; when the birdfoot violets come the south faces of the hills are a mass of pale orchid, for the birdfoot violet is never the deep violet of the woodland flower. Mounds of puccoon appear, vivid yellow, along with the yellow wild indigo that in winter turns to leaves gray and stiff, with pods and rattling seeds inside. On the hills there is lupine, blue and lavender, wild bergamot-Oswego tea, and purplish-blue spiderwort in the flat meadows; even a pale bluish-white spiderwort grows along the roadway from Spring Green to Lone Rock.

Along the roadways, also, are day lilies with orange and purple spots, and in low, marshy places and along the Wisconsin River are brilliant scarlet clumps of cardinal flowers that come in late July. Even with all this color I wonder what the look of the country would have been when it was wild and unbroken.

Of the prairies not much now remains. There were once great prairielike sections in southern Wisconsin, and the names still remain of some of them: Arlington Prairie, Empire Prairie, Barnes Prairie, Walworth and Rock prairies, Sauk Prairie, Ridge Prairie, Star Prairie, and many others. And when the early French explorers came through there were flat areas similar to prairies with great herds of game: buffalo, deer, and some elk. The Indians lived well without great effort and with almost no agricultural activity except to pick berries and harvest the Pomme-de-Prairie and nuts. In places the prairie grasses would hide a man walking upright; sometimes even a man on horseback would be almost hidden by the tall wild grasses. On the breast of the prairie were immense groves of oak, like islands.

Surely there is poetry and great symbolism in the remaining prairie elements. Of it all—the wildness, the solitude, and the sway of grasses—tiny plots of prairie alone remain. Often only a scientist can identify the prairie remnants or the prairie plants struggling on hills or "goat slopes."

Once many ancient bur oaks stood in groves in the midst of the prairie. They maintained themselves by toughness and a cork protection that prevented the many grass fires from destroying their vital fibers.

In the ground these trees of the oak openings were oak grubs, rootings that sent up annual shoots that in turn were destroyed by grass fires. Still the roots and the lower stems clung to life so that, when the settlers came, the grass fires stopped, the grubs began to grow, spoiling the beauty of the oak openings.

The settlers were stirred poetically by the beauty of the oak openings and, being "savanna" people, they made homes near the trees on the prairie. To the settlers, deep forests were full of mystery and darkness, while the open prairie had a loneliness of a different kind. They lived near groves of trees from which they might see out at the world.

I pick up Bob Graves at his farmhouse, and the Uplands country, as we drive out of the Wyoming Valley to the high ridge on Highway 23 south of Spring Green, seems to lift with the fog and open out to give a great sense of openness and freedom.

High on a point over the valley, Alex Jordan built his "House on the Rock," a strange ultramodern-Renaissance undwelling that sometimes attracts ten thousand visitors on a weekend. Nearby is the Upland Studio, which the Uplands Arts Council remodeled from a large old barn, with Robert Graves, "the Renaissance Man of the Uplands," doing most of the labor and the design. Far down below in the Wyoming Valley, where the Uplands begins, and on a bank of the Wisconsin River, is the fine Spring Green Restaurant, built by Bud Keland from original designs by Frank Lloyd Wright. Long before his death, Wright himself put up the beams of the restaurant, but the building was not finished until 1967. It was, indeed, completed on the very September evening that Lady Bird Johnson visited Spring Green, and they were still laying the last of the sod as her car rolled up the restaurant drive. The visit in Spring Green has, and will continue to become, a part of the local folklore.

Bob Graves is tall, rapid. I think I could make him up to look more like Abe Lincoln than Lincoln ever looked himself. Bob is moody, individualistic, dynamic. He is a former marine, former oarsman on the University of Wisconsin crew, and when he gets time, a landscape architect who got his training at the Frank Lloyd Wright Foundation and at the University of Wisconsin. Bob is determined that the Uplands will retain its native character and that it will somehow remain unspoiled despite the rapid commercialization that threatens to place hot dog stands, fruit markets, and sideshows all along the beautiful Uplands roads.

I have known Bob since he once invited me to Spring Green to talk about building an amphitheater when "plays better'n those up at Stratford, Ontario could be going on so folks out in southwestern Wisconsin might see the best right on their own doorsteps!".

Bob lives on the family place, formerly a part of the Wright holdings, for Bob's father, Ben, was farm manager for Wright. Himself a part of Iowa County folklore, Ben Graves was known far and wide as a man you could ride the river with—large, generous, a good manager, and a fine human being. He kept the several thousand acres of the Wright land cropped and fertilized and managed the land in such a way that it not only gave back the harvest of grain and cattle but also preserved the character of Wright and Taliesin, for it was no ordinary farm operation. Each workday at 3 P.M. work stopped on the Wright lands for afternoon tea, and the hired men as well as the architectural apprentices, who were expected to work in the fields, socialized together.

Bob Graves then is a product of both his father and of Frank Lloyd Wright. Disciple is much too mild a word to describe Bob's attitude toward Wright. Bob was one of those devoted friends who assisted in the Wright funeral in 1959 and walked in the procession that conveyed the architect's body, on a simple farm wagon, to the tiny chapel in the valley near which Wright is buried with only a chunk of field stone, on edge, to mark his grave.

On the one hand, Bob works to make the Uplands an attractive place for visitors, with fine restaurants and accommodations. But—and this is part of his tragic dilemma—though he wants the Uplands to prosper, he also works compulsively to preserve the Wright character of the land, the quiet, poetic loneliness that Wright and his architecture represented.

Bob drives the car and I listen as the university Ford clunks and chunks through slush and hole-riven roads, as we circle and come back above the Wyoming Valley. It was into this valley that the Joneses, Welsh farmers, brought a sense of education, culture, and religion. Born in Richland Center, twenty miles distant, Frank Lloyd Wright worked on his Uncle James Lloyd-Jones's farm and learned many of the approaches to nature that remained his landmarks throughout life.

But I am interested only indirectly in Wright. More, I want to hear the stories, see the people who today throw light on the patterns both past and present in the valley through memories of the past and realities of the present.

"Bob," I ask, "why do you like this country so much? You've told me many times that this valley and these hills were the greatest place God ever made. Now, why?"

"I had the opportunity to work around Taliesin," Bob said, "in the days when Mr. Wright was around, and my father was manager of the farm. I knew well many of the old-timers who worked with my father. There was something mystic about it: working in the fields of Taliesin with the students, stopping for tea, and hearing the conversations that ranged over what seemed to me then the whole field of human knowledge.

Yet there was earthiness there too, the daily farm life. The smells and feel of toil. Well, after the Korean War and after I had finished a degree at the university, I wanted to come back here. To this community."

"What about the city folks?" I asked. "All the Chicago and Madison and Milwaukee people who are buying up all the land in these hills? How about the big ski hill that Bud Keland is opening right across from your farm. How about all that? Doesn't it disturb your mystic dreams?"

"It disturbs me," Bob said, "I looked out of my window one morning and I suddenly saw a parking lot filled with cars. I know it's great for the area with the new business, and so far we've kept the signboards out; but parking lots are not what I came here to discover, or rediscover, about this country."

We are passing the Wyoming Valley Methodist Church, white, wooden frame, heartland architecture of the 1850s backed up against the hills, a symbol for the whole region. "And this church," Bob said, "where my family went every Sunday, was the center of life, almost. There was a youth fellowship of more than thirty that met on Sunday evenings when I was a kid. Now maybe there will be five come, and somehow I don't feel that my children are getting what I did out of this community. But of course a lot that I got out of it had to do with what people around here thought of Mr. Wright. The idea that Mr. Wright was here gave them something to talk about, always. He was an unfailing topic of conversation. I suppose there's excitement here now, but it's not the same as the excitement that came from his personality, and the apprentices that came from all over the world.

"Then these old codgers who lived around here. Paul Holmes, and an old guy named Ray Winch who lived over by Tower Hill Park, and a lot of others. Salty old men. I enjoyed them very much, and my father enjoyed and appreciated what they had to offer to the whole flavor of the country.

"Over where the new restaurant is, the new Spring Green, that used to be just a coffee place that also sold beer; and on a Saturday evening you could always find these old guys there, gassed up, telling yarns. And old Tracy Hickox fiddling over by the stove. And you know, it's a funny thing, but I believe most of the city people who are buying land out here are hoping to get a sense of the country, the quiet, and the flavors that I grew up with. Maybe they don't articulate it, but they're seeking something unique, and something that is really in and of these hills."

Bob Graves believes, among many other things, that the lure of the past is definitely returning to the Wyoming Valley through the yarn spinners. Somehow, he says, it's the tellers of stories that have to make the carry-over between the past and the present so the present knows how humorous, how appealing the past really was.

"It was bachelors like those old fellows who used to work for us over on the Wright farm." Bob said. "We had one bachelor, old Jeff Wilson, an Englishman. He never did wear socks. I remember that about him. He was a big, heavy-set fellow, wore one pair of overalls all summer long. He never washed them or himself either, I guess. We had a purebred Hereford bull, big, gentle . . . pretty much like Jeff. Some folks said they kind of looked alike, actually; and, well, Jeff fell in love with this bull. It was a real affair, I tell you. Every Sunday Jeff would get likkered up, and every Sunday P.M. he would come over to our barn to see that bull, and get on a crying jag. He would set there in the half-dark of the barn, right close to the bull's head. Called him Sunshine. That's what he called that bull. Sunshine. Dad would have to go down to the barn and get Jeff out of there and take him home. Used to set there and talk to that bull for hours on a Sunday afternoon."

"You ever hear him talk?"

"Oh, hell, yes."

"What'd he say?"

"Well, things like a fellow would say to a woman, maybe. Tender love things. I mean they were tender, for old Jeff. And then he'd talk about this guy or that guy and what SOBs they were. Then he would get to crying and tell old Sunshine what a terrible time he'd been having, and I swear the old bull would get to crying, too—teacups of water rolling off his cheeks! Pathetic. But it was somebody old Jeff could talk to. Only one he had. Makes a difference, especially out in the country, if you got somebody to talk to, somebody to pour it out to. Well, Jeff had old Sunshine.

"When the Badger Ordnance Works up at Baraboo opened up, Jeff went up there to work. When he had been working there about three weeks, I guess he got likkered up before he went to work one day. Jeff had him a Model A Ford, and he tipped this Ford over so, when the bus to Badger came by, old Jeff was still inside the car. It was raining and the people on the bus got off to help. The bus driver yelled to old Jeff said, 'Hey, there! Can we help you?' and old Jeff says, 'Hell, no. I'm just in here settin' out of the rain.' He wouldn't have a thing to do with any of 'em. So the bus just went on and left Jeff there in the upside down Ford. Shows how independent these old boys were.

"And even in Prohibition times, when even a lot of the best folks up in these hills were makin' moonshine, still they had a rigid set of values. Old Mabel Bennett, ran a speakeasy and made plenty of bootleg. One day Sam Stafford and Harry Pilgrim came over to visit Mabel. Sam had a model A Ford coupe, and while Sam was in the house buying some moonshine from Mabel, Harry stole two fat chickens that was sunning themselves out in the yard. He put 'em in the trunk of Sam's car. Well, Sam didn't know anything about the chickens, and Harry got 'em out when he wasn't looking. Guess there was a big Rhode Island Red chicken feed over to Harry's house.

"Yep," Bob continues, "there is a real streak of practicality in the folks hereabouts. In 1931 Mr. Wright had a whole slew of chickens, and somebody began to steal 'em. Mr. Wright told Wes Peters to find out who was doing it. So Wes and Jerry Caraway set a trap and to their surprise they caught old Joe Maxwell who was hired to be taking care of these same chickens. They caught Joe redhanded with a sack of Rhode Island Reds in each hand. Didn't bother him any. He says, 'Howdy, boys, real glad to see you. Foxes are so bad this summer, decided to carry Mr. Wright's chickens over to my place so I could take better care of 'em.' Mr. Wright laughed fit to kill when Wes told him what happened. Mr. Wright let old Joe keep the chickens. Mr. Wright was like that. Sometimes.

"The first Joneses moved into Wyoming Valley in the early 1860s. They had first settled across the Wisconsin River but found that the land wore out too rapidly there. The Valley was suited to their Welsh temperament and love of hills. It was a large family. Richard, the patriarch, [Frank Lloyd Wright's grandfather] and his sons, Thomas, John, James, Enos, and Jenkin. They were strong, hard-working, religious. They brought the first advanced farming methods into the valley; two of the daughters, Jennie and Nell, both teachers, brought the first advanced educational methods into southwestern Wisconsin. Their Hillside School offered broad, progressive education in a time when such ideas were mere whispers. The son of their sister Anna and a wandering musician and preacher, William C. Wright, was a lad named Frank Lloyd Wright who finally left the University of Wisconsin to try his luck in Chicago as an architect. He designed his first building for his aunts: the Hillside School.

"There always seemed to be a tragedy connected with the Joneses. In 1913 a threshing crew was taking a steam engine—you know, one of the old kind with high wheels at back and a smokestack in front—up the valley toward one of the Jones farms. They were crossing a little bridge over the creek. The great weight of the engine broke the bridge right in. The engine buckled and the steam scalded two of the men to death. Then James Jones climbed down over the engine, tryin' to help, and he broke a leg. Something happened. He died in a short time. They are buried down next to the chapel near Mr. Wright. The chapel was built by the Jones family.

"One of the hired men at Taliesin would never work in the field back of the chapel. They used to grow tobacco there. One day in the early 1900s they were working in the tobacco field. There was only one cloud in the entire sky. Just one. Blue sky all around. Suddenly a lightning bolt came out of that one cloud and struck one of the workers dead. So this hired man would nevermore work in that field again. He figured it was God's warning to somebody. Maybe him.

"But I tell you, there's a kind of mystery that does hang over this valley. I've heard the sounds from the hills sometimes . . . I dunno . . ."

Now we are sloshing past Trish Carroll's store at Clyde. I never yet saw a smaller place than Clyde, Wisconsin. There's almost nothing to recognize it as a place. Used to be a lot there, but now there is only Trish's little store, which is also a Shell gas station, and a few houses.

"See that parking meter out behind the store?" asked Bob.

"What in blazes is a parking meter doin' out here in the country?"

"Farfetched ideas aren't infrequent out here. One day John Miller, editor of the *DODGEVILLE CHRONICLE*, came out to Trish's store. You know, folks like to gather in certain places, and a lot of the country folks do like to come to Trish's place. Oh, they play a little poker, talk about each other. You know.

"Well, John, he drove over from Dodgeville, and would you believe, there wasn't a place to park anywhere around Trish's. John claimed he had to park about a half-mile away. He came storming into the store yelling that he was going to insist on them putting in parking meters. Parking was impossible in Clyde, and so on.

"Trish, she played right along and says that if John could get a parking meter she would put it up. So John got a parking meter, old one I guess, or maybe he stole it, from the city of Richland Center, and Trish put it up back of her store. And you know, damn fools from everyplace would park there and pay money into that fool thing. Trish took quite a little money out of it until somebody stole it one night for the nickels!

"John got Trish another one, and this time Trish had it set in two or three feet of cement. Only thing, this meter is busted and won't take any nickels."

We go into the tiny store to visit a little while with Trish. She is tall, really very beautiful, in her seventies. She speaks frankly on almost any subject and can keep up easily with the men who rely on her for advice on many things. Life in a place like Clyde can be pretty limited, at least it would seem so to me. But Trish Carroll, who has lived in Clyde all her life, has other ideas.

"I'm awfully proud of the people we have here," Trish said, "and I tell anybody that stops. Maybe this afternoon, if you'd stopped here and were going to come in here to live, you know the answer I would have gave you?"

"I don't know."

"This place is just like what you left. A community is just what you make it. If you're liked where you left, more'n likely you'll get liked right here."

"Folks still pretty neighborly around Clyde?"

"I tell you for sadness, for sickness or death, you can't beat the town of Clyde. You went to a funeral, Lutheran, Protestant, Catholic, don't make any difference. If you went to the home in the evening and looked at the crowd, you couldn't tell. Such a good neighborhood and especially in death. Can't be beat. I always say, just like my dad fifty years ago, 'Treat 'em kindly while they live and bury 'em when they die.' I try to do the same."

BEAR VALLEY IN HIGH GEAR

BOB GRAVES SAID WE OUGHT TO TAKE A LOOK AT BEAR Valley, so after we leave Clyde we come down off the hills and cross the Wisconsin River south of Lone Rock. Just by the Highway 130 bridge, beside the river on the south side, is a cliff that a lot of water drips down. Every Christmastime local folks put a few buckets of vegetable coloring up where it can run down with the water. The icicles hanging to the cliff are therefore of many colors. It's a queer feeling, in a fog, to come around the curve there and see those long, colored icicles.

Every since coming to Wisconsin I have heard about Lone Rock and the temperature. Said to be the coldest spot in the middle west, it advertises itself as "The coldest spot in the Nation with the warmest heart." Indeed, many mornings Lone Rock draws the prize for being the coldest place in the United States. Perhaps it doesn't really deserve its reputation.

Gaylord Trumbel, chief of the U.S. weather and air patrol station there, told me that one reason Lone Rock is thought to be so cold is that they keep hour-by-hour records and other places don't. "We know how cold it really is," Trumbel said. "They don't."

Some say Lone Rock—a quiet, very midwestern little town—has a seathing undercover life. I wouldn't know much about that except what Helen Silko, who drives into Madison every day from her home in Lone Rock, tells me. As secretary to the Rural Sociology Department (just down the hall from my university office), she has learned a good deal about people, and she says that what goes on in Lone Rock would make very interesting reading but that everybody knows so much about everybody else that nobody dares say a word.

One thing that most folks don't know about Lone Rock is that Charles Lindbergh landed at the little airfield there one day in 1923, when he was a barnstorming young pilot. The Wisconsin River was away up that year and the whole country was flooded. Dr. Bertha Reynolds at Lone Rock village didn't know what to do because she had emergency calls from both Plain and Clyde—really sick people in both places. She got in touch with Lindy, who was very ready to help. He cranked up his plane and took the doctor to both locations, landing in farmers' fields. All patients were saved!

But back to Bear Valley, Paul Kooiman of Lone Rock told me this story: Schumacher, who lived in the Crandal House up in Bear Valley, came into a store one day, and Baker, who was operating the store, had a big, live rattlesnake in a cardboard box. Schumacher was pretty much afraid of snakes, and Baker took his rattler and playfullike began to chase Schumacher around the store and finally out into the street. Made Schumacher so mad that he called the Richland County sheriff. The sheriff came over and says to Baker, "You got a snake, a live rattler you been keepin.'"

Baker says, "Yep."

"Well," says the sheriff, "we got a complaint about that rattlesnake and about you chasin' folks with it. So you got to destroy the snake."

"All right," says Baker, "and I know who complained about my pet rattlesnake, the coward! If he's gonna complain about me and my snake to you, sheriff, I think you oughta know somethin' about his still!'"

Bear Valley lies north of Highway 14 on Highway 130. It is beautiful farming country, and driving north, through the valley, Bob Graves chats about the region and its charms. It was settled by farmers from New York State, very progressive. For example, they had the first cooperative rural telephone system in the state.

"Are there any of the old Greek revival style places out here that were so popular in New York State in the 1820s and '30s and '40s?"

"We're coming to one now," said Bob. We passed a lovely white dwelling with the typical doorways and white columns, which I had seen so often far back in the central New York State hills when I lived in Ithaca. I have never forgotten those houses.

"There's a whole lot of fine mansions on this valley road," Bob said. "They're simply magnificent homes! Some of 'em with twenty rooms! Look at the size of that one!" he said, pointing to a rambling brick house that could almost rival some of the great country houses of England.

"Mr. Wright's father is buried up here at the old Brown Church. Interesting story about him. Time of the Civil War, Mr. Wright's father, who was an itinerant preacher, needed some money to buy his way out of the draft. You know how they were able to do that. So he sold his violin, which was reported to be a Strad, to a settler up here, and supposedly it was still floating around in the vicinity. Well, three weeks ago we found it. It is a very fine violin, but not a Strad. A gal by the name of Lorna Carswell in Lone Rock has it now. She was a teacher."

"Does she play the violin?"

"Nope."

"This next house," Bob said, indicating a charming, rambling stone one, "is owned now by a Black couple from Chicago, people by the name of Vaughn. Some tried a little, locally, to keep them out. Circulated a petition. Didn't get to first base. Folks in the valley were more than glad to welcome the Vaughns.

"Mr. Wright's father, William Cary Wright, came here from Richland Center to preach at the Brown Church. He and his first wife are buried in the churchyard. This is the church right here."

We pull up beside a charming old church, brown, wooden, well over a century old. Tall cedar trees tower over the building.

"Maybe we can see the Wrights' tombstone," said Bob.

And we did locate it—tall, red granite—from the car, but we didn't get out. The day was too messy to go through the fog and wet slush through the old burying ground.

Bob reminded me that William C. Wright's second wife was the mother of Frank, and that *she* is buried in the Lloyd-Jones family graveyard in Wyoming Valley. We drive on toward the tiny town of Bear Valley. As we went, I thought about the New York State settlers and how they came out to Wisconsin, mostly over the old Erie Canal, on to the Lake Michigan shore, and over to Bear Valley and other places in southern Wisconsin. The New York State names thickly sprinkle the Wisconsin landscape; there is even an Ithaca, Wisconsin, about eight miles from the Brown Church, a tiny place, not at all like the Ithaca at the south end of Cayuga Lake in York State so fond in my memory of Cornell University—still the product of a homesick dream, you can bet.

The bar in Bear Valley village used to be called the New York Candy Kitchen. Nobody knows why, unless it was to disguise a speakeasy during Prohibition. If it was, they carried the disguise to absurd lengths. The bar is now called the Valley Bar, and it is operated by Dorothy and Martin, friendly young folks.

A lot of citizens in the valley gather at the long, golden oak bar with a line of deer antlers behind it. Dorothy, who takes her turn at bartending, is pretty and slender; she sits on a stool behind the bar when she isn't busy with customers, exchanging gossip and information. One can view the main street through the window, but only briefly because there isn't so much of Bear Valley anyway.

Bob Graves and I have dropped in, hoping to get some intimate side glimpses of Bear Valley life, past and present. We have ordered beers, which Dorothy has drawn for us, and Bob is exchanging some remarks with Dorothy when, by some golden chance, two denizens of Bear Valley wander in. They are Otto Schultz and Rudy Dederich, both born and raised in the valley.

At first things are kind of quiet. Bob knows Otto because some time ago Otto offered Bob a chance to bid on eighty wild acres he had for sale. Bob went to Otto's house to talk about the eighty, and Otto's wife told Bob she just that day sold the eighty acres to Otto, her husband! Bob does a double take, but it is the right information. Mrs. Schultz, who is a sharp business woman, had indeed sold the eighty acres to her husband on a land contract, no less. She is collecting money from him every month!

Otto orders beers for everybody. We thank him. He digs coins out of an old-fashioned pocket book, the kind with a snap catch on the top. At 67, he has a plump, very round face and a humorous mouth. Both Otto and Rudy are wearing bib overalls, that bear the marks of honest labor. Rudy, broad faced and kindly, is larger than Otto and moves slowly, always with a firm purpose, even when he grasps a beer glass.

Rudy's grandfather was a German immigrant who came to Milwaukee and Madison in the 1850s. In Cross Plains he worked for a time as a wheelwright and bitterly left three children in the Cross Plains Cemetery. He and his wife then moved northwest to Bear Valley, where they found themselves the only Germans amidst a frontier community of Irish and Yankees (mostly from New York State, Herkimer and Tompkins counties).

When Grandpa Dederich tried to buy supplies and some straw to stuff bedticks, the Irish sold him nothing. They did not want to get a bunch of German kids started in Bear Valley. When he needed lumber to build a house, however, Grandpa Dederich pulled gold coins out of his purse to pay. At the sight of gold, which they had not seen for a long while, the Irish sold him anything he needed.

So there are Irish and more Germans in the valley. Both are Catholic and there is some contention between the groups. At the crossroads Killian Church, south of Bear Valley, the Irish tombstones run north and south across the yard, and the German tombstones run east and west. They wanted divergent ways even in the cemetery! The Protestant church is still called the Brown Church, where Bob Graves and I had stopped.

Rudy tells us these things as we quietly drink beer.

"The valley is a pleasant place," Rudy says. "You would almost think that Bear Creek was coming down through the valley like an artery of nature. And different kinds of trees! So beautiful. Pines and maples and birches, greens and browns and white! Oaks and hickory. You never saw anything like the color out here in the fall. You drive down the valley, you feel like you're in God's own paradise. At least that's the way I feel."

"Me too," Dorothy says. "It's something good and wonderful!"

"Wonderful," says Rudy. "And down south of here is Point Judith. Ever hear of it?"

"No."

"Judith was a McCloud," said Rudy. "Those McClouds. The greatest hunters and Indian fighters ever lived in this country. The early days, this valley was full of game and the McClouds got a good share of it. Even elk in here then. Once when they was coming up through here on a hunt in the 1840s they saw three Indians following them. They laid in wait and watched, and they could see the Indians was on their trail. And when the Indians come along, the McClouds shot all three. One was gettin' away, but they got him too. Then they wrote to Gov. Henry Dodge that they had kilt some Indians. Dodge he come out personally to congratulate the McClouds. Dodge didn't like the red men. But that wasn't the end of it, because the Indians didn't appreciate to have their folks being murdered that way. So one day they come upon the McCloud girl, Judith, out in the open. Started to chase her. Was going to exact vengeance upon the McClouds through the girl, I suppose. She run of course. Was a fast runner. Led the Indians a good chase but finally they was about to take her. She run to the top of a point, a big bluff down south of here, and as they was about to seize her she jumped over. Some say she jumped into a cave on the face of the cliff, but mostly they say she hopped over and was killed. Anyhow that place is called Point Judith after Judith McCloud. I knew a feller once who said he knew where Judith is buried."

Bob Graves and I listen, drinking beer. The fog outside gets thicker. We are certainly not anxious to leave. Rudy leaves for a few minutes to go to his home, which is just down the street from the tavern to fetch an item of local history. He has been collecting things and pasting them in a huge wallpaper sample book. The book probably weighs twenty pounds. Dorothy says, with real concern, "I hope Rudy doesn't lug *that* over here. He was sick not long ago."

Rudy doesn't bring the big book, but he does bring a manuscript, his grandfather's own account of his early life in Dane and Richland counties. Someone has translated it from the original German. We all bend over the manuscript, almost amazed at the spiritual strength of the pioneers that led them through the terrible hardships and bitter losses of frontier Wisconsin settlement.

Dorothy breaks the spell. "Ryan," she says suddenly.

Otto instantly swells up like an old fightin' rooster. He takes a large swallow of beer and hollers, "I'll take Ryan on any time! Yes, and anyone else he wants to persuade along! If I so much as spot that son-of-a-gun I will skin him down the front and sew buttons up the back!"

"Just what was your trouble with Ryan?" Rudy asks gently.

"Why it was that gol danged dog," yells Otto. "That no count, yeller, belly-draggin' houn' dog!"

"I didn't know there was a dog involved," says Dorothy.

Dorothy's pretty little daughter comes home from school and Otto waits courteously while the child is carefully taken care of. Then he says, "Another beer all aroun'!" He digs a bill out of his ancient pocketbook.

I have had about four beers, but to decline might interfere with Otto's story, and I did want to know about the dog. We tilt the glasses.

"That dog," says Otto, and he rolls his glass, "there was this auction over by Ithaca. Suggs was the auctioneer. Suggs is good! Can talk the fastest I ever heard except for Paul Kooiman. Well, Ryan had these cows for sale. Said they was fair milkers. Looked like it. But don't ever believe appearances, boys, not when Ryan is around.

"Suggs says, 'Boys, Ryan has got a fine stock dog, and whoever buys the most cattle can have the dog free of expense.'

"I seen the dog. Wasn't much to look at, but you can't never tell a turkey by his wattle; so I says to myself, 'Well, maybe I will get the dog. I always wanted me a good cow dog.' So I buy them cows. Bought thirteen. Was unlucky. And Suggs he says to me, 'Well, Otto, you bought the most so you can have the dog.'

" 'No, he don't' yells Ryan.

" 'Like hell,' I says. 'I bought the most cows.'

" 'You don't get the dog nohow,' says Ryan. 'I want the dog bid too.'

"That's when I seen how Ryan was. Crooked as a blackbird's girdle.

"Suggs says that *he* wouldn't auction off the dog. It was a straight-out agreement. Whoever bought the most cows was to take the dog. Ryan he put on like the dog was his best friend, and he would have to have anyway ten dollars for him to ease his pain at partin'. He put on such a show, cryin' and huggin' the dog that I finally says, 'All right, Ryan, five dollars.'

" 'Ten dollars,' says Ryan, and goes on cryin'.

"Well, I finally give Ryan the ten dollars. I musta been crazy to do it, but I couldn't stand the noise he was putting up. Suggs says it is a shame and a crime and he calls down a retribution on old Ryan. But that

Irish—don't care. He's away out on the highway to hell anyhow, so what does it matter?"

"Now you sound real bitter, Otto," says Dorothy.

"Bitter? Why I hate Ryan stronger 'n pizen. After what he done to me!" Otto raises his left hand. "See this here hand? Ain't much count. But I can whip any Ryan with my one good hand and come apoundin' him with my bad hand when I get him down."

"Must of been somethin' more to it than what you said," says Rudy.

"There was. Plenty. I taken that dog home and tied him up. And that houn' eat through the rope and run away. Back to Ryan. And I went over to get him and Ryan says I could have him but it would cost me five dollars since he had meanwhile give the dog some grub!

"Well, I called Ryan out right there and offered to fight him anyway, underholts or anyhow. He wouldn't. So finally I had to give him five dollars and I took the dog home. Thought I would try him out with the cows. And you know what? That dog wouldn't chase no cows. Just laid on his belly and howled. So I went and drove the cows up to the barn myself, and when I got 'em in there I seen that they was all dry; not a one had been bred.

"When I see Ryan, and I'm gonna see him soon, he had better look out. I am going to hand him a beatin' that'll last him all of his breathin' life! Timber! Beers for everybody! Timber!"

Listening to Otto talk about Ryan, I marvel at the extension of past into present. The Irish-German feud in Bear Valley is still in high gear!

Later in Spring Green Village we stopped at the Steele's place. Helen Steele brings coffee and good chocolate cake. Cubby Cosper feels mellow enough to change the subject from Frank Lloyd Wright to old Bill Scallam. Cubby is a well known raconteur.

"They went up at the county meeting in Sauk City, and they got to talking about divorces," says Cubby. "Old Scallam was quite a talker, and he said 'You know, the damnedest divorce I ever heard of happening up in our country. There was a feller named George Rink, had a wife named Mary, and they had a little piece of land there that they hadn't put the wheat in yet, and they wanted to get it in before it rained. One team had gone to the mill and the other had gone after a load of gravel, and they didn't have any horses to put it in with.

"Finally he got the bright idee he would take off, leave only one section on the drag, and hitch Mary up and drag it. So he says he started in the middle of the field and everything was going along fine. Finally on the last row around the outside a rabbit jumped out of the brush and, he says, scart Mary like the devil and she run away and smashed the drag all to hell, and he says now George is suing Mary for a divorce!'

"There was a man named Murphy lived up in Bear Valley. You know, there are a lot of Irish up thataway. Murphy he got powerful sick, All the neighbors got together, the doctor from Loganville was away, and the doctor from Reedsburg was sick or something. Anyway he was away, so they got together to hold a consultation to see what to do about Murphy.

"Well, Bill Scallam had been doctoring all the horses and everything around the country, and helpin' out, and so the neighbors says to him, 'What do you think we ought to do about Murphy?' Bill he thought for a spell and says, 'Well, I think you ought to give him a physic.' And so they talked on some more about it, and they asked Bill again what to do, and he says again, 'I think we ought to give him a physic.'

" 'How much shall we give Murphy?' "

" 'Well,' he says, 'why don't you go ahead and give Murphy the same as I would give a horse.'

"So he give Murphy the dose of horse physic and he went home. Bill he didn't sleep very well that night thinkin' about Murphy and how the physic would affect him, so he got up bright and early and done his chores up and he went over to Murphy's. When he got there Mrs. Murphy was out splitting wood for the stove. And Bill says, 'And Mrs. Murphy, did it work?'

" 'Oh, my God,' she says, 'it worked. Murphy went forty times during the night and six times after he died!'

"They told one day Scallam went down the road and it was sleighing time in the winter, and he was going along he noticed up ahead a wagon box tipped clear over. And he says he finally got up there and stopped and went over and up would come the wagon box a little and a voice underneath would say, 'Allllll together, Flanagan!' He said they watched that for a while and every little bit the box would raise up and voice would holler, 'Allllll together, Flanagan!'

"And there an old boy from Bear Valley, he was down underneath and he would push up and holler, 'Alllll together, Flanagan . . .' trying to tip it over. Scallam says he finally went and rolled the box off. Old man never thanked him or nothin'. Just got in the wagon and went on his way hollering 'Alllll together, Flanagan!' "

What times, what people those were!

RURAL WRITERS

HE WISCONSIN IDEA THEATER WAS FLOURISHING. THERE seemed to be a great increase of theater activity everywhere, but I was dissatisfied. Discouraged. I feared that if the University were to withdraw all stimulus in the field of the state-wide creative arts that much of the art and theater activity would stop, and that eventually, without stimulus, the whole movement would dwindle away. I was certain that the spark which might make theater and the other arts a vital necessity in people's lives had not been caught. Then one day, without warning, a small event occurred that seemed to catch a spark and that has lead to an expression that is the most hopeful thing pointing toward a deep and wide concept of the cultural necessity of the creative arts in everyday life that I have witnessed.

One day my phone rang. It was a professor from the College of Agriculture calling me. He said, "There are nine people from rural Wisconsin coming to see you."

"What for?"

"They want to talk about writing."

"What kind of writing?"

"They don't know."

"I'm pretty busy."

He said, "One of the women has thirteen children."

"A farm woman with thirteen children has time to come to Madison and talk about writing?"

"She's here," he said.

"All right, I'll see them. Where?"

"Bascom Hall. There's a classroom reserved."

I went up the hill to Bascom Hall. I found the nine people in a hot room that looked out on the slope down to Lake Mendota. There were eight women and one boy about 18 years old. One of the women was tall and gray, two were young, one was fat and jolly, one was quiet and serene, one was dark and small, two were middle aged. They waited for me to say something, and as I paused a moment looking at them, for no reason at all, I began to remember the happy and careless life I led as a kid in the Neosho River Valley down in Kansas. And it seemed that my early experience had had for me the unshackled quality of complete freedom; the gaiety; the unreasoned and complete savoring of the goodness of earth and sky; the unquestioning appreciation of neighbors, and music and dancing. And with the memory of the free wildness of my youth running through me these folks who had come to see me were transformed. I forgot that they had come to Madison on a hot June morning to talk about the technical processes of creative writing. They became, instead, a symbol of a group of my neighbors in Kansas, or people I had encountered on my wanderings, who knew a wordless appreciation of the theater that was life. I sensed, too, on this hot morning, that this whole theater that flowed around us so endlessly could be transmuted to art with only the gentlest of pushes.

I said to the eight ladies and the one boy. "You are like a group of my neighbors when I was a kid down in Kansas."

The tall, grey one said, "You remind me a little bit of a neighbor of mine up in Manitowoc County. He's a farmer. Not really a very good farmer."

"Why did you come?"

"I don't know exactly. Except that we've heard that you want people to write about their own places, and the folks they know well. I . . . I think I could do that."

I said to them, "Tell me about yourselves. Where did you come from and what kind of places are they?"

And then began one of the most unreasonable experiences I ever had. These nine persons stayed at the University for three days; and everyday about nine o'clock we would start talking together. And as we talked our lives and the struggle in them emerged to lie against the whole fabric of our native places, and as we talked, hour after hour, a kind of fantastic play that was like life itself began to emerge and to encompass us all within its spaceless and formless self. There were times when we would speak, not as ourselves, but as imaginative characters that grew from our talk of people and events that were as real as the earth itself. The whole affair was a kind of dramatic ecstasy in which we were both the actors and the audience, the dancers and the music.

When the three days were over, it was as though a kind of dream had ended, with no more explanation than that with which it had begun. The nine good people awoke suddenly, and realized that we had hardly mentioned the processes of *writing* at all, and that, instead of a partly completed manuscript tucked into pocket or purse, they had only a confused but terribly exhilarating sense of something that had stirred their lives.

When they were ready to leave Madison, I said, "I have met with hundreds of groups like this one, and I have seen hundreds of plays, but I have never had a deeper sense of theater than we have had together."

The tall, grey lady said, "I think it was because we all had something to express, and we did express it, and maybe the memory of it is somehow better than a written play."

"I wish there were more persons like yourselves."

"Mr. Gard," said the tall, grey lady, "there are hundreds and thousands of rural men and women who live on the land and love the land and who understand the true meaning of the seasons and man's relationship to man and to his God."

I said, "If that is so, the plays they send to me don't reflect such an appreciation."

"I think," she said, "that's maybe because everything is made to seem too complex, too technical, too difficult. There must be a great, free expression. If the people of Wisconsin knew that someone would encourage them to express themselves in any way they chose; if they knew that they were free of scenery and stages and pettiness that the plays we do seem so full of; if they knew that someone would back them and help them when they wanted help, Mr. Gard, there would be such a rising of creative expression as yet unheard of in this state, and it would really all be a part of the kind of theater we have had these past three days, for the whole expression would be of and about ourselves."

The eight ladies and a boy went away, but I couldn't stop thinking about them. And that same fall we launched a unique new kind of organization. An organization that was really not an organization, for then it was never really organized. But its title was "The Wisconsin Rural Writers' Association." It cost nothing to join, everybody was eligible, and the only rule was that a person must submit literary evidence of appreciation of familiar scenes and faces. City folks were more than welcome so long as they had a sincere regard for the land. The Wisconsin Idea Theater was to act as a center for the movement, and indeed, I did not anticipate that there would be a very great response to it. My judgment, based on the number of plays we had received, led me to believe that perhaps fifty persons might eventually align themselves with the "Writers' Association."

It was, therefore, with some dismay that we found our mailboxes loaded each morning with manuscripts. To the horror of my already overburdened small staff, over one thousand poems were sent in in a few days time. There were short stories, too, and a few plays. The curious thing was that the material was, for the most part, excellent. There was some bad poetry, but most of the poetry had a wonderful, honest ring. For a while, until I could get special help, we were all reading innumerable manuscripts every day, at lunch, at dinner, at night, and all of us would usually be walking from this to that task with several rural life poems or stories or plays sticking out of our pockets.

Some persons could not understand what a theater project was doing fooling around with poets and story writers, etc. But during the course of a year, nearly one thousand rural people aligned themselves stoutly with the Association, and a good effect seemed to be noted in playwriting. The plays were certainly improving and we took this to mean that the playwrights could see themselves as part of a free movement. The scripts began to be free of stereotypes and cliches and I began to see that the development of the creative impulse, no matter what its outlet, was of common benefit to all the arts.

True, we did not kid ourselves into believing that we had two or three thousand wonderful and gifted authors in the State of Wisconsin. We knew that we were working on two distinct levels, one level where thousands of persons participated in a creative program for the fun of it, or for a hundred and one other reasons, and another level where a few highly talented authors were working, who would ultimately be the ones to cast into fine art products the whole philosophy of the movement.

What the Rural Writers' movement in Wisconsin means to the individual was summed up by a writer from Baraboo, Wisconsin. She said,

"The writer's movement has focused my attention on the life I know best, and it has helped me to recognize the wealth of material right here in my own community. From that viewpoint I have acquired a greater understanding of my neighbors and their problems.

"The writer's movement has erased the inferiority I felt, arising from my limited education, and has paved the way to continued knowledge. Too, being associated with so many others in the state has removed the stigma of eccentricity from writing as a hobby, making it at least as respectable a pastime as crocheting bedspreads or hooking rugs. My 'hobby,' in turn, has given me an emotional outlet to supplement the monotonous routine of housework and has probably made me a more interesting and certainly a more contented person."

This lady's husband is a dandy farmer who always rather tended to disapprove of his wife's writing projects. But lately the stuff she had been writing has taken on a lot of personal meaning for him, because of lot of her writing is localized around their farm. Last Christmas, without saying a word about it, he went to Baraboo and bought her a new writing desk and a new typewriter.

And so, the movement grew in Wisconsin among the farm and city people. Creative writing blossomed. And I, too, was caught up in the wave. My hope continued to find and interpret the Wisconsin people, in plays and stories and to further an interest in folklife, for I considered a knowledge of folk traditions and customs very important in literary and cultural interpretation. With this in mind I proceeded toward the preparation (with my friend, L. G. Sorden) of WISCONSIN LORE. At the time of its publication in 1962 it was the only work in a single volume containing many interesting folk customs that could still be collected on the Wisconsin scene. The Rural Writers made it possible.

ARTS IN ANY SOIL

ISCONSIN DOES NOT POSSESS THE SOFT INSISTENT mystery of central New York nor the overpowering breadth of the Short Grass country of western Canada, but the state has its own appeals which, to me, are always more the result of Wisconsin traditions than of the geographical character of the land. One of these traditions is certainly the attitude with which people accept the Wisconsin Idea in education. For example, I was invited one evening "to make a talk on drama" at a crossroads town hall set at the edge of a large cornfield near Oconomowoc. The lady who invited me, Mrs. Isabelle Tremaine, the wife of a prosperous farmer, had written: "Come on for supper. Afterwards you may make your talk."

I arrived at the Tremaine farm about six and was discussing rural approaches to the drama with my hostess when Mr. Tremaine staggered into the kitchen with an ugly gash in his forehead. He had smashed into a steel stanchion in the dim barn and was temporarily hors de combat. Now, cow milking in its various forms is one of the skills one never forgets and certainly I had had enough milking in my Kansas boyhood to make a permanent impression. I offered to take over at the barn and my offer was accepted easily, naturally.

The Tremaines had a milking machine, but there were certain cows who would not stand for machinery. With my head in a warm flank I meditated about where the role of a professor from the University is as natural to cowmilking as to conducting classes in adult education. The people of Wisconsin through their tradition of the Wisconsin Idea understand the necessities of milking and adult education equally well, and professors and people are generally on common ground. After I had finished the milking and had had a bite to eat I went to the hall and gave my little talk. It was accepted by the rural audience with the same ease and naturalness and understanding that my offer to milk the cows had been. With such understanding of motives and methods I, at least, have found the strong flavors of Wisconsin places pleasant to savor. I have become familiar with Wisconsin's past, and I have found the past always adding spice to present observations. Not to know the past of a region is like viewing the setting but never seeing the drama.

How empty a trip westward from Madison toward Mount Horeb and Mineral Point would be for me if I did not know that I was traveling on the ridgeroad, the old military highway which carried the heavy lead wagons rolling slowly from the mines at Mineral Point, New Diggings, Benton, and the whole southwest. How empty my journey would be if I could not imagine the rolling wagons, the drivers, their speech, the dust, the blue jackets of cavalrymen, the settlers' rigs, and the immigrants from Europe on foot plodding along the ridgeroad, seeking new freedoms of many kinds, finding new freedoms in the valleys and on the hillsides. How empty my journey if I did not know that to the north and south of the road were valleys where Norwegian names are thickly sown with, here and there, a few Irish, English, or German shoots sticking through. I know that there are other valleys not far from the road where Swiss names are as thick as Norwegian and others where German names blanket the countryside. It is warming to know where the plantings of names lie on the land and to know how the seed came to the soil.

It adds zest to my journey to know that the ridgeroad is the stamping ground of an elusive "haunt"—the Ridgeway Ghost. In 1820 near Mineral Point, a Missouri man is said to have murdered a Virginian in a quarrel over a pretty Cornish girl. The Missouri man got the maiden, but the Virginian took up a flitting, terrorizing vigil as a ghost along the ridgeway. He is seen sometimes riding a two-wheeled rig to which is hitched a splendid team of blacks (breathing fire, some say). The team and driver appear suddenly on the ridgeway at night weaving in and out of traffic, causing squeals of terror and sudden endings to midnight romance. The Ghost sometimes is said to appear riding the cowcatcher of the occasional engine which huffs its slow way across the ridgelands on the Chicago and Northwestern branch line. The Ghost is not seen so often nowadays, since many of the Welsh and Cornish folks who lived along the ridgeway have disappeared. But an imaginative traveler can spot him. I have.

The folklore of the region is always the coloring of the region's portrait, and the responses of Wisconsin people to adult education is a part of the picture, too, an inspiring part, especially when the educational program is attached to the arts. For example, Grant County is a county of low hills, farming country cut sharply by ravines and valleys and quick flooding streams. There are towns, too, which seem to me to be very mid-American. One cold March afternoon there was a meeting at Lancaster. This was a meeting of a group of Grant County rural artists. They had been called together to see the movie the State Department in Washington had made of their Grant County art activities. Many of the artists were actors in the movie. They brought their neighbors and families to see this movie which would be shown in nations all over the world to demonstrate that rural America has a culture of its own. The meeting was held in the local movie theater where there was 35 millimeter equipment. The place held about six hundred persons and it was full. Many of the business people of Lancaster came in, too. In the lobby of the City Hall next door paintings were piled and stacked, waiting to be taken upstairs and displayed. The artist-in-residence from the University of Wisconsin was to attend the showing of the movie and, afterward, to offer criticism and suggestion on many of the paintings brought in by the people. There was to be a supper, too, held right there in the display hall, and many of the farm ladies had brought covered dishes, or pies, cakes or meats.

I drove over from Madison with Aaron Bohrod, the artist-in-residence who had replaced John Stuart Curry, Jim Schwalbach, the traveling Extension artist who had arranged the meeting, and a gentleman from the Rockefeller Foundation in New York, Edward D'Arms. He had come out to see at first hand some of the field work in the arts going on in Wisconsin. He was interested but a bit unbelieving. "Perhaps," he had said on the way over from Madison, "we are not ready for a people's art expression in America."

We sat in the back of the theater and saw the movie which had been produced by Julian Bryan who had done many good films. It was good, a work of art. The rural folk in the cast with their easy naturalness turned out to be some of the best actors we had seen. We were excited, and D'Arms expressed eagerness to go upstairs and see some of the paintings these rural folk had been doing.

We climbed the City Hall stairs and entered a long room. It was jammed with people, and there were countless original paintings lined up along the walls on tables. A passage opened before Aaron Bohrod as he went to the far end of the room. He was greeted with enthusiastic and friendly calls from every side. The people were not embarrassed. The fact that he was an outstanding American artist made no difference in their attitude toward him. He was one of their group. He believed in them and what they had been doing. He set up an easel and called for the first painting.

An elderly farm woman brought the first one. It was of a barn and cattle and a tree. Bohrod set it on the easel and commented with respect. He called attention to good points and bad, making his criticism always constructive and helpful. Then came a bachelor who had turned a corn bin into a studio; then came a high school girl, a feed store operator, more housewives, and a school teacher, a country doctor. More and more.

We watched and listened. D'Arms grew thoughtful. He made notes in a black book, asking for names and occupations of the people. Finally someone thought of food. Pictures were taken off the tables and the food was spread. We all sat down together. A grayed lady sat beside D'Arms. She said to him, "Do you see why we like to live in Wisconsin?" He said, "I think I do."

One night in 1950 I was invited to a farmers' meeting that had a double purpose. The first purpose was the discussion of an economic measure near to the community's heart, and the second purpose was to discuss what that community might do through theater to draw the community into a more cohesive body. My part was distinctly secondary on the program.

The economic question was this: The Wisconsin Legislature had recently put through a law requiring that farmers have a separate milkhouse with a concrete floor and that they haul the manure away from the barns every day. There was a date set at which time all the milkhouses must be ready. Many farmers disliked the law. They were shorthanded. They had no time to build a new milkhouse. Some of them had always let the manure pile up around the barn throughout the winter and, by Gad, they would continue to do so!

This particular meeting turned into a hot one. The chair got into trouble trying to keep order, and the county agricultural agent was almost mobbed because some of the folks blamed him for their plight. This community had also summoned its state assemblyman to be present; he had voted for the milkhouse bill in the legislature. They said violent things to him. The discussion was not getting anywhere. They wrangled for a while and then decided to call it off. They turned the meeting over to me.

I was in an uncomfortable spot, faced by anticlimax and the probable futility of trying to stimulate interesting discussion in this particular atmosphere. I knew I simply could not talk about drama in ordinary terms. It suddenly occurred to me, as I fumbled about, that the previous discussion had aspects of a drama: conflict, character, excellent dialogue. So I set about fabricating, without the people actually knowing what was going on, a comic situation in which the various factions and individuals were either for or against the milkhouse law, and before we realized it a kind of group play was actually in progress, only now it seemed in terms of comedy, exciting but laughable, for I had attempted to exaggerate the purpose on both sides and to enlarge on the innocence of the county agent and to exaggerate the well-meaning, slightly self-pitying attitude of the legislator as well as the anger of several of the more outspoken opponents of the milkhouse bill.

In the informally dramatized version of the affair that we made up there at the moment the farmer was getting his whacks at the legislator and the county agent was making his excuses but within the framework of a creative situation.

Somehow feelings seemed cleansed, purposes made clear, and actually everyone began to enjoy the situation. In fact, that particular group enjoyed it so much that they decided to put the dramatized discussion on again at a later gathering. And they did, with a big spread of good country grub, with some rural paintings hung around the walls of the hall, and with some singers from a county-wide rural chorus furnishing another aspect of the occasion.

We have tried this kind of community, or group, drama a number of times with general good success. It is, of course, a purely presentational sort of theater in which the members of the audience are actually the actors. The play, if it may be called that, is frank theatricality with the theatrical elements simplified and frankly artificial.

This kind of dramatic expression, which could find great place in countryside life, has a body of precedent. For example, during the nineteenth century Nietzsche, Tolstoi, Rolland, and Appia developed theories of "art for life's sake" and considered a kind of "communal" drama as the art of the future. The form of the group play I have described bears a slight resemblance also to the theatrical concept of Evreinov, the drama theorist and playwright who formulated a theory of drama-in-life.

The form has special value to groups of young persons, especially, who are able to free themselves from their inhibitions and from the ordinary conventional restrictions of the realistic stage. Crowd scenes, for instance, are apt to be highly dynamic and expressive, perhaps confusing to the spectator but satisfying to the participant who is the chief one involved. It is the participant's show. Within its framework is endless scope for education on the part of a leader who may aid the participants in working out more satisfying ways of self-expression through dramatic movement and interplay with other participants.

I have traveled Wisconsin in all its seasons in my search for the flavor of the state. I recall a cold morning at the University's experimental farm at Spooner, up in the northwest corner of the state. It was November, late in the month. Snow was on the ground, and a wet, chilling wind was coming across the cutover and the swamps.

The young home demonstration agent and I paced nervously about the room. We were wearing our heavy coats. She had had a lot of experience with north country economics, very little with theater. She looked continually at her watch. She was embarrassed. She said, finally, "Well, Mr. Gard, I sure hope *somebody* comes.

I said, "So do I."

That morning I had driven up to Spooner from Chippewa Falls over glass-slick roads. Earlier in the month we had written from the office in Madison: "Dear County Agricultural Agent: Spooner has been selected as a regional meeting place for a one-day drama training school. Would you please notify all persons in your area and the agents in surrounding counties so that interested people may attend?"

We had exchanged several letters. The Spooner office had written that there had never been much drama in that part of the state; folks were scattered out, sort of; and they didn't have much free time. It was hard to scrape a living out of the north country earth; so they hadn't given much thought to putting on plays, but if you want to come up we'll give your training school idea a go. Better wear your long underwear and carry a shovel in your car—guess you haven't been up our way.

So here I was, and it was time for the meeting to begin; and not a single person had arrived. The young home agent said, wistfully. "I *do* wish one person would come." She glanced at me and I knew that she sincerely hoped my trip would not be entirely barren.

I said, "Keep calm"

We paced some more, and finally she said. "There is a lady over in the eastern part of the county who put on a play once. They . . . they said it was awfully funny."

I said, "That's nice."

She said, "After all, Mr. Gard, the weather is terrible."

She heard a noise, she thought, and rushed over to the window. A car was pulling into the yard. I ran to look, too. She cried, "There are *three* in that car! *Three!*" Sure enough, there were. Two ladies and a small boy. The young home agent rushed out to greet them and I thought, "Well, three is the size of this workshop." But it wasn't. More cars pulled into the yard. Suddenly the room was full of people. They entered cautiously, some of them, glancing at me as we shook hands. There were housewives and a surprising number of men. The home agent and I got chairs and more chairs. We were excited now and she was glowing, gratified. She whispered: "They are interested! I can hardly believe it! But they wouldn't have come if they weren't interested!"

Pretty soon the meeting was started. We talked about plays and community life, about local history, legends, about what they could do with their own groups, about playmaking in their own communities. I did not need, I found, to sell them on the idea of theater. Once they saw how theater was a part of their lives they carried me along. They represented church groups and schools. Several rural schools had let the kids off for a day so the teachers could attend the workshop. There were farm men and women. "Too bad weather to work outdoors much," the men said, attempting to pass off their presence as just something to do or just somewhere to go with the wife. But they were interested and showed it, especially when we got around to discussing playwriting based on themes familiar to the region.

One lady said to me: "But, Mr. Gard, we would love to do plays in our town, but we have no stage. We have a town hall, but there's not even a platform."

I told them that although there is a vast amount of the old fashioned and ordinary process of play production going on in Wisconsin, we have become aware of numerous experiments that seem to show that a new idea of theater is evolving. I told them that to some extent the old theater realism is dying out and that many plays are being staged without curtain, footlights, or even scenery. I told them that I believed the emphasis seemed to be coming at last to a real appreciation of human character and situation basic to people's lives. When plays cannot be found to fit the needs of the people, someone or some group must make up a play; in such playmaking there is a wonderful freshness.

I told them about such a play I saw that represented life on the town square at Stevens Point. I reminded them that Stevens Point is a small city in the heart of a large settlement of Polish people and that these Poles as well as others are in the habit of bringing farm produce to sell on the square. The play, I recalled, was colorful with dancing and singing—dances and songs the people sang and danced and everybody knew. The play used characters and subjects familiar to the central part of Wisconsin.

The play was a hit, and I told the group that I believed that if we could again make our theater meaningful and joyful in terms of ourselves a great American people's movement in theater would spring to life.

I showed them how to arrange the chairs in the hall so that plays might be presented in the center of the room, and I discussed the movement in central staging that was finding popularity all over America. It was a new idea to most of the folks. We talked more theater and had lunch together.

In the afternoon a group of writers came in. Three of them had original novels. It was dark night when I got away from the farm. I said goodbye to the young home agent. She said, "You're sold on this stuff . . . plays and writing and art, aren't you?"

I said, "Are you?"

She said, "We'll have a drama festival up here this Spring."

One facet of Wisconsin that has made a deep impression on me is the selfless willingness of a few persons to assume impossible burdens in the service of the arts. One such person worked in Rhinelander.

Rhinelander, Wisconsin, is known chiefly as a small city of wood products industry and as the home of the Hodag, that fabulous and mythical white bulldog-eating denizen of the deep woods which a great local trickster named Gene Shepard captured at tremendous personal peril. Legends about Gene may be picked up by the bushel at Rhinelander, and I have often gone there with that purpose; yet Rhinelander is also to me a kind of fortress buttressing my faith in the cultural arts. A young woman named Maxine Cottrill struck the initial sparks.

It was a May Sunday night in Rhinelander, and the Northwoods Arts and Crafts Festival was due to open on Monday morning. There was a fearful amount of work to be done, and a small group of folks had been laboring almost all night at the Legion Hall. They had hung a couple of hundred excellent paintings done by artists in northern Wisconsin counties. They had carried a huge lithograph press (carted up to Rhinelander from the University) up a long fire escape and had set it up so that the

well-known lithographer, Professor Art Sessler of the University Art department, might give demonstrations. They had rigged a pottery wheel,
arranged an exhibit of the creative writings of the published authors of
the region, constructed a low stage for the presentation of one-act plays.
They had planned a "music day," an "art day," a couple of "theater
days," and a "writers day."

The festival was the first of its kind ever to be held in the woodlands
of Wisconsin. It was an outgrowth of a great local interest in the home-
grown things—an interest inspired originally by a small group of people
who had felt a great sense of responsibility to see that the arts and crafts
flourished in their northern section of the state. The art and craft work,
the plays, the music, they believed, must be put on display so that the
public might sense the importance of the arts as a vital part of community
life. There was one young lady, Maxine Cottrill, the Home Demonstration Agent for Vilas and Oneida Counties, who felt the deepest sense of
responsibility. She was a creative writer and a painter and knew the deep
personal satisfactions these things could bring. She had carried the idea
of painting and sketching, of acting and singing and writing into the farm
kitchens. She had sponsored art institutes and writers' meetings and theater one-day schools so that the people might have a chance to expand
their ideas, enlarge their knowledge of techniques; and the people had
responded.

Maxine had been one of my summer session students at the University. One day I got a letter from her asking whether the Wisconsin
Idea Theater would participate in a Northwoods Arts and Crafts Festival.
She wrote that she would undertake to see the festival through. I replied
that we would participate and I sounded out Jim Schwalbach, of the art
project, and Emmett Sarig, the music specialist, on the idea. We decided
to combine forces to help Maxine demonstrate how powerful a force the
cultural aspects of state life have become in an area remote from the
University, where, ordinarily, one might think that the major interests
of the region would be in hunting and fishing.

So plans were made with Maxine and her committee. There would be an exhibit of local painting, a crafts display, a play festival, a music festival. There would be pottery-making demonstrations, lithography demonstrations, a collection of the published writings of northwoods writers, and a collection of the folklore of the north country would be started. It was all very exciting.

No one realized how ill Maxine was, but all the work got done. The festival was a success and the seeds were sown for more creative work and a growing friendliness for the arts in northern Wisconsin. Maxine viewed it all with satisfaction and made notes on the good and bad points of the experiment. She told me that she was tired but that she had done something she had always wanted to do.

Maxine died two months later, but her faith in the arts as a necessary part of American community and individual life will not be forgotten in the northern Wisconsin country. Nor will it be forgotten by me.

There are many artists in the Wisconsin countryside who never hear of organizational programs and would not fit into them if they did. Some of these artists, rugged individualists, to say the least, contribute their own mite to my feeling for the state.

One fall journey carried me into the woods country north and east of Hayward, a country of deep swamps and timber where coarse grasses rasp together slowly in the filtering breezes. It is country where a flick of movement sensed far away through and among the splashed shadows might mean an alerted deer, a country where the moss-covered stumps and the dim trails recall the days when the forest was a setting for crawling, endless motion and echoing sound. I had heard of a man in this woodland who was delicately atuned to all the sights and sounds of the forest and whose pencil, crayon, and brush had given life to the essence of the forest itself. Him I wished to visit, for the image of a woodland artist living in solitude, sketching and painting with sensitive, intimate passion the whole of his forest reality stimulated a curiosity I must satisfy.

I found his cabin, finally, and stood for a moment looking at it. It was a shack of unpainted boards with one tiny window and a low, plank door. The dooryard was a bramble patch with a path to the outhouse. Among the brambles were the skeletons of old machines, bleak, unidentifiable. There at a far edge of the bramble I could recognize the jutting arm of an old engine piston, and in a patch of thickly matted grass I could dimly make out the outline of an ancient wheel lying flat. The whole scene was interlaced with loneliness, and ugly vestiges of human habitation filled me with uneasiness. I walked around a skimpy woodpile and approached the door.

As I came to the door I could hear a soft yet rough sound from within the shack and I paused a moment trying to define it. It rose and fell and fell and rose and was somehow echoed by the broken flow of the wind in the tops of the pines away from the clearing. I knocked at the door.

Instantly the sound stopped and a tremendous barking began. A voice said, "Quiet! Quiet, damn ye!" and the barking stopped instantly. There was motion beyond the door and suddenly it was pulled open violently. The smell came first, even before I could focus on the man who stood in the open door. It was a smell that instantly flooded my mind with memory of other bachelor shacks I had visited in Kansas and New York and Alberta, especially Alberta where bachelor living has been defined on prairie and on mountain by rigid rules of filth and convenience. As I peered at the man and at the cluttered interior I could see that he was short, that his hair was intensely black and uncombed, and he wore no trousers at all—only dirt-streaked drawers that ended in huge, thick-soled shoes. I could see at the far edge of the room his bunk out of which he had quite obviously just crawled. The bunk was occupied now by two huge hounds who looked at me steadily from the depth of human-warmed blankets.

There is a delicacy about situations such as this. Doors close so easily. Perhaps intuitively my eyes stayed on the dogs and I said, with the memory within me of dark-tan hounds in an eastern Kansas woodland on a frosty October night, "Those are fine dogs."

He moved slightly. "They are."

"They trail?"

He said, "They are good."

To break the conversational ice, I told him I had lived near a river, the Neosho, in Kansas, a great coon river, where there were mussels to be had in plenty, where there were ravines and tall cottonwood timber, where in the Fall a good dog's voice could be heard near two miles, and where when the dogs would call we would hurry through the woodlands and over the frost-stiff grass with a lantern throwing crazy shadows around us as we ran.

He moved away from the door and I went in. We fenced, jockeyed, and eventually I admitted that I was from the University, that I had heard he was an artist, and that I had a sincere desire to view his work. He quite properly denied this for a time, but eventually he reached under the bunk and pulled out a bundle wrapped in old canvas. He grabbed the hounds by the necks and jerked them off the bunk. He laid his bundle carefully on the bunk and unrolled it. There were some cheap crayons in boxes, a couple of dime store watercolor trays, some pencils and brushes and tubes of oils. There was also a roll of what looked like common white shelf paper. He lifted the roll and smoothed it out. One by one he lifted sheets of the paper and spread them on the bunk. The wildlife of the northwoods was there, suddenly, in the filthy shack, reproduced in breathtaking originality against delicate backgrounds of swamp and grasses and the dead rubble of decaying forest. I stood for a long while gazing at the pictures. Finally, I said, "I've got to be going. Thanks."

"Come back anytime," he said, and he began to gather his pictures, tenderly rolling them again for the bundle. He tied the bundle and thrust it under the bunk. As I went to the door the hounds jumped on the bed again and snuggled into the blankets.

A feeling for place, at least an instinctive understanding of the lore of the people, seems basic to the creative processes of anyone wishing to make sincere and honest interpretations of the regional scene. I have sought ballads of the north timber country in a cabin where an old lady pushed herself gently back and forth in a Boston rocker and sang "The Log Jam on Gerry's Rocks" and "The Little Brown Bulls" with such genuine flavor that I was there with Young Monroe when he broke the jam on Gerry's Rocks . . . greatest log jam the Wisconsin River ever saw. I was there beside Bull Gordon, the Yankee, when his log-skidding team of little brown bulls outskidded McCluskey's white spotted steers two to one!

I have treasured the quiet well-being of Walworth County in the south, settled by New York State People, mostly, in the 1840s and '50s. They came through the Erie Canal, bringing a feeling of New York State places to southern Wisconsin. And in contrast I have savored the central Wisconsin sand country where agriculture is difficult but where the places are warm, often, with the folk dances and wines of the Polish people. I have an intimate feeling for Taliesin, the low-roofed home at Spring Green of the famous architect Frank Lloyd Wright who believed that beauty should be a part of the everyday experience of everybody. And I have the same sort of intellectual intimacy with "The Clearing," the home of the great landscape architect Jens Jensen in Door County who believed the creative man could express himself best in terms of a deep and intimate association with nature.

THE GREAT MARSH

 NE OF THE ACTIVITIES I HAVE ENJOYED DOING, ORIGI-
nally inspired, doubtless by my Alberta experiences,
is to give talks to local groups about the Wisconsin
Idea Theater and the lore of the state. One night,
many years ago, I spoke to a woman's club at Horicon, Wisconsin, My talk that night led to interesting later developments. The local doctor's wife
told me a tale about a nearby trail tree . . . an oak whose branches had
been tied by Indians, when the tree was very young, in a certain way to
point a trail through the Horicon Marsh—one of the great wildlife areas
of America. She offered to show me the trail tree, but time ran out and
I didn't see it, and more or less forgot about the tree and its possible
symbolization.

More than twenty years later I was driving near Horicon, and suddenly remembered the tale and the tree. Something impelled me to see
the tree, and to investigate the lore of the Horicon Marsh.

I discovered that Dr. Fred Karsten, husband of the lady who told me the original tale, now owned the land on which the trail tree stood. I was able to locate Dr. Karsten that day, and he drove me, with my friend Edgar Mueller, noted wildlife photographer, out to the site. Seeing the two-hundred-year-old oak, with branches pointing out a ghost-trail across a marsh, now preserved by the State and Federal governments as a wildlife refuge, touched me off on a writing project I approached with great pleasure.

I found within the marsh itself, vestiges of ancient habitations and caves, that enlarged my deep feeling for the land and the people. "Wild Goose Marsh—Horicon Stopover" expanded my attempt to create literary landmarks within the folklife of Wisconsin, and to recall the images of the far, far primitive.

The Canada Geese which descend on the marsh twice yearly, are the great lure to travelers. Not only sportsmen, but persons interested in wildlife from throughout the world, visit the marsh in fall and spring. The thousands of geese create what is possibly the greatest wildlife show in America.

When the glacier that drove so deep into the earth had carved and worried and mutilated the form of the land to create and cause Lake Michigan, there were other, smaller, inexorable mile-high barriers of ice tearing the earth to the west. Some of the scooped-out places became lakes, and through centuries of erosion and change the lakes filled with peat and became extensive wetlands. When the white men arrived about 1640 they named the wetlands to the south and west of Lake Winnebago, the Winnebago Marsh.

Before the white men arrived the Great Marsh breathed under the leavening seasons, tossing wild tall grasses and rippled waters, floating water anemone so brilliant, and the water lily on the blue, clear water. On hummocks the wild roses knew the gentle winds that also moved the snapdragons and stirred the purple vetch; and deep in the bogs the winds turned forward and backwards the yellow thrusts of marsh marigolds.

The Great Marsh was more than a hundred square miles, in shape roughly oval, surrounded by a forest of oak, maple, ash, elm, and hickory, and to the west the prairie spread widely, with oak openings where the fires had burned away the tenderer, less hardy, growths and where the prairie grasses waved higher, at times, than a horse's back.

The red men, trailing through the grass, were often hidden in its tallness, and their traces came down from the north and the east and up from the south; and they found their campsites where there was water and game . . . where a clear spring flowed up from the inner earth. West, from the ridge that separated the Great Marsh from the boglands of the Fox River, there were the reeds swaying in the summer winds, or crackling dry in the harder bitter winds of winter. Within the marsh were the channels of clear water where the wild rice beat in the winds, heavy-headed, and the Indian women and children came in canoes to bend the rice stalks over and to pound the full heads into the canoe bottoms.

And as the red women beat out the rice heads, the birds among the willow and poplar, or clinging to the taller stems of the cattails, or from among the lower grasses, called with a hundred voices. The warblers of many varieties, the yellow headed blackbirds, the redwings, calling as they clung and swung; the orioles and meadowlarks, the grosbeak and the many sparrows, the thrush, and flycatcher and flicker. The rough-winged swallow and the barn swallow, and the martins and sapsuckers and robins, the vireo and kinglet and kingfisher . . . and the ducks which make the Marsh their kingdom as they followed their flyway in fall and back in spring. In the bulrushes the redhead and canvasback and the ruddy. The gadwall, the teal, the shoveler and pintail and the lesser scaup nesting in the whitetop grass or in the thistle meadow. Mallards in the reeds. In the shallows the great blue heron and bittern and lovely white egrets and swans: booming, waiting, or floating.

In the evening the sky above the marsh clouded with endless flights of passenger pigeons, and within the hum and the almost metalic flutter and rip of the wings was the deep throat boom of great frogs at the Marsh's edge.

Throughout the whole marsh resided the muskrats. Thousands and thousands they built their low houses on nearly every wet part, and the rat sought beneath the waters for the stems of the water lily, or other juicy stalks. He stored his food in a nearby storage house connected to the main house, and he was safe throughout the winter, unless a sudden deep freezedown blocked him from readmittance to his own dwelling and he was left to run and die on the frozen surface of the marsh.

His enemies in summer were the large pike which waited for the muskrat shadow above and struck savagely into the shining fur with sharp, terrible teeth; or the snapping turtle taking the rat swimming and dragging him to the marsh bottom. The mink was wild in savage killing of the rat and followed him into burrows, going wherever the rat went, and killing all the members of the rat household. The muskrats were prolific breeders. Two or three familes to each mating each year kept the rat population on the marsh high, until the cycle turned and thousands died and the breeding cycle diminished and for a while the rat numbers were low. Then, with the cycle turned again they came back, more than before.

On the marsh the old Indians caught the rat for his bright skin; and when the white men came, they trapped him in greater and greater numbers, even though the price of the skins was very little, less than a nickel at times.

Through the Great Marsh drifted the river. The river was called the Rock by early white men, because it cut through rocky formations. The Winnebago people say that when their people and the Prairie Indians (Potawatomi) camped on the banks of the Rock River, there lived in that stream a huge and terrible water monster. This water demon the people described as a long-tailed animal with horns on its head, great jaws and claws, and a body like a big snake. It ranged over the whole length of the stream from its mouth to the foot of Lake Koshkonong. It preyed upon both animals and men, seeming to prefer one no more than the other. Hapless deer that went to the banks of the river to drink or walked out into the water were seized and shallowed by the monster, horns and all. At the fording places of the river this demon especially hunted for victims. Indians crossing at these places were dragged down out of sight beneath the water and were never seen again. Canoes in the river were sometimes overturned by its limbs or a slap of its tail and their occupants submerged and lost. Only a few people ever saw this water monster, but its presence in the river was known by the churning and boiling of the water.

In the springtime its movement in the river broke up the ice and heaped it against the river banks. Its dens were in the deep places. There it slept and devoured its victims. Some Indians believed that there were several of these water monsters in the Rock River. Offerings of tobacco and various articles were cast into the river to appease their wrath when they were angry. These gifts preserved the lives of many people.

When the Indians ceased to camp in numbers along the Eneenne-shunnuck (river of big stones) after the white men came, these water demons also apparently left the river. The old story is also told about the Fox River, and how a great serpent writhed and crawled his way from North to South until he had wallowed out the channel of that important Wisconsin stream. In any case the Rock River swung easily south in two main branches and within the marsh the east and west arteries of the river joined, and not far to the south of where they came together at a place the white men later called "The Y" the river crossed a stony ledge and made a fast rapids. It was at this rapids that the early white settlers such as Mart Rich were later to make a dam, and very early to begin to cause dynamic changes within the life cycles of the marsh.

Nowadays the kids pile in to help keep the Rock River free of human debris. It will probably be a while yet before the name "Horicon" comes to mean what it originally meant in "clear, pure water," but the young people are working hard to achieve it. And there have been times when the pollution problem seemed too great for even the energy and idealism of youth to overcome, when the masses of detergent foam gathered at the dam and dead fish were one result.

The marsh, in winter, has a special beauty. In the early fall the wild migrating Canada geese come, of course, and they stay until late November and then they sweep down the flyway to their winter grounds near where the Ohio flows into the Mississippi. There, the geese's refuges are called Horseshoe Lake, Crab Orchard, and Union County; and the Horicon Marsh from whence the geese have departed lies quiet; the constant talking and honking of the Canadas is heard no longer, the morning blast of smokeless powder from the marsh margins has died away until next season, and the wind begins to comb the tall grasses and to bend the cattails that are now so plentiful. The farmers along the marsh edge, now that their crops are threatened no longer by the ravenous Canada geese, look ahead to the quiet winter, and to the memories that remain to some older ones, of farms that were once near, or partly in, marsh itself, and which had had to be sold to the State of Wisconsin and to the federal land buyers when the north and south portions of the marsh were taken for the wildlife refuge—beginning in 1927, the south part, by the State; and beginning in 1941—the north part, by the Federal Government.

There is some bitterness among the farmers, for the marsh, which was home to these sturdy, homeplace people, mostly of German descent on the east, and on the west side, the "Hollanders," stubborn, strong, with opinions undulled by passing time; the marsh, their home and the flavoring of their lives, drove deeply into their emotions. The present generations love the birds and the grasses and the smell of the marsh, but they remember how it was, and how their old folks spoke so nostalgically of it, and the sacrifices that many pioneers made simply to live in or near the marsh and to be a part of its seasonal change and of its always near and teeming wildness.

Most of the old-timers who lived there thought of themselves as part man, part wild bird, part muskrat, beaver, mink, fox, and raccoon for they loved and understood the animals, yes, and hunted them, and still, protected them in their own way; and most of the old-timers lived on the marsh because they loved it and would never, left to themselves, live anywhere else.

Part of my purpose was to visit the remaining old-timers . . . to hear their stories of old days on the Marsh and to get a sense through them, and of certain literary interpretations, of the continuous sweep of man through time and nature. There are not so many of the old ones left now. They have melted away into an eternal distance—along with the old Indians and the spirits of the animals and birds that were the models for the effigy mounds that abound in the marsh. But some of the old ones are living, mostly in the small marsh towns where they inhabit snug and very clean and neat retirement homes for they have evolved from a thrifty, neat, orderly tradition.

Eddie Lechner, for example, is sixty-four years old, and a very strong man. When he was young he didn't take any sass from anybody. He comes from a line of Bavarian brewmasters. His father was a highly skilled brewmaster who emigrated to the United States about 1900 to get away from army service required by the Kaiser. When his father died, Eddie took over the family tavern business in Kekoskee, a village on the edge of the Great Marsh. In prohibition times Eddie learned to be tough to survive. He made a lot of money, but he didn't keep too much of it, for personal reasons I'll relate later. He went to work for Jim Bell at the State of Wisconsin Headquarters of the Marsh, and became sort of Jim's right-hand troubleshooter, because Eddie was so expert at human relations . . . if a farmer got irate about the geese that were eating all his corn and threatened to do something violent about it, Jim sometimes sent Eddie to fix things. He was generally able to get Jim a satisfactory result. Folks at the Marsh really are fond of Eddie, and will generally do what he suggests. Jim wisely assigned Eddie to take me around the neighborhood when I was collecting the human stories for this book. We got to be good friends, and every morning when I would come up to the marsh from Madison, Eddie would have his truck ready and we would pile in and go visiting around the countryside. He knew all the older folks, and since about all of them were German and he certainly was, Eddie was in excellent ethnic rapport with them all. Some exceptionally pleasant visits were possible only because Eddie opened the local doors.

One clear, beautiful and very cold morning when the whole marsh sat still and brown where the cattails and the tall grasses waited in the soldier's places among the snow-covered marsh ice, and a couple of hawks hunted from a sky that seemed to reflect the marsh winter hues, Eddie and I set out for Mayville to visit with Mrs. Martha Krueger.

I never saw a dwelling as well swept and polished as Mrs. Krueger's. She lives all alone, doing her own housework at eighty-six, and occasionally she will still cane a chair, or meld the broken pieces of old china plates and saucers she has picked up at refuse heaps into an astonishing mosaic. Her entire life was spent on the Great Marsh in the hardest kind of labor. Her husband came home one afternoon in 1919 from World War I, and rural boy and girl married and went right to farming on the same place where Martha was raised as a girl, a farm right out on the marsh.

Martha Krueger sits with us at her kitchen table and her eyes light with her memories. She is remembering how she, a young girl, followed her father in the wheat field that he had planted and was harvesting on the Horicon Marsh. The farm was near the east branch of the Rock River which in those days, about 1900, was so full of fine fish—northern pike weighing up to thirty pounds, bass, even trout—that the settlers were able at any time to catch in any amount. No one was hungry on the marsh in those days. For centuries the old Winnebago Indians and the

Potawatomi had known that the Horicon Marsh was a land of plenty. And the fertile marsh edge lands grew fine crops.

And the girl labored along behind her father, as he swung the heavy grain cradle, and she gathered the grain and tied it into bundles. The bundles were shocked up to await the day of threshing. Later her father got a platform reaper which didn't bind the grain either, but someone had to sit and rake the cut grain off the platform, and the girl followed and tied it again, struggling in the moist heat to keep up with the machine.

After the work was done, sometimes, not very often, a young man might come in a buggy to take Martha to a dance in Mayville, eight miles away. The Bonacks lived away back in, and the road wasn't good. Also, a person had to know well how to drive the road at night, for it wasn't straight, and the nature of the land was very treacherous. There were holes that might come in the road as the wet seeped up to the surface and a wheel suddenly goes down the depth of itself, to be mired; or a horse might founder into a pothole and mire down and have to be helped out. Young people in those Marsh days didn't expect to arrive at a party immaculate. More likely they were covered with mud and dirt, and often Martha Bonack carried with her a change of clothing.

To get to the Bonack place you had to go up a high slope and down another. One time a neighbor died and the small funeral procession was stalled for many hours while the hearse that carried the casket was struggled with, for it had sunk floor deep in the middle of the road. But the marsh settlers were used to that sort of thing, and they made up for the struggle with the joy that they took in life, and in the songs and dances and the neighborly ways of helping each other, and in the mysterious presence of the great duck flocks that were everywhere and the plenty of the good earth and the fish-teeming waters.

The Bonacks lived well. Hog butchering, when the meat was prepared; salted, smoked in a special smoke house that Martha's father had built and the hickory wood he got from the Marsh timber, and cut and seasoned and used for smoking the meat. And in the kitchen her mother fried down a supply of the pork, and put it away in large crocks, or made delicious country sausages, large cakes, fried and put down in crocks in deep lard; and on the winter mornings, early when her father would go to the kitchen and start the fire in the cookstove, one by one the family would assemble in the kitchen, hugging up to the stove, and the mother would come from the pantry with a stoneware vessel of sausage and dig the hard, frozen cakes out of the lard, and into the smoking skillet she would plunk the large cakes. The smell of them as they browned, while she made the pancake batter—buckwheat, with the starter she had kept all the winter, and the way the cakes rose, and the bubble of the brown sausage fat in the skillet and the brown sides of the light cakes, with sorghum poured over them. They made coffee from barley which they roasted and ground up.

They worked very hard, though the wild game was so plentiful they never had to worry about something to eat. Wild duck got to be so common it was considered a second grade food. Mother Bonack prepared wild duck by frying it; sometimes it was roasted but much more often was just cleaned and put into the skillet. And they played hard. Father Bonack squeezed the concertina very gaily and sometimes the neighbors would come to the Bonack house for a party. The party would usually last all night, and the dancing was vigorous and very rough. Everybody could dance. The schottish, the waltz, the two-step, the polka—everyone knew them and they danced and laughed, and usually the whole neighborhood was there. There was always something to drink—it depended on who had it, and how much—but they did have homemade beer and wine and moonshine, and there wasn't any Puritan self-consciousness about using these good things, because almost all the neighborhood was German and they were folks who had been used to having beer and liquor all their lives. Nobody got drunk, but everybody had a delightful time.

One time a neighbor boy, Albert Clark, went hunting in the marsh and he stayed out too late. He didn't come home, and finally his family knew that Albert was lost out there. Father Bonack had been working in the fields all day and he was very tired, but when the Clarks came and told him about Albert he immediately got ready to go. Father Bonack knew the marsh better than anyone living along it, and he led the men in to hunt. It was a very dangerous expedition, because dry-year Marsh fires had burnt deep holes into the peat and these filled with water, and were extremely dangerous. If a man got into one of these he might easily be lost, for the vegetation that had collected in the potholes was impossible to support any weight. It sank, like the surface of a bog, and whatever was on the surface went down.

Many a woman, that night, wished that her man did not have to go. But she knew that he must go. For everybody helped one another.

The boy, meanwhile, had made his way north, mistakenly thinking that he was coming out on the south edge; he came out instead away north and east at Stooks Point, and there someone found him, and sent word back that he was safe. The men in the marsh didn't know this, however, and all night they searched. No one else was lost.

If a person is lost on the marsh the way things are nowadays he can always find his way out by simply following one of the ditches. They will always lead him out. In those days, though, the vegetation grew very tall . . . sometimes taller than a man's head, and if one were in the marsh and were lost, he might not be able to recognize the marks that were even very familiar to him. There was something mysterious about the marsh, and it took hold of a person's imagination someway, and twisted his thoughts and made a kind of confusion, the old-timers said, that could dismay a mind and lead a person to have fanciful visions.

One time an old settler had become lost and confused in the marsh and wandered around for a long while and eventually came upon his own farm, and didn't recognize his own buildings. He went to the door and asked his own wife how to get home! She didn't swing the skillet she was planning to bash him with, but saw instead that he was bewitched by the marsh and led him into the house to introduce his family all over again.

There were two hermits who once lived in the marsh and they lived over near the Rock River under the hill. Their names were Julius and Herman Stroede. They lived there alone in an old shanty for years and years. Herman worked quite a lot helping thresh and doing general chores, but Julius was in bad shape and didn't do much work at all. Herman always wore a lot of badges on his coat: Civil War badges and a lot of other kinds. He always walked to Beaver Dam, about fifteen miles, and once he walked clear to the St. Louis World's Fair in 1906. To St. Louis and back! He wouldn't take a ride with anybody. He was that independent.

Martha Krueger said: "I know that when Herman would walk to Mayville, he would stop off in the garbage grounds, and there he would pick up all kinds of stuff. There was a Lutheran minister in town name of Gerhardt Schrectner. Herman would agree reluctantly to take a ride with this preacher once in a while. Sadly the end of brother Julius was that once, during a cold spell, he was climbing through a barb wire fence, and he got hung up there. He couldn't get the barbs out of his clothes. And he froze, hanging there in the fence. It was awfully sad, because Julius was a good man, and he believed that man should only act natural and do just the things that God had provided for him to do. And Herman also, unbelievably, froze to death when he ran out of wood and was not able to get out to cut more.

"When I was a girl I went to school, but it was always walking. I went to school, walking five miles, and in bad weather we couldn't go. But the little school was a good one. And we worked so hard all the time, too. My father couldn't make a complete living on the unpredictable marsh. He had to go working. The marsh was too wet some of the time. If it was dry, then you could get the hay, but it was never knowing what would happen. But the land was good grey ground out there. We raised all kinds of vegetables. We had always nice watermelons, and good corn and oats. And we built us a stone silo so we could have silage for our cows. It was nice living out on the marsh but there was a lot of thinking sometimes: how to make a living.

"My father was a great hunter and we always had ducks to eat. Once in a while we would have a goose, too, though there weren't then so many geese as now. Mother would pick the ducks dry, and then we would nearly always fry them in a skillet. Fried duck was very, very good, because the ducks then were always fat. Quite different from the wild ducks today.

"The geese always migrated through the marsh in the spring only. Never in the fall. The geese never stopped at Horicon really, until after the refuge was established. My father, when he went duck hunting, had a special suit made of hay. He looked like a straw man! He would put this long hay coat on and it reached clear down to the ground.

"Out in the Marsh, especially on the islands, there was great patches of raspberries. And there were beds of wild strawberries. The wild berries were sweet, and when the children gathered them and took them to the house, Mother Bonack sometimes made a shortcake, and the small, sweet berries on the hot biscuit cake with fresh cream poured on and running down and filling up the plate around the red berries—that was one of the maximum thrills of childhood. My sister and I, when we were quite small yet, had to carry the butter into Mayville for market. We had eight cows and each of us girls had a basket with some pounds of butter in them. We were little and the day wasn't very good. It was raining. We got to town, delivered our butter, and started home. But the Rock River bridge had been taken out. They were afraid the high water would wash it out. They had simply tied teams to it and pulled the bridge out! That was near our home and our father, who was afraid that in the darkness we would miss the bridge and plunge into the swift-running Rock River, was waiting there on the opposite bank for us to come. When he heard our little voices there on the far bank he shouted that the bridge was out and that we would have to walk two miles upstream to where there was another bridge. We were very small, and very tired; but we set out, and finally, hours later, we did get home. I have never felt anything so good as the way the clean sheets felt that night."

THE LAND TRANSFORMED

THE LAND ITSELF DEFINES THE WISCONSIN WAY OF LIFE as I have seen it. I can never escape the pull of the land and the peoples' pride in it. The Norwegian emigrant who walked onto his land in 1845, planted his black locust staff deeply into the earth, *his* earth and cried; "This is my land, my home, my Wisconsin" and he left his staff sticking in the earth and it took root and grew, some said, into a beautiful tree that stood near the dooryard of the dwelling this settler built. Wisconsin is a kaleidoscope of change—the land transformed.

It is the human struggle that is important in Wisconsin: the devotion of families to the welfare of the Wisconsin land. The course of the struggle is not hard to follow: from the earliest settlers with their homestead problems, the stubborn sod, the loneliness, the hard labor, often the advent of death from disease or overwork. It is easy to appreciate the man with the simple farm instrument, toiling to make his home, his place, and a future for his children. Out of that struggle came the Wisconsin spirit, and the Wisconsin Idea . . . a better life for everybody, a chance at books and education, at a cultural side to life, an inspirational side, a religious side, certainly a fun side. The struggle can be seen in earlier parts of the story of the Wisconsin farm. But what did the struggle mean? What did it become? Were the settlers successful? Did they achieve what they worked so valiantly to accomplish? What of the family? What of the land? Are the values of determination, hard work, regard for land and for neighbors still there?

In answer, there is a kaleidoscope of achievement, of development, of meaning. First the youth left the farm. The cities were the benefactors. The farm and family life suffered. And there were the machines that grew larger and more efficient, spawned from the simple ones made by Wisconsin inventors in the days of the primitive reaper, the plow. One man could ultimately do as much as twenty, using the machines. And the cattle improved to purebred herds on every side, and the farms grew larger, with fewer farmers. Was all this what the early settlers had in mind? What has happened is fascinating and paradoxical. Wisconsin has become the leading dairy state and is known far and wide as a home state, a neighbor state, a state of beautiful farmlands; and the kaleidoscope, in order to understand, is put together from the memories, the statements, the hopes of many persons from all parts of the state. The spirit seems to be there still, though the pioneer cabins are mostly all gone now. And there is something else, a sense of largeness, as though the land has taken on a mysterious dimension that is bigger than life. Wisconsin is the land where the image of rural America grows, waxes, and spreads itself in the eyes of the world as *the* state where achievement of the farm has grown almost beyond belief. But now it is a different world and we search for motifs from the past, cherishing them:

The prairies now are nearly all gone. Along old railroads are some prairie plants, undisturbed; and the wild growths are not trampled. In a country cemetery on an old prairie acre, there is still a bit of the tall, tall grass, and at times the winds weave it into patterns of strange memory.

The valley below where I stand is one where settlers arrived on a June evening in 1845. The Norwegian who led them carried a staff of locust wood. This he suddenly thrust deeply into the sod and cried, "We have here our home! It will be here, in this valley! Here I'll leave my staff until it takes root in the good soil." And, as they say, the staff took root and became a shade for the old man when he reached ninety.

I do not know who lives down there now; or whose cattle are upon the hillside. I know that once a family of seven arrived on that flat by the creek, and built a cabin and broke sod for a crop of Indian corn. Now the hillside herd is large; great black and white Holsteins with swelling udders. On that hillside there was once only one beast; a thin, bindle cow newly dried of milk.

When you envision the people coming from Europe and from New York State and New England and Virginia and Ohio, and you stop a minute to remember what they went through, how they worried through the wheat-growing era, and got dairying started, and raised hops, and improved the cattle and horses and sheep and hogs . . . all of that, struggling all that time. And they learned about better seed and more economical ways to farm, then struggled through World War I and the Depression and finally achieved the success story, where you can be successful on the farm if you follow the right prescriptions and have the right machines and cattle. It isn't hard to identify the struggle, the clearing and breaking of the land, but are the people still there? The struggling people, the family people, the ones who created state and national strength and traditions. Are they, or the spirit of them, still there?

They do live on, for the spirit of Wisconsin grew out of experiences of the early families and their descendants who found their strength in the land. Generation after generation, leadership in the community and the state has come straight from the family, the home, the values of home.

Farm homes were gathering places. New methods developed at the university were synthesized and exchanged there when, from time to time, the Extension people would drop in . . . Soy Bean Briggs, Jim Lacy, Ranger Mac, Tom Bewick, Verne Varney, Warren Clark, Henry Ahlgren, Rudolph Froker, Dave Williams, Bruce Cartter, Nellie Kedzie Jones, Abby Marlatt, Almere Scott, Edith Bangham, L. G. Sorden, Walter Bean, Ray Penn. . . . Many others of the great ones who took a personal interest in the farm people would just drop by the home place to see how things were going. That was the way it was done; the whole thing evolved in one crucible—experts, farmers, all devoted to the same end: the betterment of a condition, of the land, of personal life. Community problems, farm problems, and community culture were what concerned them.

When meetings were held in the schoolhouse or the town hall, folks came from all over the countryside to discuss matters important to the farmer, or to the farmer's wife, or to his kids. Sometimes their concerns were expressed in the form of plays, usually obtained from the university, that told about the problems of the dairyman producing milk and cheese, or about a farmer raising chickens or geese or marketing produce, or about the farm wife saving up her egg money to buy a piano or organ.

The plays were done with lots of humor and fast action. Sometimes "Old Brindle," the all-purpose cow, was portrayed onstage by boisterous farmers covered with a large cloth and holding a painted cow's head. The plays were entertainment and more. They furnished a good reason for the busy farmers and their families to get together. The men would come in the evening to build a stage in the school or in the hall or outside. To some it was a great honor just to pull the stage curtain, to make the simple scenery, or to put up the lights—often just bulbs in tin cans, if there was nothing better. It was all part of the rural community spirit.

In the background of the entire rural Wisconsin way of life was what *had* happened. To understand the Wisconsin of today, one must appreciate the courage, determination, humor, and awareness of home and home place that accompanied the transformation of the land.

In working on this book, I talked to many farm people who helped shape this agricultural setting. All of them found it necessary to speak of the past before they could put the present into any perspective. All agreed that a world of work, suffering, and idealism lies behind the way it is now in rural Wisconsin. Henry Acten, of the Watertown area, put it like this:

"When I was twelve years old dad hired me out. He collected what I earned; I got a dime a month. I got a quarter, or something like that, later on. That was the goal them days. They came from the old country. That was the way it was done. Dad raised eleven kids. I never had any resentment. I pray to this day for him; he did the best he knew how, and here I am a healthy boy, eighty-seven years old, and feelin' fine. He did good for me, huh? And he gave me plenty to eat, he saw to it. He didn't believe a man should milk a cow. A woman should do that. When mother was pregnant, sometimes he'd have a neighbor woman come and milk. She set right out in the barnyard and done the milking.

"I started my milk business in 1920. In no time we had a big route, three hundred stops. Bottle milk—we bottled it, washed those bottles every day. Five o'clock milking time, hired man and me, and I was peddling it at first myself. My wife would see that the milk run over a cooler, cooled and bottled right away. And that milk that was milked at five o'clock was delivered the next morning at four-thirty. They got it for breakfast. Then I came home and the morning milk was done, and it was bottled and I'd go out peddling again. I peddled milk in Oconomowoc for eighteen years. It was successful. I was going to retire in 1927. I was going to sell my business out to my hired help and live high on the hog myself; but the Depression set in in '29 and the hired help backed out on the deal and milk went down to a nickel a quart. Lost everything. So I got a job selling milking machines and hammermills and cattle spray and I done good. Little over a year I was in that business and had over two thousand dollars on the books. And then they stopped paying. Like that. Stopped. No money. My wife was running the milk business and that stopped, too. Nobody could pay. I had to bear the whole loss from the milking-machine company because I was taking the whole commission. Borrowed the money and backed my own business. Lost the whole thing. Hadn't been for the Depression I'd of been sitting on top of the world.

"In the thirties we went into several years that were the slimmest and the hardest to get through. The farmers had food to eat, but it wasn't always what they had planned. Gardens were planted but the drought was bad. Gardens died. Eggs sold for ten cents a dozen. Feed for cattle was high. Milk sold for a dollar ten per hundred, then went to seventy cents, or lower. That's what caused them strikes by farmers. Calves about ten dollars. We hesitated to spend twenty-five cents. The slogan was make it do, do it over, or do without. It took all year to earn enough to pay the interest on the mortgage. Many farmers lost their farms. Nowadays we spend whatever we have, and sometimes it's a lot. They say, 'Hey, there'll never be another depression.' I sure hope they're right.

"Recall how it was when the Great Depression was deepening. All the farmers in our neighborhood were complaining about the low, low prices of milk. Finally they got together, it was in 1934, and had this 'Farmers' Holiday'—a big strike. They banned all the deliveries of milk and picketed the roads leading into the cities. Governor Schmedeman called out the troops, four thousand sheriff's deputies. Took into the farmers with billy clubs. Guess the farmers dynamited milk plants and trucks, dumped milk out all over the railroad tracks. Never forgot how the farmers gathered along the roads there in the dark."

There is still this seed of discontent in rural Wisconsin when the prices are low and the level of debt is high. A while ago young calves were shot in protest against farm prices. When something like that happens it is pertinent to recall the troubles of the 1930s when the milk strikes reflected the desperation of farm families. Milk was lowest at sixty-five cents per hundred-weight. A two-hundred-pound hog brought two dollars. A carload of sheep didn't net enough to pay their freight to Chicago.

Low prices were not enough; drought and swarms of grasshoppers added to farm misery. The hoppers could devour a ten-acre field of corn in a day. Railroad crews could not propel their handcars over the greasy, hopper-covered rails. Farmers couldn't meet their debts; banks and other mortgage holders foreclosed on many.

The government was confused. The National Recovery Act was launched to regulate prices. President Hoover, whose slogan was "Prosperity is just around the corner," supported a $500 million loan to help start farm cooperatives. Much of this money was never spent. Under the clouds of the early depression, the country was on the brink of an agricultural revolution.

Practically all of Wisconsin was involved in the strike. Roads were blocked with spiked planks, and strikers guarded the roads and railroads to prevent delivery and shipping of milk. They would not market milk at the low prices. Farmers who tried to get their milk through the lines were stopped; strikers dumped milk from the trucks. There was mass sabotage in milkhouses. Heads were cracked with clubs. Sometimes truckers carrying guns ran the blockade. There were stories about rural school children being stopped for inspection of their lunch boxes and for confiscation of their lunch milk. Near Madison a man was shot.

Henry Acten said that he guessed he was a damn fool in 1934 when the milk strike was on:

"I stuck my neck out. I stuck up for them farmers. My customers in town started to quit me because I was going with the farmers. There was this guy name of Walter Singler. Boy, when Walter stood up to talk you had to listen. He got the farmers all going on this Farmers' Holiday. Them trucks stopped, milk dumped out all over. Farmers mad and burnin' angry. Why not? Milk seventy cents per hundred. I was a leader in that and just about lost out."

The tendency to use the past to interpret the present is a favorite pastime for many rural Wisconsin folks. The women can recall hard times, too, as did Minna Breitsmann, retired homemaker. "I had a little doll, one of these with a china head, you know, and pink cheeks. Well, that was my Christmas present in 1900. And the next year mother'd go and put a new dress on it and just keep on handing it down to the next girl in line. There were fourteen children in our farm family. We had wonderful times—on just nothin'."

Or Elizabeth McCoy, of Dane County, who believed that the trees planted by the early settlers symbolize much about the past:

"At one time the whole frontage of the farm was a line of elms and maples, planted alternately. The Dutch elm disease began in the area about four years ago, and it took the elms along the road one right after the other. At the same time they said that the silver maples were about through, and were about to fall across the highway. They took them all out then. I have a few elms and maples in the yard, but the great line of trees is all gone. In the beginning there were some Douglas firs that the early settlers had planted. They were along the drive as you came up to the house. There is a unique thing on the place, white lilacs, and the white lilacs have a very interesting history. Over near the fish hatchery, on the hill, the Lakeland family had their first log cabin. They later built their house down on the crossroads. But up on the hill there is one white lilac bush. Still doing well. The white lilac I have was transferred from that in 1874. The Lacy family came in territorial days, before 1848. The lilac is still blooming. And other cuttings have been placed around. At the front of the house there is a hedge of lilacs. Probably the first bush was planted because the pioneer wife wanted some flowers."

In the memories of their beloved elder relatives, the women find the values of an earlier generation. Bess Bartlett told us about her husband's mother who devoted her whole life to hard work: "When she and grandpa got old they moved into town. But she wasn't ever very happy. There just wasn't enough for her to do. It got to working on her mind, I guess, and she just had to get back out on the land, so she and grandpa came back to the farm and lived with us. Grandma worked hard till the day she died. She was happy that way."

The women hark back to personal landmark events that set the course of their future: "I was a fifteen-year-old farmgirl when I had my first date. I had met this young man for the first time at a dance at the crossroads dance hall, and he said, "Can I come to see you Saturday evening?' And I said yes. And when he came he drove up to the house with a beautiful open carriage and a snow-white and a coal-black pony. It was the most beautiful team! I was just flabbergasted. I thought he'd come with an old farmhorse. And here he came with that beautiful team. I'm married to that man now. Fifty-four years!"

The men remember the more boisterous social events that had a kind of splendid energy and good humor. Roger Green, retired farmer from Grant County, said: "Usually the night of the wedding, if the young couple stayed home, or if they didn't and went on a little wedding trip, they'd wait until the bride and groom got home and then as many as wanted to go they'd take washtubs, or plow discs, or anything they could pound on to make a noise, or shotguns. They'd just surround this house, and beat all that stuff and keep it up hollering and hooting until that couple came out. And when they came out it usually meant a half-barrel of beer, or the money to buy one. Sometimes if the poor guy couldn't supply the beer the gang would demand the bride! They called this nonsense a shivaree."

And Bert Jones, Columbia County, recalled another typical prank: "We had a right splendid outhouse in our neighborhood. One of our farmers built it for his wife. It was a real ornate affair, six-sided, and it was plastered inside. One Halloween night the local boys tipped that over and that was a cryin' shame. It just collapsed. It would have been a showpiece and should have been sent to Washington or someplace. We tipped over an outhouse one night and there was a feller in there. Later on a few years after, I was telling how we had pushed it over and how the guy inside hollered and all, and a feller who was listening says, 'So you're the guy that done that to me, are you?' And he took out after me and we run near a mile, but I outfooted him. I never saw him again, and I never wanted to."

Carl Munz offered some humor from threshing days: "Years ago, before every farmer got a threshing rig, there were certain people who owned the rigs and they would go around threshing for everybody else. They'd leave home on a Monday and they'd not get home again maybe for a week. The person who owned this threshing rig was my brother-in-law's dad. There was one certain place that was in their round. This place wasn't known to be too clean and one thing and another, and there was a saying they used when the threshers went there: 'If you wanted to go out to the backhouse, go out there during mealtime, because then the flies were all in on the table.' "

Or, more seriously, Don McDowell, Future Farmers of America executive, found great nostalgia and meaning in family get-togethers: "My grandparents on both my mother's and father's side lived fairly close together. Brothers married sisters, in the neighborhood, and about every Sunday the entire families would gather, at one of the grandfathers' houses which happened to be right across the road from a little rural church, eight miles out of the little town of Montello. We had a family gathering every Sunday, a potluck dinner. The women got together and gossiped and talked about their families and what had happened during the week, and the men would talk about farm matters and tell stories. The kids ran wild all over, all around the farm, in the woodlot, up in the hayloft. And the dinner was spread out on the lawn when the weather was good, and it was a great time. Until late afternoon, or when it was milking time, the neighbors were there in family groups."

Wisconsin farm people know where they have been all right, but there are paradoxes in the present that trouble them. When some old-timers were on the land, thirty-five percent of the population were farmers. Today only four percent of America's population is engaged in farming, although the worldwide figure is eighty percent. As the science of technology became a more important part of farming, and as the farms began to get larger, the nation's agriculture required less and less manpower.

Farm folks speak with regret of the passing of the old values of rural life but generally find comfort of this sort: "There are so few of us left on the farms we just can't have the same kind of effect on human values we used to have. But then maybe there is something good happening that will change that, because a lot of urban folks are moving back out to the rural areas to raise their families. I guess they will become conscious of the fact that the human values of people on the farms instill good character and good patterns of living."

Until recently these same values were found in the urban areas because, to a large extent, the people living in cities came from the farms. Now, though, many folks in urban areas have never even been on a farm. A teacher in Milwaukee asked her little pupils, "Now if a cow produces four gallons of milk a day, how much milk will she produce in a week?" Every one of the pupils got the wrong answer because they were all figuring on a five-day week. They thought a cow was on the same schedule as workers in the cities. On the old farms, of course, it was work, work, work, seven days a week.

Henry Ahlgren, long important on the American farm scene, former U.S. Assistant Secretary of Agriculture, and Chancellor Emeritus of Wisconsin University Extension, commented to me, "If I were going to try to write America's Horatio Alger story, her greatest success story, it would be the story of American agriculture. There is no greater success story in this nation.

"I would think, however, that we have paid something of a price for it. I think of the kinds of people that have come out of rural America, who grew up in this hard work philosophy, the religious, family-loving people who struggled and had faith. We don't see so much of this kind of person in rural America any more, at least not to the extent we saw them in earlier parts of our history. I happen to be one of those people who thinks that that's too bad for our country. It's a part of the price we have had to pay for technology on the farm.

"The important measure of each one of us who grew up on the family farm was not *how* we worked but how *hard* we worked. Success was a matter of long hours of hard work. This was how my father operated. We used to come home from school in the wintertime and I ran all the way. I was a pretty good runner and my dad was all for it because I could stay at home later in the morning, do more work, and then run home from school at night to get the chores done. I've got some medals in a trunk that I earned in track. That was how I trained.

"Dad would have seven or eight trees marked for cutting, too, and as soon as we got home we had to go to the woods and cut trees, all winter long. Hard work. Long hours.

"My parents both came to this country from Sweden. I doubt that either one of them ever went as far as the eighth grade, but one thing my parents wanted above all others was the chance to give their children an education. Not only that, but the children in our family *wanted* an education. The parents didn't have to twist our arms and make us go to school. We considered it a privilege to have an opportunity for education. I guess folks now may look at education not so much as a privilege but as a right. Maybe this is some of the difference between the culture of today and back then.

"Now as you look at things today the farmers are college graduates. It's no longer a matter of how hard you're willing to work. Now it is a matter of how you do it. It means the application of all these discoveries that have made agriculture scientific. When I grew up on the farm we planted our corn when the leaves on the oak trees were the size of a squirrel's ear, and we planted our potatoes in the dark of the moon; and my dad planted everything he grew just like his dad had in Sweden, I think. Well, that's no longer true. Today just about everything you do on a farm has a scientific base. You wonder about some of the great, great developments that have taken place in our agriculture. I think the most dramatic one of all is hybrid corn.

"When we were growing up the kind of corn we grew on our farm was the tallest corn we could get. We had contests among the neighbors to see who could bring in the tallest corn stalks. Well, this corn seed always came from Iowa. It just didn't adapt very well to my part of the country, Polk County, and almost never, maybe just a couple of years, when the corn got ripe. But we always had this tall corn from Iowa. It went in the silo and it made poor silage even, because it was usually too green at the time it froze.

"Then hybrid corn came along. My dad used to laugh at me when I talked to him about planting alfalfa, and maybe getting some hybrid corn, and things to improve his crop production. Well, now we have taken the major hazards out of farming. It's kind of amazing, but during these golden years between the thirties to the fifties, we learned to write prescriptions. We just told a farmer that if he'd do this, and this, he'd get a hundred bushels of corn next fall. We just learned to apply the kinds of science and technology that got predicted results. All of this came out of our land grant universities."

But if the old families and the older citizens remember the lessons of the past, the same spirit of family and of love of land seems to be present in the youth of today. My observation is that the values that guided the older ones are still important. Looking at the 80,000 Wisconsin 4-H Club kids and the 27,000 Future Farmers of America members, we simply have to admit that it's the rural youth who have their feet on the ground. Part of it is the nature of the way they were brought up. It was a family affair: Father, mother, the kids, all shared and shared alike, cared about the land and the animals, and kept up the traditions of the family. It's a proud thing to think about—the people came to settle the land at such great sacrifice and with such hard work, and now their families, their young people, are carrying on in the same spirit, even though the way they *do* it on the farm today is vastly different.

The young folks do have definite pride and interest in the folklore of the earliest Wisconsin settlers. Engrossed in getting back to nature and in living close to it, today's youth seem to understand the fascination that weather and signs had for their forefathers. Feeling close to earth and sky, many can understand how the early settler, living much of the time out of doors and close to nature, came to rely on weather signs to guide his activities, from planting crops to preventing lightning from striking. The advent of rain, and particularly of a storm, was always of interest. Having no radio broadcasts or reliable information, he made up his own; it was passed along from neighbor to neighbor and from grandparents to grandchildren.

A storm was surely on its way under the following conditions:

When the wood fire in the old iron stove roared as it burned.

When the water drawn from the well looked cloudy.

When the ground-up feed that was mixed in the swill barrel rose to the top of the liquid instead of staying "mixed."

When there was a circle around the moon.

When the cat slept with her head "turned under and her mouth turned up" instead of in the usual curled-up position.

There were other signs to show changes in the weather and what to expect from the skies:

When the potatoes boiled dry, it was a sign of rain.

When the leaves on the trees curled up or blew wrong side out, it was a sign of rain.

When the chickens ran for shelter in a shower, it wouldn't last long. If they stayed out in it, it would rain for a long time.

When there was a ring around the moon with stars inside the ring, the number of stars indicated the number of days before a storm.

When the sky was flecked with small clouds, called buttermilk clouds, it was a sign of rain very soon.

When your feet burned, it was sign of rain.

When there was a heavy dew in the evening, the next day would be hot.

When the smoke from the chimney settled to the ground, it was a sign of rain. When the smoke went straight up, it would be colder.

When roosters crowed before midnight, it meant a weather change.

When a dog ate grass, it was a sign of rain.

When six weeks had passed after crickets began to sing, you looked for frost.

If streaks could be seen from the earth to the sun, which looked as though the sun was "drawing water," it would rain.

Wind in the south—blows bait in fish's mouth. Wind in the east—fish bite the least. Wind in the west—fishing is best!

When the kitchen range was being used, and sparks clung to the bottom of a frying pan or pot, it was supposed to storm.

The weather on the last Friday of a month predicted closely what the weather would be like during the following month.

A good time to plant hotbed seeds was on Good Friday.

If rain fell on Easter Sunday, six weeks of rainy Sundays would follow.

If the sun set behind a bank of clouds, there would be rain tomorrow; when the sun set "like a ball of fire," it would be a hot day, or at least a bright sunny one.

> *Evening red and morning gray,*
> *Sends the traveler on his way.*
> *Evening gray and morning red,*
> *Brings down rain upon his head.*
>
> *Rainbow in the morning*
> *Sailors take warning*

Rainbow at night
Sailors delight.

And here are some other weather jingles:

A snow storm in May
Is worth a load of hay.

A swarm of bees in May
Is worth a load of hay.

A cold April the farmers barn will fill.

If Candlemas Day be mild and gay
Go saddle your horses and buy them hay;
But if Candlemas Day be stormy and black
It carries the winter away on its back.

If Candlemas Day be fair and clear
There'll be two winters in a year.

A year of snow
A year of plenty.

Much damp and warm
Does the farmer much harm.

When the morn is dry,
The rain is nigh.
When the morn is wet,
No rain you get.

When the grass is dry at morning's light
Look for rain before the night.

The bigger the ring
The nearer the wet.

When the cats played in the evening or the fire popped in a wood stove, the wind was going to blow.

If the Wisconsin moon shines on you as you sleep, there may be a death in the family, and if you dream of something white it may be a sign of death. Rain falling in an open grave means a death within a year. Three knocks at the door and nobody there means a death in the family. Dream of the dead, hear of the living. If a death occurs at the end of a week, so that the corpse is held over Sunday, some relative is going to die within three months. To set two lighted lamps on the same table means certain death to someone close to you.

It is the custom in some parts to announce to the bees a death in the family, especially the death of the father or the head of the family. The bees will then bring consolation to the family members. If a swarm of bees settle on the dead branch of a live tree in the yard, a death will occur in the family within a year.

It is unlucky to plant a bed of lilies of the valley, as the person who does so will surely die within the next twelve months. Cows forecast the future. If they moo after midnight, it is warning of an approaching death.

Granddaddy Longlegs will give the location of the cows in the pasture when asked, and witch hazel will cast spells on its encounterers. Moonstones are good-luck charms, but an opal is an unlucky stone portending injury and mental or physical trouble. An agate insures its wearer health, long life, and prosperity. A diamond may disperse storms, and a topaz prevents bad dreams. Rubies are said to discover poison and correct evil, but the finding of purple hyacinths can only denote sorrow. Broken straws or sticks foretell a broken agreement, and in summer, if you are not careful, snakes may milk your cows dry in the pasture. If your nose itches you will hear some good news. If you drop your comb while combing your hair you are in for a scolding that day; also a scolding if you button your dress the wrong way. If the teakettle sings there is sure to be trouble, or an argument—the only remedy is to keep putting cold water in the kettle! If it rains on your wedding day you will shed many tears during your wedded life; but if you eat raw cabbage on New Year's Day you will have plenty of money in your pocket all year.

But, still, with all the appreciation of folk ways, there is something missing. As we approach the end of this story of the Wisconsin farm, we almost expect a crescendo to build toward a crashing finale to illustrate the beauty and dignity of man on the land. Although the potential of the big chords is there—we have the bigger farms, larger machines, better cattle, and an understanding of how it all came to be—we can't quite hear the great stirring music that would represent the tremendous victory of Wisconsin men and women on the farm. The struggle of the past we can see—the man with an ox team breaking prairie, building a new log house, or wresting a subsistence living from the land. But the drama of ultimate success—well, where is it?

Is it one lone man in a vast milking barn with a line of a hundred fine cows and a multitude of hoses and wires and pipes? That has some visual interest, but it isn't quite as emotionally satisfying as an old lady sitting at a cow's flank on a three-legged milking stool, a kerosene lantern hanging above her in the barn on a winter's night. The modern picture is almost too big, too perfect, too technical.

The one thing that is not technical in itself is the Wisconsin family. As we recall the past again, we see that the family depended on horse power and manpower. The machines on the farm were quite simple and there weren't many of them. An average family looked upon forty acres of land as just about all it could possibly handle. In one typical family whose surviving members we talked with, there were three boys and a girl. The father's game plan each year was to clear and to bring into production an additional five acres. That product seemed to take about all the time the family had, beyond chores and the work with land already cleared. Even in the first decades of the twentieth century, agriculture was often reminiscent of pioneer days. Most farmers still had walking cultivators, some of the more affluent farms had riding ones, and the boys contested to see who could cultivate five acres of corn in a day, or who could plow one acre of land with a walking plow. The father depended upon his family much more than is true today. It took all the boys to clear those five acres. There just were no shortcuts.

The country itself—in this instance, northwestern Wisconsin—was heavily timbered. It was virgin timber, basswood, maple, hickory, elm. Father and sons blasted the stumps with dynamite. The blasting was almost continuous at times. Both stumps and rocks had to be cleared away. The Scandinavians who came to settle in Polk County were attracted by trees, rivers, and lakes. They got those, and rocks!

As the family grew, the farm expanded to about a hundred acres. By the time the boys were grown, there was a stone fence all the way around the farm, and every stone came from the field. The boys used stone boats to move those rocks, and every field was crisscrossed with the sledge tracks.

Although the family possessed very little material goods and by today's standards would even have qualified for welfare programs, they didn't think of themselves as poor. When the father and his sons and daughter and wife struggled with the task of clearing the land, their income was perhaps four hundred dollars per year or less. When there was no money at all, they simply took eggs to town to trade for sugar and coffee. Everything else came from the farm.

But no one suffered from lack of food. Before the boys did morning chores and went to school, they'd have a cup of coffee or milk and perhaps a piece of bread. About seven o'clock there would be breakfast: always oatmeal and thick cream, fried potatoes, fried meat, a slab of pie and sweet bread. There was always a coffee break at midmorning with cookies brought to the field by mother or daughter. The big meal of the day was at noon: potatoes, meat, other vegetables, nothing very fancy but lots of it. There would always be afternoon cake, rolls, and cookies. They'd have supper around five, usually before the chores, and before bedtime there would likely be another snack. Seven or eight meals a day! At least that's what this Swedish family did.

But that kind of struggle on the land is mostly over now. The land in Polk County has all been broken. The farms there are good. People have a lot more material wealth. When they look back and try to put it all into perspective, they sometimes do so in football terms. Folks in Wisconsin used to know that the Green Bay Packers talked a great deal about pride. It was pride, they said, that made the Packers the kind of team it was in the Lombardi days. Certainly the one thing that all the Swedish, Norwegian, German, the other ethnic groups and old American families in that part of Wisconsin had was pride. They wanted to prove to the world that they could make their own way without help from outside agencies.

And this attitude led to faith in themselves and faith in the land. Faith in the rural area is still very strong. The urge to have an education, to struggle for it, not just have it handed over free, is still there. And there is pride, too, because the farms in Wisconsin are still family ones, and the same family values operate there. The farms are bigger, and there aren't nearly so many of them. The whole family may not be involved in the operation because it simply takes a lot less manpower than it used to. In 1930, to produce one bushel of wheat by hand took about four hours. Today, with a four-wheel drive tractor and combine, it takes one-half minute.

Remember that it was the land that originally drew the people to Wisconsin. People left Europe because they had no opportunity to own land. They came to have their own place. They lived through the pioneer struggle, they attained education for their children, and finally they became better off and were able to buy machinery and to put up silos and have superior cattle. They created the farm state we have today.

The farm family is what made Wisconsin a friendly, neighborly, tradition-conscious state. The family is the important thing about Wisconsin, far more important than the cow, or nutrition, or animal husbandry or agronomy. The meaning of this book lies in the kind of people who came to Wisconsin, and in their families. They played together and worked together and evolved a whole social structure. They arranged social gatherings to help one another in the harvest, to raise barns, and to support one another in times of illness, death, and disaster. Many a farm today is in the hands of its Depression-day owners because the neighbors came to the 1930s auction and "bid in" the farm for a dollar . . . and dared the local authorities to say otherwise. The folkish proverbs by which our forefathers sowed and reaped, the songs they sang, the religions they practiced—all are a part of the Wisconsin way of living, and of the spirit of this state. In many families these traditions have been passed down generation by generation.

Certainly one of the wonderful aspects of the rural "Wisconsin Idea" is that young people really are returning to the land. It's basic with Americans to want land, to have it, to farm it, to love it. They do actually say, in Wisconsin, *This is my land, my home, my Wisconsin,* because the land is so essentially theirs. And the young folks are coming home again. On many farms there is still an old dooryard tree standing, where the families once gathered on Sunday afternoons in summer. And when families come home now the old tree, perhaps a hundred years old, will mean a special thing: that the young people and the old are coming back to the homeland where their folks started it all.

This is the great meaning and the mighty crescendo, the Wisconsin theme repeated again and again. Wisconsin is still a family state. The farms large and small are mostly family farms. It isn't just a woman and a man and a plow any more. Things have gone way, way beyond that. Yet the spirit is the same, and we sense that the spirit that arose from struggle will become stronger, more prevading. Technology? Sure, we've got that in abundance, and far fewer farms, but faith is there. It is faith in the land, faith in man and man's strength and his will to survive. It is faith in the past, and faith that the Wisconsin farm country still has a potentially powerful future. It is also faith in god and in the nation. That hasn't really changed.

A lot of the farm places are really beautiful. The desperate human struggle isn't there any more, not like it used to be. But then, maybe that's good. The thing that does remain is the "spirit of Wisconsin," or as the preachers used to say: "Lord, we are neighbors. We have a duty to one another." If times are changed, so be it, but the faith of people has not changed very much. Not really. We are doing different kinds of things, no doubt, but the spirit of the family on the farm, the home, the whole knowledge that Wisconsin is a home state, a neighbor state, and that people here are home folks. That's the great thing, and a thing we'll never lose. It is too deep in our bone and muscle and our blood. There is the climax of the story . . . the swelling of the symphony . . . us, as people . . . a farm state, a farm people, a Wisconsin *people!*

AFTERWORD

I RECENTLY FOUND DOCUMENTS IN OUR ARCHIVES RE-lating to my establishment of the Rural Writers which became the Regional Writers, and the friendship of the great volunteer leader, Fidelia Van Antwerp; to the founding of the Wisconsin Idea Theater Conference; the Wisconsin Regional Writers; the Council for Wisconsin Writers; the National Community Theater Training Centers. I found abundant correspondence with the officers of the Rockefeller Foundation; with David Stevens; with Les Paffrath of the Johnson Foundation (always a backer of my programs); plans for Wisconsin Folk Drama tours that David Peterson, L.G. Sorden and I launched; the fine program in behalf of minorities, the handicapped and incarcerated; "The Arts and Human Need;" the Upper Middle West Professional Playwright's Laboratory with Dale Wasserman; with the founding of the Rhinelander School of Arts; programs of cooperation

with the countries of Finland and England; the forming of the Wisconsin Arts Council and Foundation; work with Native Americans; with rural communities; with the Wisconsin Academy of Sciences, Arts and Letters; with state folklore and folklife; work with the elderly; with the Wisconsin Bicentennial Commission; with book publishing and scores of letters to and from my good friends, Cap Pearce and Charlie Duell in New York at Duell, Sloan and Pearce; projects with August Derleth and other writers; with Allen Crafton and Alexander Drummond; with a hundred graduate students and assistants, with the Arts and the Small Community; the National Endowment for the Arts; with 4-H Clubs; with the National Theater Conference; with national surveys of the American Theater; with national and international organizations; conferences with thousands of writers eager to realize themselves . . . and the establishment of the Robert E. Gard Wisconsin Idea Foundation at Aldebaran Farm at Spring Green. All these things I have done, or caused to be done.

My life in Wisconsin has been a rich one; yet overall the whole experience has taught me how necessary it is to probe deeply into the life and background of a region if the feeling of what has really transpired is to be important. It is something beyond the superficial, and even beyond the bitter necessities that a land imposes upon its settlers; it is more the spirit of a place and its distillation in human lives. That theory applied now makes me sure there must be great writing about the development of American regions. I do not mean more history, often already splendidly done. What I mean is a great and dramatic portrayal of the spirit of the people, in terms of their epic arrival, struggle, the design of their nationalities. A magnificent canvas ought to be created. I am familiar with the scope of the Wisconsin land, and how the land beckoned to people. I know what happened when they converged upon Wisconsin, freedom seeking, land seeking, their families destitute for the most part, their women self-sacrificing and humble, but with terrible pride and courage. I have read the epic novels of Rolvag, the novels of Moberg; I have read the novels and the stories of Hamlin Garland, but in all of them something is lacking that is implicit in the Wisconsin story. It is a vision that was here; a great responsibility to self, to future, that ended, finally, in the concept of the "Wisconsin Idea." If a writer could catch that flicker of world greatness . . . buried in so many, many humble and seeking hearts . . . there it would be. It was, of course, this elusive thing, this heartrending idealism of simple people and also the terrible intellectual necessities that helped bring about free education and libraries; the gift, at least in part, of early free-thinking German intellectuals, who beginning in 1848 brought and maintained the search for a world betterment. It seemed to congeal, to focus, to become inevitably a part of Wisconsin, the soul, the spirit.

All of this, with the smell of the land on the spring air, the way the rivers look in April, the dark of forest tracks, the far flung University that spreads its influence into every home, the farm girls and boys with multitudes of hard-won fair ribbons, the great cattle herds, the brown of fall corn, the silos, the barns so large, the fields so many, seen from above. The green of summer, the contours, and the wish for the cold green of primitive eras. All of this drew me, draws me, and makes the Wisconsin sensation real for me. It is a sensation that "comes home" to me everytime I realize this is Wisconsin and that I am at home here with all of this.

So what does it all mean?

Our aim with the Wisconsin Idea Theatre was to make the arts in grassroots places particularly, the great frontier they can become in America.

It is so hard to distill a wish above all. But if I could do this I think my wish might be something like this: that I might live long enough to hear the music of the American spirit emerging from hundreds of fine orchestras and choruses in large places and small; see good plays joyously presented and viewed in many communities, using themes deeply felt by many new writers; know that fine pictures by American artists, hang on the walls of a multitude of American homes of every economic status;

and to feel secure that the folklife and tradition of American regions is being written about and preserved.

I have tried sincerely to make Wisconsin a proud territory of the human spirit; of the sensitive approaches of man to home, nature and to the arts. Through the arts, through so many cultural summations of the Old World to New, I have tried, tried, tried; visited so many communities, done so much teaching, travel, seeding. Success? Looking backward now, the state as I conceived it, appears somewhat like a battlefield. The debris of conflict is everywhere; discarded dreams lie helter-skelter like thrown shields of ancient warriors; yet a sense of unique Heartland civilization is there, too, and above the plain, some monuments.

Like many another writer trying to sum up total meaning in ideas that developed over a lifetime, I have discovered that life eddies and circles around and around, and that ideas return finally to their places of origin.

In what I have called "Prairie Visions," where first glimpses led on to a search for deeper meanings, I am now often conscious of the great circle sweeping me back to my Kansas boyhood, and sweeping onward to a multitude of adventures there and elsewhere which there has not been space enough to fully recount.

And I keep remembering the importance and coincidence of the strangers who appear in human lives, to straighten ideas and purposes. I recall the faces and hear the words of Allen Crafton, of David Stevens and Alexander Drummond and have somehow enshrined their images on the side of a personal mountain which will forever remain for me, one of the monuments of my search.

The importance which I attach to the scope and personality of regional arts development has not been shaken by what I have done; nor, though I fully realize how minor my contribution has been, have I become in the least discouraged. I do fully believe that the greatness of American arts must lie in the seeding ground of the homeplace, and in all that the homeplace can mean in its first, faint realizations, and then seen again and again from many places and viewed through many visions.

More and more I have become an interpreter of the State of Wisconsin. I attempted many things, of course as developments of the Wisconsin Idea Theatre. I only hope that the remembered figures of my mountainside know that I have worked hard to make their dream of a land-conscious and arts-conscious America a reality.

COLOPHON

Edited by Tom Klein, Ashland, Wisconsin

Designed by Moonlit Ink, Madison, Wisconsin

Calligraphy by Linda Hancock, Madison, Wisconsin

Type set in Trump Medieval Book by Impressions Inc., Madison, Wisconsin

Printed and bound on 50 lb. Warren Sebago, cream white by R. R. Donneley & Sons, Crawfordsville, Indiana

Published by Heartland Press, an imprint of NorthWord Inc., Ashland, Wisconsin

Also from NORTHWORD INC

ALL-SEASON GUIDE TO WISCONSIN'S PARKS
Jim Umhoefer
"There are more than 70 state parks, forests, and trails in Wisconsin, and author Jim Umhoefer has visited them all. The guide is useful, informative, fun to read, and suited to all seasons, melding together commentary, maps, and photos. A browse through the book reveals the state's highest falls, best fishing holes—enjoyable regions to spend a few days. Bikers will find indispensable maps of the state's bike trails; hikers, campers, picnickers, vacationers, and anyone wanting to be outside will find this guide more than worth their money."
—Wisconsin Trails
$9.95 • 8½ × 11, 80 pages, paper • ISBN 0-942802-00-4

ALL-SEASON GUIDE TO MINNESOTA'S PARKS
Jim Umhoefer
"To assemble this information-rich guidebook, Jim Umhoefer traveled 12,000 miles in Minnesota. He camped, hiked, biked, backpacked, swam, canoed, sledded, skied and snowmobiled in discovering his adopted state. His book captures that intimacy, revealing little details and recounting anecdotes that underscore the charm of Minnesota's lakes, streams and forests. In Itasca State Park, for example, he pinpoints the bison kill site, locates bald eagles' nesting spots, and shows sunset fanciers where to watch the sun disappear as the haunting melody of loons drifts across the lake."*—The Milwaukee Journal*
$9.95 • 8½ × 11, 104 pages, paper • ISBN 0-942802-06-3

CALKED BOOTS & CANT HOOKS
George Corrigan
Through Corrigan's eyes you can follow the evolution of the logging industry from horses to tractors and from cross-cuts to chain saws. Having worked dozens of woods' jobs, he describes the evolution with detail and accuracy as well as compassion. He loved the woods and the assortment of people who worked with him. With an ear for language, he has captured the character of the lumberjack.
$11.95 • 6 × 9, 288 pages, paper • ISBN 0-942802-14-4

FIRE & ICE
Don Davenport and Robert W. Wells
Combines two deadly disaster epics under one cover. "These are shocking tales of nature's fury: the 1958 killer storm that sent the big ore carrier *Carl D. Bradley* bubbling to the bottom of Lake Michigan, and the 1871 holocaust that charred bodies and blackened the landscape in Peshtigo, Wisconsin, the most disastrous fire in American history.
"*Shipwreck on Lake Michigan*, by Don Davenport, a Great Lakes scholar, is the kind of story a reader can't put down. Robert Wells tells the searing story of *Fire at Peshtigo* with the sure hand of a veteran newspaperman."*—The Milwaukee Journal*
$13.95 • 5½ × 8½, 450 pages, paper • ISBN 0-942802-04-7

LUMBERJACK LINGO
L.G. Sorden & Jacque Vallier
Over 4,000 terms and phrases fill this unusual dictionary. "*It's five a.m. and the gabriel blows. The bark eaters fall out of their muzzle loaders and head for the chuck house to bolt down a pile of stovelids with lots of blackstrap, some fried murphys or Johnny cake and maybe some logging berries.*" That's the colorful language of the lumberjack. Anyone with an interest in forestry or forest industries will enjoy reading this reference work, page by page.
$9.95 • 6 × 9, 288 pages, paper • ISBN 0-942802-12-8

UP COUNTRY
To the 17th century explorers, the great wilderness surrounding the Great Lakes was known simply as the "Upper Country". *Up Country*, a compilation of journals, letters, and memoirs is a book of firsthand experiences, offering pure impressions of primeval landscapes and of initial contacts between the European explorers and Native Americans. Edited by William Seno.
$11.95 • 6 × 9, 242 pages, paper • ISBN 0-933437-00-5

To receive our free color catalog or order any of these books call toll free 1-800-336-5666 (in Wisconsin 1-800-922-2460). NorthWord Inc., Box 128, Ashland, WI 54806.